Mel Gibson's *Passion*

Shofar Supplements in Jewish Studies

Mel Gibson's *Passion*

The Film, the Controversy, and Its Implications

edited by Zev Garber

Purdue University Press / West Lafayette, Indiana

The following essays appear in this volume with kind permission of the publishers that printed earlier versions:

Irving Greenberg, "Review of *The Passion of the Christ,*" reprinted with permission of *Commonweal* magazine.

S. Scott Bartchy, "Where Is the History in Mel Gibson's *The Passion of the Christ?*" reprinted with permission of *Pastoral Psychology* and its publisher Springer Science and Business Media.

Printed in the United States of America.

Library of Congress Cataloging-in-Publication Data

Mel Gibson's Passion : the film, the controversy, and its implications / edited by Zev Garber.
p. cm. -- (Shofar supplements in Jewish studies)
Some essays are from a symposium held Mar. 30, 2004 at Purdue University.
Includes bibliographical references and index.
ISBN-13: 978-1-55753-405-7
1. Passion of the Christ (Motion picture) I. Garber, Zev, 1941- II. Series.
PN1997.2.P39G37 2006
791.43'72--dc22

2005028575

Contents

Mel Gibson's *Passion*

Introduction

Zev Garber

The unprecedented biblical-cinematic debate on the merits and demerits of Mel Gibson's controversial Jesus movie, *The Passion of the Christ,* began long before its release nationwide in 2,000-plus American theaters on Ash Wednesday, February 25, 2004. A combined group of Christian and Jewish scholars convened by the United States Conference of Catholic Bishops' Advisory Committee on Catholic-Jewish Relations and the leadership of the Anti-Defamation League met in the spring of 2003 to evaluate the film's biblical accuracy in conformity with the Catholic Bishops' Guidelines on Passion Plays.[1] Their judgment was two thumbs down in both categories and they offered corrections to balance history and scripture and strong suggestions to purge the anti-Judaism motif in the script. Though Gibson and his film company, Icon, were knowledgeable and initially supported this ecumenical review, they rejected vehemently the scholars' advisory, threatened lawsuits, and informed the media that the script was "stolen and outdated."[2] The rest is commentary.

Gibson's *Passion* has produced in its wake a flurry of opinion pieces, syndicated columns, and cover stories in major newspapers and literary magazines (e.g., *Forward, LA Times, New York Times, The New Yorker, The New Republic, Washington Post, Village Voice*), Catholic and Jewish Journals (e.g., *America, Commonweal, Commentary, Tikkun*) newsmagazines (e.g., *Newsweek, Time, Vanity Fair*), movie reviews, and study guides[3] in how to make sense of the willful death of the suffering savior of the Christian faith. The first response made it abundantly clear: the film has shocked and divided Christians and Jews, between and among themselves, in how to view and review the traditional Jesus of the Gospels. On one side there are Jewish literati Frank Rich, Charles Krauthammer, and Leon Wieseltier, who opined that the film's cinematic exaggeration is intoxicated by blood, bloodthirstiness, and blood libel;[4] religiously observant and politically conservative Jewish radio talk-show hosts, Michael Medved, Dennis Prager, Rabbi Daniel Lapin, who see Jewish criticism as a mistake and misrepresenting Gibson's conscientious attempt to portray a non-antisemitic Jewish Messiah and his sympathetic Jewish followers; and Jews and Christians who express a deep concern that Gibson's dark portrayal of Temple leaders and the Jewish crowd, renders asunder the good work done in Jewish-Catholic-Protestant dialogue post–Vatican II Council. On the other side, there are Pentecostals and other evangelical Christians rediscovering a centralist Reformation theology that a suffering savior crowned with thorns, caused by our sins, is willed by God. What traditionalist Catholics never lost, born-again Christians are discovering, and both streams are returning to scriptural basics, a bloodied Christ on the cross is necessary for the salvation of mankind.[5]

Mel Gibson focuses on the passion, not the life nor resurrection of Christ. By doing so, he leaves out most of the elements of the Jesus story familiar to Christians and consequently he adds non-biblical gruesome details foreign to the Gospels. Case in point, the mean-spirited visions of the nineteenth-century Sister Anna Katharina Emmerich detailing the arrest and flagellation of Jesus eked out by shouts from a crowd of bloodthirsty Jews. Her problematic diaries, *The Dolorous Passion of Our Lord Jesus Christ,*[6] added to other distressing historical and linguistic inaccuracies, make a sham of Gibson's claim that he was striving for historical accuracy.[7] Nonetheless, countless Catholic and Protestant church leaders maintain the oft-quoted but disputed papal review: "It is as it was."[8]

The incredible box office success and the overwhelming amen-appeal to millions of denominational Christians (and others) world-wide reaffirm the necessary work of Jewish-Christian dialogue: confront the anti-Jewish bias of *contra-Judaeos* found at the crossroads of Christian preaching and teaching; and expose the dreadful and shameful replacement thinking that Christian have projected on the Jews for the past two millennia as errant scriptural reading and bad theology from the writings of Jerome, Augustine, Aquinas and Luther on the Jews as eternally banished and cursed by God and man, to the writings of contemporary evangelical Christians, many of whom believe that the Shoah signified that Jews' non-acceptance of Jesus as their savior is partly responsible for their suffering and genocide during World War II. This may well explain why countless European Christians saw no distinction between Christian verities and Nazi slogans. What happened to Jews during the Shoah was the word of the Lord. But Jew and Christian in dialogue reject this replacement theology and eschatological myth as neither the teaching nor the way of the historical Jesus. By stressing the importance of the Israelite religion ("Written Torah") and the centrality of rabbinic interpretation ("Oral Torah") in the life and instructional aspects of the Teacher from Galilee, Jewish-Christian dialogue assesses correctly the positive value of Pharisaic-Rabbinic Judaism, rite and law on the nascent Jewish Christian movement and on the later history of Gentile Christianity.

Despite annals of Christian teaching of contempt and supersessionist theology, many Christians in dialogue with Jews are discovering that contemporary biblical scholarship and the depth of Jewish biblical teaching and rabbinic tradition—what makes the Children of Israel a Holy People—do not disrupt their loyalty to the Cross at Cavalry. What emerges in scholarly interfaith encounter is that Jesus did not teach what was to become the church's understanding of him and his mission; traditional negative teachings about the Jews associated with the Crucifixion have been used to justify great acts of evil against them; and that Jesus our Lord points the way to God, meaning that the God-man of the hypostatic union is metaphorical and not the ultimate God-as-God. Correcting the theological errors blatant in Gibson's *Passion* is to welcome Jewish/Hebraic hermeneutics in teaching about Jesus' love and compassion. That is to say, by focusing on Jesus as a Pharisee, the believer properly recovers the oral traditions preceding and following from the Jesus way. More importantly, it places the moral and spiritual message of Jesus in a sound Jewish context, which underscores a salient message: demythologize the Jewish guilt in the death of Jesus and demystify dogmatic Christology.

Neither option is entertained by Gibson. His cinematic *Passion,* overflowing with *Heilig Blut* and driven with cadences of Satanist Temple priests and demonic shrieks from the Jewish street, is assailing, not advocating, Christ in a post-Shoah cross-cultural world. Gibson claimed that a religious conversion motivated the making of the *Passion* and that the Holy Spirit was felt everyday in shooting it. But given the plethora of historic inaccuracies, religious stereotyping, and doctrinal misrepresentation, we wonder, *Was würde Jesus sagen?* The silence of the Lamb suggests a box-office debauchery.

This monograph embraces a special section of *Shofar* 23.3 (Spring 2005) on *The Passion of the Christ* and has added additional essays, discussion questions, and an annotated bibliography. The contributors reflect on a plethora of issues that show that concerned and informed Jews and Christians together can assess dis/misinformation, monitor dissent, alleviate community fears, and reassure that the solid rock of Jewish-Catholic-Protestant dialogue, though assailed, has not become chipped. The passion over *The Passion* has proven to be a blessing, not a curse. In summation, this book is construed to diffuse errant viewpoints in portraying the Passion story by separating the real from the reel. The respect of two ancient faith-communities demand and deserve this.

A special thanks to Nancy Lein for her technical assistance in preparing this manuscript for publication. Her interest and support in this learning venture is very much appreciated.

Notes

1. See the document "Criteria for Evaluation of Dramatizations of the Passion (1988)," in *The Bible, The Jews, and the Death of Jesus* (Washington, D.C.: United States Conference of Catholic Bishops, 2004), pp. 72–81.
2. P. Fredriksen, "History, Hollywood, and the Bible: Some Thoughts on Gibson's *Passion*," SBL Forum http://www.sbl-site.org/Article.aspx?ArticleId=225 Fredriksen reports that Gibson and his representatives "characterized our suggestions as 'extortion' [and] our evaluation as 'attack'."

3. Noteworthy are "Facts, Faith, and Film-Making: Jesus' Passion and Its Portrayal: A Study Guide for Viewers and Reviewers" (2004), created by the Christian Scholars Group on Christian-Jewish Relations affiliated with the Center for Christian-Jewish Learning at Boston College, and the complementary essay by Philip A. Cunningham, Executive Director, "Gibson's *The Passion of the Christ:* The Challenge to Catholic Teaching." Also, Eugene J. Fisher's "The Bible, the Jews, and the Passion" (*America*, February 16, 2004) and the symposium papers published online in the *Journal of Religion & Society* (2004), which can be accessed at http://www.creighton.edu/JRS.
4. C. Krautheimer, "Gibson's Blood Libel," *Washington Post* (March 5, 2004); L. Wieseltier, "Mel Gibson's Lethal Weapon: The Worship of Blood," *The New Republic* (March 8, 2004); and several of Frank Rich's Sunday columns in the *New York Times* (January–March 2004).
5. The *Roman Catechism* (1566) of the Council of Trent extends the responsibility for the trial of Jesus from the Jerusalem Jews then to the contemporary Christian/Man of the ages: "Since our sins made the Lord Christ suffer the torment of the cross, those who plunge themselves into disorders and crimes crucify the Son of God anew in their hearts" (cited in E. Fisher, "The Bible, the Jews, and the Passion").
6. Many scholars believe that the "19th-century German Romantic poet Clemens Brentano, who recorded and then embellished Emmerich's mystical vision, wrote the diaries" (*Forward*, June 11, 2004).
7. Gibson's ABC interview with Diane Sawyer, February 16, 2004.
8. Attributed to Pope John Paul II by his longtime private secretary, Archbishop Stanislau Dziwisz. However, senior Vatican officials acknowledged that "The Holy Father saw this film, but did not express any opinion on it" (Cindy Wooden of the Catholic News Service, December 24, 2003).

Section 1

Reflections on the Film

Review of *The Passion of the Christ*

Irving Greenberg

Mel Gibson has fashioned the most successful Passion play of all time. His film, *The Passion of the Christ*, is weak in its presentation of Jesus' teachings, but is a powerful retelling of the Gospel stories, complete with miracles, cosmic portents, and signs—though bloody and bordering on the sadomasochistic. The film is gripping and emotionally wrenching, but it focuses one-sidedly on the suffering and death of Jesus and hardly deals with the Resurrection.

The Passion will be seen by tens, perhaps hundreds, of millions of people—that is, by far more viewers than all previous Passion plays combined. The audience will therefore include many more people than have participated in the laborious, painstaking task of rearticulating Christian theology to stop it from spreading hateful images of Jewry. The film is likely to reach many more clergy and active Christians than were reached by all the statements, books, films, and conferences held to end stereotypical, demeaning interpretations of Judaism—one of the main foci of Christian dialogue with Jews for more than half a century. Whether the film will roll back sixty years of effort to theologically reconstruct Christianity in order that it no longer serve as a source of hatred (or justification for hatred) against Jews remains to be seen. One hopes that the American spirit of democratic respect for fellow human beings and disdain for hatred will defeat the film in this regard. In America, hopefully, even those devout Christians who love the film's telling of the Passion will mentally distance themselves or block out the rage at the Jews that the film evokes.

Like the classic Passion plays, *The Passion* is primarily built on Gospel accounts, but combines differing elements from all four Gospels to heighten the hatefulness of the Jews. The Gospels refer to Jesus' flogging but do not portray it. In Matthew and Mark, Pilate has Jesus scourged and hands him over to be crucified. In Luke, Pilate offers to let off Jesus with a flogging but is shouted down by the crowd, which insists on crucifixion. (The text gives no indication that Jesus is actually flogged.) Only John separates the flogging from the crucifixion, and portrays Pilate again offering to let off Jesus with that first punishment only—but Pilate is overruled by the shouting Jewish mob. Gibson follows John. However, Gibson first represents and expands the horrific beating and torture—to make all the more cruel the Jewish insistence that Jesus be further tormented to death by crucifixion.

The external source material in the film systematically heightens the culpability and the inhuman hardheartedness of the Jews and their leaders. Gibson inserts an androgynous Satan into the Jewish group urging Jesus' death, literally putting Jews in league with the devil. Only Matthew has Pilate's wife urge the Roman governor to "have nothing to do with an innocent man." (The other Gospels do not mention her at all.) Gibson turns this fleeting reference into a portrait of Claudia, a good Roman who pleads with her husband to save Jesus, anguishes over Jesus' suffering, and brings a white fabric to wipe up his blood—all to highlight Roman compassion for Jesus and their reluctance to kill him, as compared to the Jews, who are hard and unyielding. Only John—and Gibson—have Pilate declare to the Jews who wish to execute Jesus, "Take him away and try him by your own law." Only John and Gibson have Jesus console Pilate by stating, "It is he who has delivered me to you [that is, the Jews] who has the greater sin." Only Gibson (borrowing here and in other places from Anna Katharina Emmerich, a nineteenth-century teacher of contempt) outdoes John in graphically heaping up Jewish responsibility and absolving the Romans. Gibson alone has the Jews fling Jesus off a cliff in chains as another of the hideous torments inflicted before the crucifixion.

The whole film is a flagrant violation of Vatican II's declaration "Nostra Aetate," which declared that "what happened in his Passion cannot be blamed upon all the Jews then living . . . or upon the Jews of today." Furthermore, as Professor Michael Cook has pointed out, the film violates the U.S. bishops' conference 1988 "Criteria for the Evaluation of Dramatization of the Passion." That document states that the Jews should not be presented as bloodthirsty or as Jesus' implacable enemies; that Gospel elements with potentially negative impact or the image of the Jews should not be used; that modern scholarship should be employed; and that, above all, Jesus and the apostles should be clearly portrayed as Jews. With countless uses and abuses of iconographic techniques, Gibson's *The Passion* represents Jesus, his apostles, and his family as "Christians" (that is, better looking, kind and compassionate, sensitive to pain, trusting in God), whereas the Jewish leadership and the Jews are depicted as "Jews" (that is, long- or hook-nosed, diabolically cruel and unfeeling, driven by power, and oblivious of God). Despite the fact that the Roman soldiers do the dirty work, on balance, the Jews in the film are less human than the Romans.

Under the circumstances, the failure of the U.S. bishops to condemn the film is disappointing. One understands that they may have been preoccupied with the church's current internal scandal, or fearful of Gibson suing, or reluctant to get in the way of a box-office juggernaut. And, to be sure, the French

Roman Catholic bishops as well as important American Catholic scholars have spoken out against the film's portrayal of the Jews. That contrast makes the U.S. Conference of Catholic Bishops' official review of the film truly troubling. By calling *The Passion* "a deeply personal work of devotional art . . . unflinching in its brutality and penetrating in its iconography of God's supreme love for humanity," the conference sanitized the film. The review's statement that "concerning the issue of anti-Semitism . . . Jewish people are at no time blamed collectively for Jesus' death" is wrong. Rhetorically, this statement may be true—no one condemns all the Jews verbally for doing the dastardly deed—but the dramatizations, highlighting, body language, and images communicate, in sum, the message of Jewish culpability.

Admittedly, Gibson caught a break from America's culture wars. Many devout Christians—even some Jewish Orthodox rabbis and conservative cultural spokesmen—defended the film. They read the public argument over *The Passion* as a struggle between film evangelism and secularists. They believe that antireligious filmmakers and cultural tastemakers hate *The Passion* because it is devout in attitude and powerful in its presentation of Scripture. Apparently some of the bishops themselves viewed the film through that lens. But the essence of pluralism and the moral challenge of the promise made in "Nostra Aetate" is to preserve the powerful articulation of God's presence in the Christian narrative without letting it extend into teaching contempt or serving as a cover for hatred. *The Passion* willfully crossed that line in order to degrade Jews; sadly, the official Christian leaderships in the United States failed to defend that line.

Dramatization without degradation is the fine line that all Christians will have to draw in order to repent for past mistreatment of Jews. Remember, the only true repentance is one that prevents recurrence of past evil behavior. Perhaps this means that sometimes Christians must pass up a powerful tool for preaching Christianity if that tool might harm innocent bystanders or repeat past crimes against Jesus' family and people. Therefore, no simple republication of the general guidelines to teaching the Gospels (in which the bishops call for every attempt to avoid the type of treatment of the Passion that Gibson actually gives) can atone for the sin of silence in addressing the film itself.

This brings us to the three theological challenges posed by the film to all Christians who witness their faith in this postmodern world, as well as to Jews of goodwill who are striving to undo almost two millennia of hostility and hatred. *The Passion* is an assault on the half-century effort to prevent the gospel of love from serving as a sanctuary for hatred of Jews, in order to create a partnership of these two Abrahamic faiths going forward.

The fact is that the film is substantially based on the Gospels. The Gospels themselves, literally understood, generate hatred (and worse) vis-à-vis Jews, living and dead. The consensus of modern scholarship agrees that the Gospels are not eyewitness accounts but rather poetic/theological renderings. They are the outcome of historical revisions reflecting the painful separation of the two faiths, and an attempt to whitewash the Romans in order to make the new covenant faith more acceptable to gentiles. The scholarly consensus also discounts the extreme anger in the Gospels' language as reflecting an overheated, overstated inner-Jewish contentiousness (which is distorted out of context when exploited by gentile Christians to portray Jews in this cruel way).

The Holocaust dramatized how these vicious portraits can be utilized to set up the Jews for genocide and to justify mass murder; at the least, these degrading accounts encouraged Christian bystanding. After the Shoah, the leadership of the various mainstream Christian churches in the West determined to remove this cancer of hatred and began what is surely one of the great religious purifications of all time. Vatican II's "Nostra Aetate" was the bellwether of that movement.

There were two choices before the assembled bishops. The council could have communicated the polemical aspects of the Gospels and the facts of modern Gospel research. But the council (and to this day, the authorities) was afraid to undermine the simple faith of the masses. Alternatively, the council could have directly challenged the Gospels' own *adversos Judaeos* tradition as an example of the texts of terror that every religious tradition carries from the past–and distanced them. The opposition of the traditionalists and the fear of disillusioning the faithful led to a third choice. The council declaration hinted that the Jews never forfeited their election, and combined this compliment with a call/promise to teach the Gospels in such a way as to present the Jews not as cursed or reprobates of God. This tack left the Gospels' authority untouched. However, it left open the door for people like Mel Gibson, Tridentines who reject Vatican II's reforms, to continue to use the Gospel story to portray Jews as the hateful, spiritually decadent, and blind people who killed God, albeit not fully knowing what they did.

The bishops' failure to check this misuse puts the spotlight back on the Gospels. Read literally, they are primary sources of hatred and anti-Semitism. In order to atone for past sins and to prevent future evil acts based on Gospel writings, the bishops and the leaders of other churches must confront the New Testament (via modern scholarship or theological critique) or stand convicted of continuing the evils of the past.

The fact, as I believe, that most Americans will not act on the Gibson/Gospels' portrayal of the Jews does not get Christianity off the hook. Thank God, there are hundreds of millions of democrats, secularists, etc., who resist the uncorrected, pejorative aspects of the narratives in the Gospels. Among such people, awareness of the Gospels/Gibson as the source of a recurrent virus of hatred will hurt Christianity's credibility. The equation is simple but devastating. The more devout you are, the more likely you are to ignore modern scholarship and condemn a whole people unjustly and generate hateful images of others.

The second question is that the film overwhelmingly concentrates the Christian message on the crucifixion, that is, the suffering and death of Jesus

Christ. The Resurrection is hardly dealt with and barely referenced—although clearly the triumph of life is the central message of Christianity (and Judaism). Were we in the polemic stages of relationships between Jews and Christians, I could argue that this film turns Christianity into a faith focused on death. The Evangelical and conservative Catholic approbation of this movie derives from the film's glorification of Jesus' suffering for the sake of the forgiveness of human sins. But the psychology of a religious focus on the crucifixion glorifies martyrdom as against religious living. Historically, the focus on suffering privileged religious asceticism and led to denial of this worldliness, placing the emphasis on human sinfulness and the inability to repent. Is that where Christianity wants to go at a time when the chance to savor this world, to improve it, and to empower humans to serve God out of strength is at an all-time high? Dietrich Bonhoeffer, where are you when we need you!

Do Christians really want to insist on the centrality of satisfaction theology, the teaching that God demands the tortured death of God's son as the price of forgiveness of human sin? What does this say about the God of love of the New Testament that such infinite suffering is the divinely required payment for forgiveness? Ah, you say, but God takes on this suffering voluntarily out of love for humans. But what kind of love tortures one's self and one's beloved son out of love for another? I must add that it is truly chutzpah to hold this model up while speaking disparagingly of the God of the Old Testament as a God of wrath—when according to Jewish understanding, this God accepts the individual's wholehearted repentance willingly and lovingly, without demanding sacrifice or the torture killing of animals, humans, or the son of God.

Finally, the film distorts the Christian faith in yet another way. Despite the extended cruel lashings and sadistic crucifixion, Jesus is portrayed as almost untouched. He not only says the words of forgiveness with equanimity as if he were not in pain; he says the words "My God, my God, why have you forsaken me?" as if he were stating a triumphant praise. The film comes close to reviving the old Monophysite heresy—that Jesus is totally divine in nature. Neither his faith, his capacity for suffering, nor his serenity is touched by the supposed agony he is undergoing. It is almost as if, as a divine being, he looks on this breaking human body as a foreign object.

Gibson has managed to obscure the deepest, most powerful teaching of the Gospels on the crucifixion. The Gospels of Matthew and Mark (but not Luke or John) reveal the dark, bitter truth and the true lesson of the crucifixion. The agony was so intense, the pain so unendurable, that Jesus broke under the strain. To religious Christians this means that even God on the cross cracked under the pain and cried out in utter despair that God had forsaken him and that faith is lost. Then the true lesson is *not* that God is above all this pain and that human suffering in imitation of God is to be glorified as heroic. On the contrary, the lesson is that all who love God and love the human being in the image of God must do everything to prevent any more people from being put on the cross. We must revolt to overcome evil and take people down from the cross, lest future suffering servants be so overwhelmed by torture as to lose the faith and hope in God for whose sake the servant underwent the ultimate agony in the first place.

Christians—and all believers—should reject the glorification of suffering and rise to protest. With God, they must labor to correct a world in which too many innocents are crucified by poverty, hunger, oppression, war, and sickness. On God's behalf, all believers must strive to take away the power of tyrants and nations to abuse the innocent. True, suffering may sometimes ennoble. When there is no choice, the innocent may bear up under the strain and take refuge in the everlasting arms of God. But this response should always be a last resort. That Jesus returned love for hatred and blessing for torture should not be allowed to obscure his message. In life and in death, one should love, heal, rescue, and protect humans first—for as Jesus said, what you do unto the least of these, you do unto me.

Discussion Questions

1. Greenberg argues that the film is anti-Semitic as proven by its heightening and exaggeration of the Jewish bad traits portrayed in the New Testament. He suggests that nevertheless the New Testament Passion narrative itself is anti-Semitic. Some Christians argue that it is anti-Judaic, not anti-Semitic. What do you think?

2. Greenberg argues that the satisfaction theology of the film (i.e., Jesus as God's son is sacrificed to appease the Divine wrath against sinners) is bad for Christian theology and not just for Jews. What do you think? What other interpretations of the crucifixion might be offered?

3. It has been noted that despite wide viewership the film has not unleashed any visible wave of anti-Semitism. Greenberg attributes this to the strength of American democratic values and secular thinking and faults the bishops for not condemning the film. What is your explanation of this phenomenon? Do you think there has been negative fallout?

Gibson at the Crossroads

Penny Wheeler

Mel Gibson's *Passion of the Christ* is a cinematic tour de force which manages to humiliate both Christians and Jews. It humbles Christians by having their Christ—as well as his mother, apostles, and disciples—speak an incomprehensible Middle Eastern language, the language spoken by *his* people, the Jews. Jews, in turn, are embarrassed by the sight of some Jews kicking Jesus when he is obviously down, having offered no resistance to his captors. Gibson's insistence on Aramaic implies getting back to the original sources: the four Gospels of Christian scripture. From the outset, however, it is apparent that the filmmaker has sought other sources, some of whose contributions are highly questionable or outright erroneous, in order to flesh out the details. Finally, the viewer cannot help but conclude that this celluloid passion is as much about Gibson's differences with his own Roman Catholic Church as it is about the sufferings of Jesus.

The principal source that Gibson utilizes in addition to the four Gospels is a book entitled *The Dolorous Passion of Our Lord Jesus Christ.* This is an account of the visions of a nineteenth-century German mystic named Anna Katharina Emmerich, an Augustinian nun. Emmerich, however, did not write this volume. The actual author was Clemens Brentano, a contemporary who sat with Sister Anna Katharina and wrote down her visions as she described them to him. How does it happen that Anna Katharina Emmerich had incredibly detailed visions of the Passion of Jesus Christ and had to rely upon a scribe in order to record these visions? The answer to both queries lies in the fact that Sister Anna Katharina bore the *stigmata*.

To the non-Catholic, the very concept of stigmata seems at best morbid weirdness, at worst psychotic masochism. A stigmatist is one whose meditations upon the Passion and in particular the crucifixion of Jesus has resulted in physiological phenomena—usually bleeding lesions—situated in approximately the same areas as were the wounds received by Jesus during his actual crucifixion. The first person known to have received such lesions as a result of intense meditation was Francis of Assisi. A number of persons have since received these wounds, most of them women. The only priest known to have born the stigmata was the late Padre Pio, an Italian mystic who seems to have been able to "read souls," and who died in the late twentieth century. The Catholic Church is understandably reluctant to proclaim this phenomenon, and subjects mystics with such lesions to rigorous physical and psychological scrutiny. In any case, such phenomena result from deep meditation upon the details of the suffering of Jesus. From whence come these details? The point of departure of the individual mystic undoubtedly is an image from a book, from a statue, or from a stained-glass window that provides the first impetus to the imagination, upon which meditation depends.

One might well ask how it happens that Mel Gibson chose this particular source to fill in the details of the Passion in his film. There have, after all, been many accounts of the sufferings of Jesus, only a few of these emanating from stigmatists. The history of Christianity abounds with outpourings of pious literature. Why this particular source? While the presence of the stigmata definitely seems to lend authority to Sister Anna Katharina's vision, there is yet something else about her account that recommends it. The visions of this nun have a quality that is decidedly literary. Her account of the events leading up to the crucifixion are highly readable, yet the choice of vocabulary in no way panders to a poorly educated readership, as is so often the case in this genre. Despite the stylistic niceties of Emmerich's *Dolorous Passion*, however, there remain curious gaps—literally lapses of memory—in which the mystic cannot recall details of her vision. In these cases, which occur rather frequently, the first-person narrator simply states that she cannot remember various particulars. Some of these details seem inconsequential, but others are not, and the reader is often nonplussed to encounter Emmerich's frank confession of memory failure. The fact that Emmerich's vision has been recorded by a second party sets the narrative apart in yet another way: the near absence of the first-person pronoun, which abounds in other examples of the genre. Readers are not bombarded with descriptions of Emmerich's feelings. The narrator describes what she "sees," and the reader intuits her sentiments through her choice of adjectives.

What makes Emmerich's *Dolorous Passion of Our Lord Jesus Christ* so very readable even in the twenty-first century is the literary acuity of the man who transcribed it: German poet and novelist Clemens Brentano. A convert to Roman Catholicism, Brentano found his romantic soul stirred by reports of a local woman who bore the wounds of Jesus Christ and had visions of first-century Jerusalem. Intrigued, Brentano arranged for an introduction to the nun. Weak and sickly by nature, Anna Katharina became an invalid upon receiving the stigmata a year later. Fortunately a benefactor provided her with a room. Apparently persons from all sectors of society sought her counsel. Clemens Brentano—the pious convert—found Anna Katharina a beacon of spirituality, and was delighted to discover that they shared a birthday, the eighth of September. Fascinated by her detailed visions, Brentano asked her to relate them so that he could write them down. After her death Brentano withdrew to a monastery, where he lived for awhile in strict seclusion. He was to spend the latter part of his life in Frankfurt and Munich, where he devoted his literary energies to the propagation of the Catholic faith.

If Mel Gibson chose to heed Emmerich's visions—as opposed to the visions of others—it is because of Brentano. Similarly, it is due to Clemens Brentano's editing that Emmerich's *Dolorous Passion* opens with her vision of Gethsemane. It is more than a curious coincidence, then, that Mel Gibson's cinematic *Passion of the Christ* opens precisely where Emmerich's literary *Passion* opens: in the garden of Gethsemane. Gibson's is a monochromatic Gethsemane, whose shapes and textures layer blue upon blue upon blue. Gibson's Christ is heavily beset by the knowledge and fear of what is soon to transpire. As in the accounts of Mark, Matthew, and Luke, the apostles provide little moral support. They fall asleep. At this point one of Gibson's more interesting characters is heard from. Gibson introduces the character of Satan as a voice heard by the praying Jesus and by the viewer. The voice asks Jesus, "Who is your father?" The voice persists, pressing relentlessly: "Who are you?" Critical questions indeed are these, whose deceptive simplicity yet plumbs the depths of teleology and eschatology. And how skillful Gibson is to start with only the *voice* of Satan—that nagging of doubt that pries insistently at chinks in the armor.

Only after hearing the voice with its calm, seductive tones of sweet reason does the viewer see for the first time the androgynous being whose lack of eyebrows emphasizes the eyes that never once blink. Viewers see this creature, but if Jesus does, he pays it no heed. The only indication that he has noticed the intrusion of Satan into the velvety blue recesses of the garden is the sudden crunch of his foot upon the head of the serpent that seems to issue forth from the hooded figure. Whence comes this satanic image? Not from any of the four Gospel accounts. On the contrary, this evil intrusion into Gethsemane comes straight from the mystic whose visions so heavily influence Gibson's *Passion*. Indeed, Luke's Gospel presents quite a contrary image, that of a heavenly helper—an angel of God—whose presence in the garden is to console the suffering Jesus, whose achingly heartfelt prayer has brought about a phenomenon known to medicine as *hematidrosis:* the sweat of blood. Gibson, however, chooses to represent only the bloodshed inflicted from without—in this case by members of the temple guard—and avoids that which originates psychically. There is a strange paradox here, for that which recommends his nineteenth-century source so highly to pious Catholics is the presence on her body of the stigmata, lesions originating psychically. And Anna Katharina Emmerich's Satan "let loose his fury against Jesus, and displayed before the eyes of his soul increasingly awful visions"(100). Having presented Jesus with these scenarios,

Emmerich's Satan asks him: "Takest thou even this sin upon thyself? Art thou willing to bear its penalty? Art thou prepared to satisfy for all these sins?" (100). The notion of Satan's seductive query in Gethsemane carries over into the Gibson *Passion* word for word. Unlike Gibson, however, Emmerich also places angels in the garden; only Satan far overshadows them! Gibson evidently preferred a Gethsemane less cluttered with preternatural visitors, hence the single cloaked persona of the unblinking androgyne.

The inclusion of the Satan scene shows that Gibson is certainly not averse to going against the conventional portrayal of the Passion. He was definitely willing to break with tradition in some areas: the visible Satan, for instance; or having Jesus jostled off a bridge en route the headquarters of Caiaphas; having Jesus' mother and Mary Magdalen—accompanied by John—follow Jesus to the courtyard of Caiaphas, thus enabling a weeping Peter to confess to Mother Mary that he denied her son three times; having Claudia, the wife of Pilate, present Jesus' mother with two large pieces of white linen; and so forth. These innovations Gibson uncritically incorporates directly from Emmerich's visions. Of these, the confession of Peter serves a dramatic purpose and ties up a loose end. While all four Gospels mention Peter's denial of Jesus, no such confession is reported. The confession, however, gives devoutly Catholic Gibson the opportunity to show Blessed Mary at her most forgiving, truly "the Mother of Mercy." The introduction of the satanic androgyne and its occasional reappearance adds drama. The bound Jesus being shoved off a stone bridge underscores the brutality of his treatment at the hands of his captors, but this is gratuitous: the film has plenty of violence without adding more unnecessarily. As for Pilate's wife bestowing two large pieces of linen upon Jesus' mother, the scene comes out of nowhere and seems to serves no purpose. Indeed, the scene has exactly the same effect when it occurs in Anna Katharina Emmerich's vision narrative. However, this unwarranted intrusion into the nineteenth-century narrative does have a certain curious antecedent. In Clemens Brentano's *Life of Anne Catherine Emmerich,* which precedes the narrative of her visions, the reader learns that when Sister Anna Katharina professed her solemn vows at the age of twenty-nine, her father—who had been much opposed to his daughter's entering the convent—gave her two pieces of cloth, which, she said, constituted "the winding-sheet used for my spiritual burial in the convent" (13). Somehow the two pieces of cloth found themselves translated into a deep meditation upon events in first-century Jerusalem, and from there they were seized upon by Mel Gibson and thus make an appearance in his *Passion of the Christ.* The route may have been circuitous, but some very pedestrian details of life have found their way into mystical visions. It is the commonplace, after all, that fuels the imagination, enabling it to soar to faraway places and times far removed from the here and now. Why Gibson includes this strange scene, in which the two pieces of cloth undergo a highly unlikely transfer of ownership, has to do with his preoccupation with blood—not just with any blood, but with

The Blood. Jesus' mother and Mary Magdalen use this linen to soak up the blood of Jesus from the cobblestones of the courtyard where he has been scourged. The essence of Jesus' Passion, according to Gibson, lies in the blood.

Because of Gibson's fixation upon the blood of Jesus, one might be tempted to assume that he consulted medical sources during the planning stages of *The Passion of the Christ*. Indeed, Roman Catholic columnist James Bemis writes of a work which supposedly exerted great influence upon Gibson's film project. This was *A Doctor at Calvary*, written by French surgeon Pierre Barbet after a painstaking examination of the Shroud of Turin. To be sure, Gibson incorporates Barbet's description of the facial wounds of Jesus, including an abrasion below the right eye which causes it to swell shut early on. Barbet also describes the scourging with the *flagrum*, an instrument of torture consisting of a handle to which were bound several leather thongs with balls of lead on the ends that bit into the flesh of the victim, a detail which Gibson faithfully reproduces, over and over. Furthermore, Barbet states that normally the corpses of the crucified remain on their crosses, to be savaged by birds of prey and wild beasts, another detail that Gibson includes, to the horror of squeamish viewers. Gibson picks and chooses which details he wishes to incorporate from Barbet's scholarly treatise. In keeping with the blood theme, Gibson tends to accept that information from Barbet, who depends solely upon the Shroud of Turin—the ultimate Testament of Blood—for its verification, for example the facial lacerations, or the location of the wounds of the scourging.

Aside from his acceptance of the shroud—whose authenticity is another matter not within our purview here—Barbet sets forth two major theses, both of which run contrary to the traditional portrayal of the Passion, and neither of which depend upon the shroud for verification. Gibson rejects both of them. Barbet's first proposition is that Jesus did not carry the entire cross, but rather the *patibulum*, or crosspiece, in keeping with the imperial custom. The *stipes*, or upright, awaited the condemned at the place of execution. The English expression "to carry one's cross" is a synecdoche for the Roman phrase "*patibulum* ferre"—"to carry one's *patibulum*"—literally, to carry the transverse bar, or in a figurative sense, to accept one's punishment. This is why a condemned man was referred to by the Romans as a *patibulatus*, "he who must carry his *patibulum*." Quite apart from linguistic evidence, logistical considerations alone would indicate that Jesus bore only the one-hundred-pound *patibulum* rather than the complete cross, which would have weighed nearly two hundred twenty pounds. In his physical state, to carry one hundred pounds would have been quite a feat. It is interesting to note that Roman and Greek texts use the word *portare* or *bastazein* ("to carry"), respectively, and never *trahere* or *surein* ("to drag") (Barbet 48). In the case of slaves, for whom this punishment originated, the hands of the condemned were bound with ropes to the *patibulum*, which he would bear on his shoulders in the procession to the *stipes*. Gibson's two thieves bear their crossbars in this manner. Why does his Jesus not do the same? Perhaps Gibson was loathe to contradict centuries of pious Christian art depicting Jesus dragging the complete cross. In this regard it is important to remember that Constantine had banned crucifixion in the early fourth century. The crucifixion—a symbol of opprobrium—was never depicted in early Christian art. When the first crucifixes finally did appear at the end of the fifth century, it had been nearly two hundred years since the last such executions were carried out. People no longer understood the logistics of the process. Gibson had the opportunity to set the record straight on this matter. Perhaps he felt that to alter such a traditional visual effect would be too much of a gamble. Unfortunately, the viewer cannot help but notice the difference between the treatment of the thieves and that of Jesus. The less sophisticated viewer might well assume that it was the Jews—perhaps the high priest himself—who had insisted that Jesus, in his incredibly weakened condition, nevertheless be compelled to drag a weight twice as heavy, because of who he claimed to be. After all, had not Anna Katharina Emmerich envisioned that a Pharisee had dispatched seven slaves to fetch five pieces of wood to construct Jesus' cross? According to the nun's narrative, the slaves obtained these pieces of wood from the temple's fuel supply. Gibson mercifully does not go there, avoiding Emmerich's entire preparation of the cross scenario.

Pierre Barbet's other major argument has to do with the nailing of the hands of Jesus to the cross. In essence, he demonstrates conclusively that had the nails been driven through the palms, as is usually depicted in Christian art, they would not have been able to support the weight of Jesus' body, but would have ripped out between the fingers as soon as the body assumed an upright position. Barbet maintains that the nailing was done not through the palm, but through the carpal region at the base of the hand, in other words, through the wrist. Having performed a number of experiments, Barbet concludes that the radio-carpals actually separate when penetrated by a nail. The nail thus introduced ruptures the medial nerve, producing horribly agonizing pain. If Gibson did study Barbet's treatise, he chose to ignore this major segment, again opting for the more traditional depiction of the nailing through the palms of Christian art. This, however, would not have been nearly such a drastic visual departure as the more correct enactment of the carrying of the *patibulum*. Remember that Gibson dared to have his Jesus speak in Aramaic. It is odd that a filmmaker daring enough to present the dialogue in Aramaic—because it was *authentic*—would not also have wished to reenact the nailing in the only manner in which it possibly could have been accomplished. Did the influence of Sister Anna Katharina overshadow that of the French surgeon in this regard? One can only speculate. One thing is clear, however: Gibson the filmmaker consistently favors details with emotional appeal as opposed to those details supported by rational evidence.

The *patibulatus* of the Roman Empire normally faced a long and terrible death. This cruelest of tortures brings about a slow and agonizing death by asphyxiation. The outstretched arms bearing the weight of the body prevent the lungs from exhaling, hence normal oxygenation of the blood cannot take place. Severe muscle cramping occurs. Body temperature rises dramatically. The victim sweats profusely as he slowly suffocates. Abolished under Constantine as a means of punishment in the Roman Empire, crucifixion-style torture was employed by the Austrian and German armies during World War I and revived by the Nazis in the *Aufbinden* of Dachau. In a perverse paradox of history, the Jewish victims of the Nazi broken cross share the fate of the Jewish Jesus: crucifixion. Does Mel Gibson the moviemaker acknowledge the Jewish Jesus? When viewers hear Mary Magdalen ask Jesus' mother, "Why is this night different from every other night?" they realize that Gibson does indeed acknowledge the Jewish Jesus. But later in the film, when they hear, "His blood be upon us, and upon our children!" viewers realize that while Gibson may indeed *acknowledge* the Jewish Jesus, and actually accept him intellectually, Gibson still cannot *embrace* him, at least not at this point in his life.

However, there is one fact about Jesus that the filmmaker makes abundantly clear: Mel Gibson's Jesus certainly does have a Jewish mother. How is this possible? It comes about because Gibson evidently has read Anna Katharina Emmerich's visions cover to cover. The nun's narratives are curious in this regard. Her visions of the Passion are filled with fulminations against the Pharisees, who apparently rival Satan in their capacity for wickedness. After the death of Jesus, however, the mother of Jesus visits the temple. Emmerich's narrator paints a poignant picture of a Mary who is incredibly saddened by what has happened to her temple. As she examines the damage, her distress is palpable, and the reader cannot help but feel for this Jewish woman whose sanctuary has been desecrated. Twenty-first-century readers must remember that when Emmerich's account was written, German Jews were still ghettoized. They were truly *the* Other, especially for someone of so little sophistication who led so sheltered a life as Anna Katharina Emmerich.

Fast-forward two centuries to Mel Gibson, filmmaker—who, like his fellow Traditionalist Catholics, is all about "Us against the world." It is entirely possible that when he reads Emmerich's faultfinding with the Pharisees, he understands it not as invective against the infidel, but rather as the grumbling of a rebel against the intransigence of a well-entrenched religious hierarchy. Whiten his robes, and Gibson's high priest becomes the bishop of Rome, complete with a mitre that bears the cross! Often front and center, his gaze is steady and serious, yet not unkindly, although some of his underlings appear vituperative and cruel. The title of his film is *The Passion of the Christ,* but throughout the entire enterprise viewers sense the passion of Mel Gibson, seeking vindication in his struggle with the Catholic Church. He has offended a number of Jews and Catholics. As a *mea culpa* of expiation to those adversely affected by the Passion of Jesus, Gibson might well consider offering the passion of Judas—Judas Maccabaeus. The saga of the Maccabees would provide a most fitting and provocative *quid pro quo* that would unite rather than divide the children of Abraham.

Discussion Questions

1. How can one's religious beliefs color his/her view of a major event? Describe how one's religious beliefs might cause one to see
   a. a natural disaster such as a tsunami
   b. a closely contested presidential election.

2. This article mentions certain physiological manifestations that have been psychically induced. What were the author's examples? Can you think of additional examples ?

3. Imagine you are a moviemaker. What kind of source materials would you consult in order to make a film about
   a. the life of Anne Frank
   b. the life of Malcolm X
   c. the life of the Dalai Lama
   d. the life of Madonna
   e. the life of Martin Luther
   f. the life of Martin Luther King, Jr.
   g. the life of Francis of Assisi
   h. the life of Gandhi

Gibson's *Passion*

Yvonne Kozlovsky-Golan

Many critics claim that Mel Gibson's *The Passion of the Christ* is a violent movie, whose main theme is not Christ's vision of Christianity, but Gibson's vision of violence for its own sake.[1] A careful viewing reinforces this impression and identifies aesthetic, contextual and format-related flaws in the film. Yet this is not all; as we examine the movie and its context more closely we find subversive elements that reflect not merely a violent vision of pure sadism, but narrative and methodological contradictions that blatantly disregard the text of the Gospel according to Matthew and its historical connections and religious messages.

The subversive current in the film defies both the Gospel according to Matthew as accepted by most Catholics since Vatican II and the belief of Protestant Evangelists who see the King James Bible as the sole interpretation of the scriptures. The most important and conspicuous subversion appears in the sly criticisms that Gibson—the film actor and director America has embraced—expresses against American culture, the importance it assigns to law and order, and the sources of its faith and ideas.

The narrative and subjective aspect of the film most familiar to—and, some claim, most beloved of—the American viewer is the court and its legal proceedings.[2] In earlier research I have claimed that the American motion-picture industry's most outspoken and useful narrative has always been that of law and order, a narrative that has spawned innumerable films dealing with courts, laws, prisons, crime[3]—and lynching, which, although contrary to the legal system, somehow presents the American spirit of the time and place. In *The Passion* Gibson has cleverly used situations very familiar to American viewers as a result of their average four and a half hours a day of television-watching. During those hours Americans presumably see not just a screen but a reflection of their culture.

In *The Passion*, as in his previous movies, *Braveheart* (1995) and *The Pa-*

triot (2000), Gibson consciously caters to the American viewer's tastes. In these films we recognize a few familiar scenes from beloved old movies by such creators as Billy Wilder and Steven Bochco. Three main scenes in *The Passion* contain the juridical substance of the movie and encompass some of the elements mentioned above. One is Jesus' trial before the Sanhedrin; the second is the Sanhedrin's delivery of Jesus to Pilate as a traitor to be dealt with; and the third and decisive scene is the verdict and the transfer of blame for the crucifixion from the Romans to the Jews: "His blood be on us and on our children."

American cinema's normative conception of the American legal system tends to show in its emphasis on that system's orderly conduct and efficiency. No matter what the plot, the mistake is always the individual's, and justice is explicitly embodied by the All-American system. This is evident in the contrast Gibson builds into the scene of Christ appearing before the Sanhedrin. In it Christ, a symbol of virtue and honesty, stands against the anachronistic Jewish Sanhedrin. The Sanhedrin, as Gibson sees it, is the primitive relic of an unorganized, obscure, mob-driven system. This Jewish body, although historically a council of seventy, is portrayed here as small but noisy and emotional, swaying with the mood of the proceedings, in stark contrast to Christ's calm, stoic peace. This is the Jewish law system according to Gibson: A system in which Jewish racial motivation contrasts with the composed demeanor of the Euro-American Christ figure and his post-modern association with the Hellenistic commonwealth. Gibson's trial scene inevitably evokes anti-Semitic claims about the Jewish thirst for blood, the sacrifice of human innocents for religious rituals, and especially the creation of conflict and controversy in order to glorify Judaism and discredit any objector as "sick."

While early on, following a scene that supposedly represents an internal quarrel in the Jewish community, the educated viewer may accept Christ's Jewish origins, imagining that he may actually belong to the noisy, grotesque group blabbering about his deeds, the next scene undercuts this impression by creating a dichotic division between the protagonists: The Jews are ridiculous, dressed in Muslim burkas (unsurprisingly similar to those seen in televised broadcasts from Afghanistan), while we civilized Westerners are dressed in Roman haute-couture and bare-limbed, just like Christ standing in the midst of an angry Jewish mob, swathed with rags and hatred. We believe in due process and an orderly trial, as opposed to the stammering Hebrew law system, which is turned into a pseudo lynch-party. The cognitive impression that Gibson creates seeks to glorify the "new-generation" savior, but at the same time it ridicules and degrades not only the Jews but also the Protestant believers who see in the Old Testament a strong infrastructure of faith and ideas based on divine law. This faith is the heart of the religious concept held by the Anglo-Saxon society that Gibson lives in and from, and Gibson's muckraking approach to this ancient world, unsupported by any real evidence from the New Testament, does injustice to the believers in both New and Old Testaments.

One example is the cruel beating of Jesus depicted in the scene of his capture. As Matthew describes the scene with the Sanhedrin, "Then did they spit in his face, and buffeted him; and others smote him with the palms of their hands, Saying, Prophesy unto us, thou Christ, Who is he that smote thee?" (Matt. 26:67–68). Beyond this, there is no scriptural evidence of physical abuse by the Jews. They do tease and taunt him about his prophecies and his Father, who cannot help him. Even the Roman abuse and beatings are not explicitly described in the Bible. Jesus was flogged and handed over for crucifixion. He was ridiculed in front of the legion and told: "Hail, King of the Jews! And they spit upon him, and took the reed, and smote him on the head. And after that they had mocked him, they took the robe off from him, and put his own raiment on him, and led him away to crucify him" (Matt. 27:29–31). This describes the usual treatment of condemned men at the time. Gibson gives it a cinematic representation and demonic vision that could be called arrogant, since he has taken it upon himself to play the role of the last prophets. To further the plot, Gibson exploits the audience's identification with screen heroes—a magic formula that is one of the cornerstones of Hollywood cinematic technique. It is based on a sophisticated script that is shaped by the producer's social and cultural criticism.

How does Gibson absolve the Roman governor? Ultimately, it was he who, in a few words, pronounced the Messiah's sentence, had him flogged (despite having inquired in puzzlement shortly before: "Why, what evil hath he done?") and sent him to the cross: "Then released he Barabbas unto them: and when he had scourged Jesus, he delivered him to be crucified" (Matt. 27:26). The answer is Gibson's identification with the aggressor; however innocent Pilate may be, his soldiers were obeying his command. To reconcile the Christian audience's conflicting feelings of anger and pity, Gibson calls on their personal knowledge of legal trials and government.

Pilate, judge and final arbiter of the accusations against Christ, finds himself politically squeezed between, on the one hand, his commitment to the local population (the Jews) who demand a "just trial" according to their faith, and, on the other, his commitment to preserve political and social peace in the province he was sent to govern on behalf of the Roman Empire. To illuminate Pilate's complicated position, Gibson evokes associations to which the viewer can relate from personal experience. Pilate plays the same role as an American judge, who is often an elected official with a responsibility to public opinion and morality. It is clear to the American viewer that in Pilate's day, like today, the judge's commitment and expected verdict are political and voter-influenced rather than motivated by any personal aspiration to justice. The civilian government, claims Gibson, is essentially cruel and blind to truth. Accordingly, the man who does see the truth (Pilate) is granted a forgiveness on celluloid that the Scriptures do not seem to warrant.

But Gibson's anarchistic "truth" is a cinematic cliché: Birds flying free above the condemned man, skies covered by the clouds that seek to envelop the tortured martyrs, a plagiarized series of quotes copied exactly from Karl Drier's *The Passion of Joan of Arc* (1928) and John Ford's *Mary of Scotland* (1934), and even colorful replicas of the dawn portrayed in *The Chamber* (1996) on the day the racist hero is led to his death. Unexpectedly, the role of conscience is portrayed by Pilate's wife, representing, in Gibson's vision, the primary Christian concept of compassion and love for all men, which is focused on the body of the Jew brought to trial by her husband. It is Claudia, with her white robes and towels, and the white skin of the master race, who demonstrates a pure, unbiased faith that represents, according to Gibson, basic Christian purity. The fleshly Judaism represented by Mary, Jesus' Jewish mother, and Mary Magdalene fades in Gibson's version; their role is merely symbolic, consisting in following Jesus, wiping up his blood, and crying tears of love on the day of the crucifixion. A similar but opposite role is played by the devil in Jerusalem, who follows Christ with a sense of satisfaction, very pleased with himself. (His image is not described by Matthew, but derives from Gibson's imagination and the writings of a nineteenth-century German nun, Anna Katharina Emmerich, that Gibson translated into a cinematic manifestation claimed to be "true to the source.")

Another Gibson criticism is directed at "government violence" in the United States, implemented by the death penalty. Here he is obviously targeting the fundamentalist Christian community in America, which is the only major religious community in the Western world that still supports this irreversible form of punishment. The story of Jesus of Nazareth, the holiness of the innocent man walking to his death, and the price he pays for his faith are the main arrows that Gibson aims at the fundamentalist society in which he lives. Gibson uses a heart-breaking story, full of pathos, to impress upon the American viewer the Catholic view that supposedly forbids the death penalty as an arbitrary punishment imposed by man upon man.

However, Gibson's manipulation of this audio-visual sequence shows up the ignorance of this would-be educator: the Catholic Church accepted the principle of capital punishment as an option, and even recommended it to a leadership whose authority was derived from Scripture.[4] For centuries, in fact, the Christian world used capital punishment and torture as tools of control, on which it based its political, social, and religious agenda. Only since the reign of John XXIII and the Second Vatican Council—which Gibson opposes—and especially during John Paul II's time has the Church shown any opposition to capital punishment.

Moreover, the argument over the death penalty is apparently far from over, since fundamentalist Protestants in the U.S. insist on following religious law. Unlike Catholics, however, they have anchored it in a secular legal framework, while giving the Constitution a more flexible interpretation. The early argument for capital punishment was based on the Scriptures. The pro-death-penalty camp based its argument on the Old Testament's "eye for an eye"; opponents cited the New Testament exhortation to "turn the other cheek."[5] Although the dispute may seem to have waned in some eras, the idea that a man must pay for his sins has always endured. "Social" or "logical" factors were secondary.

Another religious element derives from the Protestant interpretation (as expressed in the King James translation) of Jesus' "the law of the kingdom is the law." When Jesus was asked whether tax collectors were to be paid, he held up a coin and asked, "Whose picture is on the coin?" "The Emperor," was the reply. "Then," said Jesus, "render unto Caesar what is Caesar's." This interpretation also applies to capital punishment, according to Protestant clergy who support it and serve as spiritual leaders in jails. In their opinion, even if we oppose a penalty and view it as contrary to the law of nature, we must accept the edict of the sovereign, the secular law maker (as opposed to divine law), and obey it. The Papacy today does not accept this interpretation, asserting instead that God is the sole arbiter of human life. And Jews—whose law gave rise to these ideas—have opposed the death penalty since the time of Jewish independence between the Greek and Roman occupations.

The Catholic Church, until recently a proponent of capital punishment, returns to its sources, basing its opposition to the death penalty on the same principle as the Jews: because man is made in the "image of God." More than once the Vatican has pleaded for clemency on behalf of a condemned American, in the name of Christ and the sanctity of life. Such papal appeals are sometimes accompanied by similar pleas from Jewish traditional and religious organizations. Their opposition derives from early Jewish thought on the subject of capital punishment, as developed during the Second Temple era (500 BC to 70 AD), when the biblical interpretation evolved from the "*pshat*" (literal interpretation) of "an eye for an eye" to the "*drash*" (rational and imaginative adaptive interpretation). This was the era when verbal interpretations and laws were beginning to form and to govern day-to-day life—the beginning of the process that formed present-day Judaism. The main elements of the *drash* from the Torah came from the "death" laws that had been used by previous generations. These evolving laws contradicted the Bible's literal "eye for an eye" and replaced it with rulings that "eye for an eye" meant material compensation. The apparent contradiction was explained by the belief that both the written Torah given to Moses on Mount Sinai and the oral Torah, as its updated interpretation, are equal in importance. By Christ's time, the Sanhedrin was rarely asked to consider the death penalty. Jewish literature claims that a Sanhedrin that pronounced a death sentence once every seventy years was called a "murderous" Sanhedrin.

If the occasion did arise to bring the deadly dilemma before the Sanhedrin, then the Talmudic principle of striving to find grounds for exemption applies.[6] First, in order to save the accused from death, the Sanhedrin tried to establish points in his favor (including trying to find defects in testimony and increasing the number of witnesses needed to convict from two to four, so that the decision could be made with a pure conscience and clean hands). Second, if a decision was reached unanimously (all seventy judges) then a mistrial was declared, since it was inconceivable that not a single point in favor of the condemned could be found among seventy judges. Moreover, the Sanhedrin restrained itself as much as possible, since it wanted to prevent massive loss of life. The fear was that a license to kill might become "second nature" and the death penalty would be widespread. The Sanhedrin prohibited the establishment of norms and values that injured human dignity; it feared the indifference to human life that might arise, both in the taking of one person's life by another and in the state's use of capital punishment against its citizens.

Gibson, uninterested in such "minor details," is blind to this difference between Jewish thought and Protestant beliefs. He prefers to view both as one and attack them simultaneously, the first for inventing capital punishment and the second for adopting it into the American way of life. Although the Catholic Church only began to object to the death penalty in the last few decades, Gibson apparently has no qualms in attributing it to the Jews and attacking the Protestants who endorse it, while portraying the Romans as true Christians with no blood on their hands. For Gibson, the Jews chose the death penalty, and the Jews support untimely human death. This covert yet blatant defiance never relinquishes the anti-Semitic elements that underlie it.

First, the unconcealed intolerance here emphasized as a main Jewish theme, is actually the director's intolerance for the Jewish subjects of the film. He creates a visual dichotomy, in color, form and substance, between the good and the bad, between martyrs and assassins. A second point is that the film is anti-Semitic not only in its grotesque imaging of the Jews, but also in the way the Jewish trial is portrayed. The barbaric disorder of the exchange with Pilate, the noise and shouts, are all stereotypes of Jewish character. The priests' self-interested call for the death of Christ is the "kosher" imprint that allows Gibson to build scenes in which Jews are portrayed with the traditional stereotypes and biases. The *Ordnung*, the European order so cherished by Gibson, is gradually lost, scene by scene, while the Jewish trial prevails: with no separation between defense and prosecution, all is made in sin; the sin of Jewish barbarism, religion, tradition and people.

In the Passion that Gibson has invented, one does not die for one's sins as is taught, according to him, by the death-penalty-supporting Jewish and Protestant fundamentalist faiths. The crucifixion—that is, the killing of multi-humanism incarnated in one body in order to proclaim the salvation of humanity—was the mother of all sins. And the burden of this sin will be borne by all those, Jews or fundamentalist Protestants and their children, who believe in crucifixion as a punishment for sin. The condemnation of Christ's execution in modern terms strengthens Gibson's thesis concerning the guilt of those advocating the "Jewish" concept of the death penalty and their involvement in the fatal decision and responsibility for the death of the Christian Savior.

Thus, religious and legal narratives are used concurrently and support each other. Moreover, the juridical scenes are validated by cinematic experiences already present in the mind of the viewer, derived from such films as Drier's *Joan of Arc* (1928), Wilder's *Ben-Hur* (1959), Kubrick's *Spartacus* (1960), and others. All Gibson does is rearrange them and present them in a different light. In *The Passion,* Gibson places the priests and the crowd on the steps of the Roman governor's palace, in a scene remarkably reminiscent of pre-lynching scenes in such well-known Hollywood movies as Fritz Lang's *Fury* (1936) or Robert Mauling's *To Kill a Mockingbird* (1962). In these scenes, a bloodthirsty mob confronts the law (usually the sheriff) on the steps of the local jail or courthouse, demanding that the (usually innocent) defendant be handed over to them. Most of these mobs come from the American "Bible Belt," an area inhabited largely by fundamentalist Protestants whose intolerance towards such outsiders as Jews, African-Americans, and Catholics is infamous. Most lynchings took place in these states. Today, the support for capital punishment in these states produces a fair crop of executions—218 during George W. Bush's administration as governor of Texas, for example.

For Gibson this is enough to subvert all that represents America and to attack an issue that is important to 30 percent of Americans. He stages a known and accepted story, played by actors, while at the same time showing the viewers their own wretchedness. On the one hand, he challenges the basic American concept of law and order, based on the Protestant approach to dealing with serious offenses: an eye for an eye, and dying for one's sins. On the other hand he confronts his audience with the cruelty visited on the innocent martyr. The death of a saint, Gibson claims, is an indictment of all those who believe in the death penalty, Jews and Protestant Americans included. Yet he glorifies the Catholics (or the future Catholics—the Romans) and their objection to the death of a martyr. Gibson might seem to be offering a sophisticated, faith-based interpretation, but he trips over his righteous intents. As a fanatic believer who has rejected Vatican II, and perhaps as a myopic producer, he is unable to portray Christ's vision and universal values in either the subtext or the actual dialogue of the film. The true danger lies in his eagerness to present his own vision. Gibson's influence over the viewer's senses, achieved by force of the visual impact of the narrative he chooses to describe, presents the American and Western viewer with a clear and coherent conceptual framework. Thus, a false and deceptive framework is convincingly shown as raw truth.

The cinematic text is also problematic in an area that might be thought to pose no danger: the public execution. There is considerable debate among researchers and legal and media experts as to whether the process of execution should be revealed to the public. The debate centers on four main issues:

The public's right to know;
The privacy and anonymity of the condemned;
Public peace and welfare; and
Deterrence.

Although one might assume that the controversy over these points is between those who approve and those who oppose the death penalty, in fact it crosses boundaries, proving that the debate over capital punishment is much more complicated than it appears, and revealing how easy it is to manipulate audiences through cinema. Ideologically, capital-punishment proponents support publicity, since it has a deterrent effect. Opponents claim that public punishment not only does not deter, but actually encourages violence. Past experience has shown that public executions are not only ineffective as deterrents, but create controversy and attract disorderly crowds. For this reason, executions were brought indoors in 1937, away from the public and with a minimal number of witnesses. There is no written documentation of these executions—only a handful of witnesses and audio recordings of the closed-circuit communications between jail officials.

Prison executives, in the name of the government, justify all this on the basis of the right of the condemned to privacy and anonymity. Intellectual objectors to capital punishment, however—usually liberals who sanctify the right to privacy, ironically enough—have demanded that executions be public, so that citizens can see them. They claim that the decision to hide executions from the public eye from beginning to end fosters distrust of the government: "In executions there is an act of government hidden completely from the public."[7] Given the public's "right to know," the execution should be widely broadcast in order to influence viewers' intellectual perceptions.

In this respect it is interesting to note the attitude of two liberal researchers. Media expert Wendy Lesser criticizes the presentation of capital punishment on television and in films.[8] She claims that instead of simply imagining the infliction of the punishment, viewers are made to feel they are there. Since they know they are not, their perception is clearly unrealistic, and they have no real sense of the cruelness of the punishment. In contrast, Austin Sarat claims that the death penalty should be public.[9] His reasoning is that when it is held away from the public view, it becomes invisible, absent from the public consciousness. The public, Sarat claims, must see the infliction of capital punishment and realize the cruelty involved. Then it can make a more balanced judgment on the punishment than it could without seeing the effect of its stance. Gibson adopts this view and takes it further. Death and its cruelty receive full public recognition in *The Passion.*

Christ's torture by Pilate demeans both men more than it immortalizes them. Under the pretext of reliving the Gospel, Gibson attacks and subverts both mainstream Christianity (Catholic and Protestant) and America and its most precious jewel, its legal system. He does this by demonizing the Jews and their legal system, while in fact insinuating the American system's resemblance to the barbaric proceedings—much as Shiite rites are portrayed on global news today.

The ugliness of the blood takes on a barbaric, fundamentalist significance, turning Jesus' Christianity into paganism. The love of torture and its acceptance as part of a death ritual is in no way part of Christianity, but in complete contrast to Christian teachings of love. Gibson's decision to make Christ's noble death a gory portrait of man's cruelty to man is completely opposite to Christ's belief in man. It makes a mockery of Christianity in general and the teachings of Christ in particular. Christianity, and the American legal system, are turned here from divine ideology to an earthly depiction of gore, concerned mainly with the flesh and the visual impression of pain.

Discussion Questions

1. What are the article's main points of criticism against Gibson's *Passion?*
2. What tools does Gibson use to convey his criticism, overt and covert?
3. Can we assume that Gibson reconciled the methodological and theological conflicts of the script with the reality of the New Testament?

Notes

1. Leon Wieseltier, "Mel Gibson's Lethal Weapon: The Worship of Blood," *The New Republic*, 26 Feb. 2004.
2. Yvonne Kozlovsky Golan, "'Until You Are Dead': The Death Penalty in the USA and Its Representation in Motion Pictures" (Ph.D. diss., University of Haifa, 2003).
3. Anthony Chase, *Movies on Trial: The Legal System on the Silver Screen* (New York: New Press, 2002).
4. Bryan Vila and Cynthia Morris (eds.), *Capital Punishment in the United States: A Documentary History* (Westport, CT: Greenwood Press, 1997).
5. The "eye-for-an-eye" argument is based on: "And he that killeth any man shall surely be put to death. And he that killeth a beast shall make it good; beast for beast. And if a man cause a blemish in his neighbor; as he hath done, so shall it be done to him; Breach for breach, eye for eye, tooth for tooth: as he hath caused a blemish in a man, so shall it be done to him again. And he that killeth a beast, he shall restore it: and he that killeth a man, he shall be put to death" (Lev. 24:17–21). It is countered by: "Ye have heard that it hath been said, an eye for an eye, and a tooth for a tooth: But I say unto you, that ye resist not evil: but whosoever shall smite thee on thy right cheek, turn to him the other also" (Matt. 5:38–39), as well as "Thou shalt not kill" (Exod. 20:13).

   Other arguments for capital punishment that are often cited:

   > A. Whoso sheddeth man's blood, shall man shed his blood: for in the image of God made he man (Gen. 9:6).
   >
   > B. Let every soul be subject unto the higher powers. For there is no power but of God: the powers that be are ordained of God. Whosoever therefore resisteth the power, resisteth the ordinance of God: and they that resist shall receive to themselves damnation. For rulers are not a terror to good works, but to the evil. Wilt thou then not be afraid of the power? Do that which is good, and thou shalt have praise of the same: For he is the minister of God to thee for good. But if thou do that which is evil, be afraid;

for he beareth not the sword in vain: for he is the minister of God, a revenger to execute wrath upon him that doeth evil (Rom. 13:1–4).

C. He that leadeth into captivity shall go into captivity: he that killeth with the sword must be killed with the sword. Here is the patience and the faith of the saints (Rev. 13:10).

All the biblical quotations are from the Authorized (King James) Version.

6. Babylonian Talmud, Masechet Makkot, 7A.
7. Austin Sarat, *When the State Kills: Capital Punishment and the American Condition* (Princeton, NJ: Princeton University Press, 2001).
8. Wendy Lesser, *Pictures at an Execution: An Inquiry into the Subject of Murder* (Cambridge: Harvard University Press, 1993).
9. Sarat, *When the State Kills.*

Where Are the Flies? Where Is the Smoke?

The Real and Super-Real in Mel Gibson's The Passion

Bruce Zuckerman

First of all, I have to make confession: I really did not want to see this film. I wasn't reluctant because I thought that the message conveyed about Jews and/or Christians, ancient and/or modern, might prove "problematic" (as we scholars like to say when we want to choose a polite word for something we do not like for one reason or another). If anything, the problematic potential of Mel Gibson's *The Passion* was more of an inducement to go see it than a disincentive. Truth be told: I'm squeamish. I do not like depictions of blood and gore, nor do I get much of a charge out of graphic violence, gratuitous or otherwise. I never could sit through all of *Schindler's List,* and as for *Jurassic Park*, my lack of intestinal fortitude sent me ducking and cringing every time some evil raptor began to rattle its cage. I don't even go near a slasher film. Early word from those who boldly rushed in where I feared to tread confirmed my worse fears: If I were going to see this movie, I would have to endure a veritable *Nightmare on the Via Dolorosa.* I knew myself better than that: No question—I would rather sit this one out.

Still, as I began to read and hear more and more about the movie from its fans and critics, certain prominent, salient themes came to the forefront that began to pique my curiosity. In particular, I kept hearing about how authentic everything was: This was no "greatest story ever told" in the Cecil B. DeMille manner with a white-berobed, somewhat prissy Jesus and with Romans clothed in flashy armor, short-shorts and stylish red capes who all speak with the distinct accent of the British upper-crust. No indeed. Careful research had been done—and the result was a film more concerned with history than histrionics. For example, Romans spoke vernacular Latin, Jews intoned the local dialect of Aramaic, the scenes in Jerusalem and its environs were designed to depict the gritty look and feel of a hard-scrabble first-century town at the ragged edge of the Roman Empire.

In particular, I was told that the scenes depicting the scourging of Jesus, his march to Golgotha and his crucifixion were hard-core to the point of being brutal. No aspect of Jesus' suffering was left to the imagination, friends told me (either in awe or in horror—sometimes both). You were compelled to witness *everything:* every blow struck, every welt raised, every wound, every bruise, every nail driven into writhing flesh and especially every aspect of the slow torture and strangulation on the cross. Granted, there were a few quibbles about the accuracy of some of the realism. A few friends who know about these things carped in emails about small, perceived grammatical errors in the spoken Aramaic while others complained that the Romans improperly used "Church Latin" and ought to have been speaking *koine* Greek, anyway. Still, as far as I could gather, everyone I talked to pretty much conceded the main point: That every effort had been invested by Mel Gibson and his team into making this story of the last hours of the life of Jesus Christ as authentic as such things can be. Even the Pope, according to published accounts, conceded as much when, after a private viewing of the movie, he was overheard to say "It is as it was."[1]

Of course, I (Mr. Squeamish) had no way of judging or weighing just how realistic *The Passion* was in terms of its portrayal of the suffering and death of Jesus. All I had to go on was the testimony of those brave souls who had borne witness on my behalf. Still, I began to wonder just how real *The Passion*'s realism really was and, upon due consideration, I came up with what I decided might be a good way of testing its authenticity without actually having to see things for myself. So the next time someone came up to ask me if I had seen *The Passion*, wanting to know what I thought of it, I responded by saying, "No, I haven't seen it; but maybe *you* can help me decide what I think of it." Then I asked the question I had been saving for just this precise, opportune moment:

"Tell me," I said, "were there any flies?"

After the predictable look of surprise in response to this apparent *non sequitur*, my companion answered, "Yes, well, I guess so. I seem to remember some flies on a dead carcass, maybe on a dog or a horse or something."

"No," I persisted, "let me be more specific. Were there any flies at the crucifixion scene, any flies of *any* sort crawling over the crucified body and face of Jesus?"

Again this brought a look of consternation, followed by puzzlement and finally (to judge by the way my companion screwed up his brow) an effort at recollection. "No," he finally replied. "I suppose not. I can't recall seeing any flies on Jesus, himself."

My question about flies and Jesus was hardly random. One of the most gripping descriptions of the crucifixion of Jesus—one that has indelibly marked the way I see that scene in my mind's eye—comes from the creative imagination of the great Russian novelist Mikhail Bulgakov, in his most famous work, known in English as *The Master and Margarita.* And what makes his death-of-Christ scene always seem so utterly and completely real to me is the prominent role he ascribes to the insect-population of Golgotha. The climactic scene of Jesus' last moments, hanging between the two thieves, unfolds in Bulgakov's laconic narrative as follows:

> Yeshua had been more fortunate than the other two. In the first hour he had had intermittent fainting spells, and then he lost consciousness. His head, in its straggly turban, hung on his chest and he was, therefore, so covered with flies that his face had disappeared beneath a black, heaving mask. Fat horseflies clung to his groin, stomach and armpits, sucking on his naked yellow body.
>
> In response to a sign made by the man in the hood, one of the executioners took a spear, and another brought a bucket with a sponge over to the post. The one with the spear raised it and ran it along each of Yeshua's arms, which were stretched out along the crossbeam on the post and fastened to it with ropes. The body with its protruding ribs gave a shudder. The executioner ran the end of the spear over his stomach. Then Yeshua raised his head and the flies took off with a buzzing sound, thus revealing the hanged man's face. Bloated from bites, and with swollen eyelids, his face was unrecognizable.[2]

There are a number of reasons why, when I first began to hear about Gibson's *The Passion* and the ambitions of its creators, I immediately began to make a connection with *The Master and Margarita*. In many respects Bulgakov and Gibson shared much the same goal: to portray a tough, no-holds-barred depiction of the last hours of Jesus. Like Gibson, Bulgakov underscored the genuineness of his depiction of the times in every way he could. For example, he eschewed the Hellenized names one finds conventionally in the New Testament in favor of more authentic, Semitic versions: Thus "Yeshua ha-Nozri" in lieu of "Jesus of Nazareth," "Yerushalaim" for "Jerusalem" and so on. While Bulgakov allows his characters conventionally to communicate in Russian, he nonetheless makes sure that the reader understands that, when Yeshua speaks, he does so in Aramaic, while the Romans talk to each other in Latin and to the local population in Greek (which, as noted by my linguist colleagues, would certainly have been the preferred case in Gibson's film, too). Bulgakov's descriptions of Jerusalem are meticulously detailed and filled with technically correct, contemporary terminology, based, in so far as I can gather, on solid, historical research. Like Gibson, Bulgakov has spared no effort to convince his readers that when they read about the last hours of the life of Jesus in *The Master and Margarita*, this is the *real deal.*

In this respect, Bulgakov's tour de force, in my opinion, is his depiction of the crucifixion scene with so prominent an emphasis placed on the flies. What makes this so brilliant is that—as soon as he introduces flies into the picture—the reader instinctively grasps that, not only is this *right*, but, by the same token, *any* other crucifixion scene that lacks a cloud of insects feeding on Jesus' flesh—and that, of course, means just about *every* other crucifixion scene depicted in art, literature and film for the last 2,000 years—is *wrong*. Of course there were flies! Flies would have been the first arrivals at the feast routinely served up by the executioners on Golgotha. By the time Jesus was crucified, the insects would have been very well trained.

Because Bulgakov is so masterful in his narration of the story of Jesus, his readers believe in the reality he labors so long and hard to depict; more than that, they *want* to believe. On the other hand, if we step back from the immediate moment of Jesus at the point of death with his accompanying cloud of flies and look at *The Master and Margarita* in a broader perspective, we might well hesitate to take Bulgakovian reality at face value. For one thing, the actual Jesus-narrative is portrayed in the novel as a story within a story—in fact a work of fiction first narrated to us by none other than the Devil himself, then continued as a dream materialized from the frenzied imagination of an apparent maniac locked away in a psychiatric ward and finally written as a flimsy typescript manuscript of a novel, soon to be burned up by it despairing author. None of these venues for the reality of the crucifixion could be considered models of fixed and certain reliability.

Moreover, the story of Jesus presented by Bulgakov does not attempt carefully to mirror the Gospel accounts. In fact, on almost every level Bulgakov subtly endeavors to subvert the "authentic" biblical narratives and substitute for them his alternate version of reality. We are told that the "official" versions all stem from the misguided efforts of a former tax-collector, called Levi Matvei (the Gospel's Matthew), who had somehow gotten an obsessive fixation on Jesus. In fact, it was Matvei's fanatic promotion and misrepresentation of Yeshua's teachings that had attracted the attention of the Roman authorities in the first place and had led to Jesus' arrest, condemnation and execution.

According to Bulgakov Matvei created the "official" Jesus we find in the Gospels out of his own guilt and hero-worship. But the *real* story, Bulgakov tells us, the *lowdown*, actually went rather differently.

Thus, in *The Master and Margarita* Bulgakov seems to take particular delight in bending reality—making "gospel truth" appear to be a pious, sanitized fiction: a pale substitute for the fly-ridden authority of his own account—even though his novel is self-evidently purely the work of his imagination. This is, in fact, Bulgakov's major objective throughout the novel: making reality seem imaginary while the imaginary is made to seem all too real. The question he leaves open for his reader to ponder is this: Where, then, is one to find The Truth? Is it to be found in what is "real" or in what is "imagined"?

Another recent film also makes a close examination of this same question—*The Matrix*, especially the first movie in the series, as opposed to the far more inferior and derivative second (*The Matrix Reloaded*) and third (*The Matrix Revolutions*) installments. Curiously enough, I found I had no difficulty watching and even enjoying *The Matrix*, although, ostensibly, there is far more violence in it than in Gibson's *The Passion*. I found the violence of *The Matrix* far easier to take because it is remarkably free of graphic, gruesome carnage; when people get blown apart, they die cleanly. To be sure, buildings of glass and stone as well as the bullets and bullet casings fly around everywhere but hardly anything in the way of blood and guts. Indeed the way people are dispatched in *The Matrix* might best be described as artistic, even ballet-like, as both killers and killed engage in choreographed duels of elegant homicide, lovingly depicted, frequently in stop action and slow motion.

Recently, I had a chance to see *The Matrix* again, and I found that I my reaction to it—and particularly the way it depicted violence and death—had profoundly changed in the world we now live in, under the shadow of the horrific events of 9/11. First of all, I realized there was something fundamentally wrong about the movie, something that did not jibe with what I now knew, indeed, what I had eye-witnessed on TV about unfolding, urban disaster. The scene in the movie that particularly stands out in this respect seems now a prescient foreshadowing of the destruction of the Twin Towers of the World Trade Center. It involves a helicopter that careens into a modern glass building (once again depicted in slow motion). In one respect, the depiction seems dead on: like the planes that hit the Towers, the helicopter at first almost seems virtually to be swallowed up by the building which then erupts in a ball of fire and shattered, flying glass. Against this backdrop of a building disintegrating before our eyes, the heroine, Trinity, is clearly outlined zooming Tarzan-like across the screen as she uses a cable held by the hero, Neo, to swing out of the helicopter miraculously to safety. Outside of the fact that she emerges from this "perils-of-Pauline" escape with scarcely a bump or a bruise (a cliché that the James Bond movies have made so much a Hollywood staple that I was therefore preprogrammed readily to accept it), I realized that there was something *else* that was not credible, something that my eye-witness knowledge of 9/11 no longer allowed me to accept as a valid part of the scene.

For a little while I was not quite certain what it was, and then, like the flies at Golgotha, I suddenly *knew* what was missing: Where was the smoke? One thing that watching the Twin Towers collapse had taught me was that, when modern buildings of steel and glass crumple into a heap, they generate an all-encompassing cloud of debris-filled smoke that billows out like a tidal wave of destruction, covering everything, obscuring everything, blasting aside everything and everyone in its way. But in *The Matrix* there is no such cloud of smoke: Neo and Trinity don't even need to dust themselves off. There is another scene of similar smokeless destruction in the movie. A bomb is set off in an elevator shaft, and we watch—more in fascination than horror—as a bright orange fire undulates in slow, fluid motion to fill and then incinerate the entire first floor of the structure. The fire seems to reach everywhere, but again: There is no smoke, no debris. The destruction somehow seems to leave everything clean as a whistle.

Mind you, it doesn't take much imagination to understand why the creative artists who produced *The Matrix* preferred their fireworks to be smokeless. First and most obviously, smoke is not particularly photogenic. How are you going to see the actors do their heroic acts of daring-do, their "stunts," if smoke gets in your eyes? Perhaps even more to the point, we should remind ourselves that, according to the guiding premise of *The Matrix,* nothing that happens in the Matrix is *real* anyway; it's just a simulation created by dastardly machines to lull away the human populace whose life energy is being sucked out of them as they wile away their existence in a cyber dream world. Such a world does not need necessarily to follow the rules of physics or combustion or anything else. It can simply be what one imagines it to be. In this respect, one recalls that in a crucial scene in *The Matrix* a child, who, like a mentalist can bend a spoon at will with his mind, explains to Neo how it is done. His explanation—"There is no spoon"—neatly sums up everything you need to know about how the real and unreal interrelate in the film. Perhaps here the movie's creators have created their own tour de force: a fantasy movie that the audience takes to be real, in which there exists a fantasy world that has inhabitants who also believe it to be genuine. As in the case of *The Master and Margarita,* one finds oneself facing the question: Where is The Truth in all this? In the fantasy or in the reality?

For me, *The Matrix* and 9/11 well illustrate how imagination shapes reality and how then in turn reality can reshape fantasy. I and millions of others sat in the TV audience and watched thousands of people die before our eyes in *Matrix*-fashion: lots of stone, steel and glass flying everywhere, but no apparent blood, no carnage. After 9/11 (but not before) I found myself asking: Doesn't anyone in *The Matrix care* that people are getting blown up left and right? This, in turn, led me to consider an even darker trend of thought. I realized that the reason no one seems to get upset about wholesale slaughter in *The Matrix* is because nothing in the Matrix is supposed to be true to life. Real people live (in so far as they live at all) in an entirely different realm of existence. While the Matrix has a definite, if tenuous, connection to this reality, it is better characterized as a realm of super-reality: both more and less than genuine existence.

But this led me to a further thought: Is this not in essence the mentality of the religious zealot who can blow him/herself up in order to send as many victims to their deaths as possible? Perhaps they too believe in a world that is super-real—a matrix where the lives we live are both more and less than they appear to be. It's much easier to kill off people if they are not really *there.* It is much easier to rationalize violence, if it only occurs on an imaginary plane of existence that is but a pale, smokeless imitation of the world-to-come, the true paradise where all martyrs receive their just reward.[3] I suppose I would have liked the successive *Matrix* movies to have explored the implications of the shoot 'em/blow 'em up mentality its characters (both the good and the evil) embrace without much apparent fore or after thought. The fact that these latter movies seem most obsessed with special effects rather than root causes is, for me at least, one of the great, recent cinematic disappointments.

Yet, by the same token, I hesitate to dismiss the rest of the *Matrix*-trilogy out of hand. After all, we are dealing with *movies* here, and movies by their very nature are super-realities that always have a tenuous connection with the world we live in. The fact that the creative minds who imagined *The Matrix* have stimulated me—just one of the millions sitting in the audience—to really think about matters to the extent that I am writing about them in this essay is about as high a compliment as I can give to them.

Which brings me to a final confession: I still have not seen Gibson's *The Passion,* and I am doubtful if I ever will do so. You may therefore chide me and further conclude that you can dismiss this essay as lacking in credibility because I am only imagining what it is that I am writing about. But then, in this respect, I stand in good company. After all, the Gospel writers—Matthew, Mark, Luke, and John—also wrote about events that, as best we can now judge, they also never eye-witnessed. Moreover, let us further recall that the desire of these early story-tellers was not to give the most accurate, historical accounts of Jesus' life. They were not, nor did they ever imagine themselves to be historians, at least in the modern sense of the term; rather, they were evangelists intent on giving everyone who would care to listen a proclamation (in Greek *kerygma*) that would turn them away from a preoccupation with this world so that they could be better prepared to be saved in the world to come.

Certainly, the most famous and oft-quoted line from *The Master and Margarita* is "Manuscripts don't burn."[4] What Bulgakov meant was that the spark of creative imagination can never be extinguished—even in the repressive world of the Stalinist Soviet Union—as long as artists are ready to fold, mutilate and bend reality to reshape it in their own, respective images. In the final analysis I see Gibson's *The Passion* in this light. I doubt very much that he ever intended to depict the last hours of Jesus' life in an absolutely authentic fashion. Like Bulgakov and like *all* talented, creative artists, his true aim was and is to manipulate and to move his audience—to get them to live, if only for a short period of time, in a world as he and his collaborators have imagined it. The Gospel writers did no less: If it required a little less smoke or fewer flies to create their respective super-realities, the aim was much the same: to imagine the truth of what is real in the super-real.

Discussion Questions

1. Although depictions of the crucifixion are often gruesome, just how realistic are they?
2. In what manner do movies bend reality to make events "super real"?
3. How does one demarcate the fine line between reality and imagination?

Notes

1. This was extensively reported in the press; see, e.g., CNN.com article of Dec. 17, 2003 (http://www.cnn.com/2003/SHOWBIZ/Movies/12/17/pope.gibson/); although the Catho-

lic News Service in a release dated Jan. 19, 2004 denied that the Pope made this statement and papal authorities were quoted as stating "the Holy Father made no judgment of the film" (see http://www.catholicnews.com/data/stories/cns/20040119.htm). For further consideration of what the Pope may or may not have said, see, e.g., B. Blakemore, "Controversy Brews Over Pope John Paul II's Reaction to the Passion." (http://abcnews.go.com/sections/WNT/World/pope_passion_040122-1.html).

2. M. Bulgakov, *The Master and Margarita* (D. Burgin, K. O'Connor, trans.; New York: Vintage, 1995) p. 151. All references to Bulgakov's novel are taken from this edition.

3. For further consideration of the mind-set of the religious terrorist, see Z. Garber, B. Zuckerman, "The Rabin Assassination in the Long View and the Short View: Biblical Radicalism in a Modern Context," *Haqirah, A Journal of Jewish & Ethnic Studies* 1 (2003); pp. 69–88; now revised and reprinted in Z. Garber, B. Zuckerman, *Double Takes; Thinking and Rethinking Issues of Modern Judaism in Ancient Contexts* (Studies in the Shoah vol. 26; Lanham: Univ. Press of America, 2004), pp. 79–104.

4. See chapter 24; p. 245 in the Burgin-O'Connor edition (note 2); as noted, e.g., by E. Proffer, this is "a phrase that went into Russian literary history" (ibid., p. 354).

How Austrians Viewed *The Passion of the Christ*

Klaus Hödl

Mel Gibson's controversial film *The Passion of the Christ* hit European movie theatres six weeks after its release in the U.S. By that time, a large segment of the population was already familiar with the content, whether they read film reviews or not. This was due to the fact that all major newspapers covered the controversy in the U.S. over the movie's potential anti-Semitism. The polemics surrounding the film were not paralleled in Europe. It may even be argued that the American reaction to the movie was of more interest to Europeans than the movie itself.

As much as research on the differences in the American and European reception of *The Passion* might be worthwhile, this article focuses primarily on the Austrian context, with some references to Germany. It is a descriptive study, based on an examination of printed sources, particularly the country's most important newspapers. Magazines or journals dedicated to specific religious or ethnic groups, such as Jews or Catholics, are not included since they do not have a substantial readership outside their respective communities.

The Passion in Austria

In Austria, the running of Gibson's movie occurred in an overall calm, sedate atmosphere. No fierce debate preceded its release, and no excoriating altercations took place in the weeks it was shown all over the country. This might be explained by the absence of Christian fundamentalists promoting *The Passion* and, conversely, of decisive attempts by critics of the film to dissuade people from watching it. Minor conflicts, such as a dispute between Klaus Küng, the ultra-orthodox bishop of the Austrian diocese Feldkirch, who recommended the movie, and the director of the Jewish museum in Hohenems, Hanno Loewy, who publicly criticized Küng for this enunciation, did occur.[1] But they were more of local interest and did not have any lasting repercussions.

By and large, Austria's media coverage of *The Passion* was rather restrained. Although the newspapers reported on American reactions to the film and attempted to elucidate the context in which the various lines of argument were put forward, the country's intellectuals and opinion leaders remained largely quiet. This is surprising since *The Passion* displays images of Jews which correspond to the way many Austrians think. One might have expected the film to encourage a debate on the "guilt of the Jews for the crucifixion of Jesus." According to the Spring 2004 EUMC-Report on anti-Semitism in Europe, the Austrian variant is characterised by "diffused and traditional stereotypes."[2] To put it more concretely: The Austrian perception of Jews has its roots in the views found in the Gospels and revived in Gibson's movie. Interviews conducted with people who watched the movie confirm the thesis that the stereotypes of the Jews conveyed by *The Passion* resemble typical Austrian images of Jews. The interviewees asserted that the movie merely shows "how it happened in reality."[3] But these views were rarely made public and were only scantly reflected by Austrian newspapers. In this sense it could even be argued that most of the media played an "enlightened role" in reviewing the movie from a more complex perspective. Yet, upon closer examination, it appears as though the media's restraint in advocating or even fanning anti-Jewish views was not entirely due to enlightened or ethical motives, but rather because they did not consider anti-Semitism to be a central issue of the film. This stance, however, could be interpreted as a lack of sensitivity towards this topic.

In order to appraise the media coverage of Gibson's movie in Austria, one first has to understand Austria's "newspaper world." It is important to recognize that there are only two "quality" newspapers, aimed primarily at a national audience. These newspapers don't have to be considerate of foreign readers and/or worry about portraying a "nationalist" view, but may write from an "Austrian perspective."[4] Thus, articles on *The Passion* can be regarded as largely reflecting an "Austrian standpoint." Both these newspapers serve as important forums for debates because they also print the opinions of intellectuals and professionals not affiliated with the newspaper. The two newspapers in question, *Der Standard* and *Die Presse*, therefore, play a major role in shaping public opinion.

Their influence on the populace is only dwarfed by *Die Kronen Zeitung*, Austria's major tabloid. If one considers the percentage of Austrians who buy the paper, *Die Kronen Zeitung* has the world's largest readership. Its popularity may be attributed to its reductionist views of complex issues. Its popular and simplistic reporting render the newspaper an extremely powerful factor in Austrian political and cultural life. Moreover, *Die Kronen Zeitung* is well known for its anti-Semitic tendencies.[5] Other newspapers, such as *Salzburger Nachrichten*, the *Kurier,* or *Die Kleine Zeitung,* can be placed somewhere in between the "quality" newspapers and the tabloid.

All Austrian newspapers published articles on the *Passion.* Most of them, however, dealt solely with the controversy about the movie in the United States. Those few articles which reviewed the movie itself, and thereby expressed the view of the newspaper, have been analyzed for this study.

The Coverage of *The Passion* by Austria's "Quality Newspapers"

Die Presse steers a conservative course. In the past it defended Kurt Waldheim against the accusations of the World Jewish Congress that he lied about his activities during the Nazi era, advocated the formation of a coalition government between the Austrian People's Party and the rightist FPÖ under the leadership of Jörg Haider, and is not loath to print articles which at least tamper with anti-Semitic codes.[6] Concerning the Gibson movie, the stance of *Die Presse* merits particular attention, since it belongs to a publishing company which is partly owned by the Catholic Church.

Die Presse published a few articles on the *Passion.* The most important coverage contrasted two different views on the film. Neither of those views took an equivocal stance on the movie, nor did anyone consider the movie outspokenly anti-Semitic. Whereas the critical perspective concedes that the film might strengthen existing stereotypes of Jews, the favorable view holds that the *Passion* was less anti-Semitic than the Gospels. These two assertions were the only references to the issue of anti-Semitism, and they do not differ widely from each other.[7]

Other comments, however, revealed a strong difference between the two approaches. This was especially true regarding the amount of violence shown in the film. Whereas the appreciative position interprets it as a display of suffering designed to trigger a process of soul-searching among the viewers, the critical view deemed the violence an unnecessary display of brutality, matching, however, the simple characterizations of the main figures. The one-dimensional portraits transformed them into caricatures. According to *Die Presse,* these aspects of the movie, in combination with the brutality, made *The Passion* come close to an outright assault on modernity.[8]

The oversimplification of the complex figures involved was also criticized by *Der Standard.* Although it was more outspoken against anti-Jewish tendencies than *Die Presse,* the major reason for dismissing the movie was its anti-modernist tendencies. *Der Standard* contended that the movie ignored historical consciousness, played havoc with the tradition of Bible and religious criticism, and undermined the legacy of the Enlightenment.[9] The author of *Der Standard* article also muses on positive reception of the movie in the United States, arguing that *The Passion* was emblematic of the present, in that it showed how ignorance and powerlessness manifested themselves into terror.[10]

Die Presse and *Der Standard* stood in sharp contrast to *Die Kronen Zeitung*. Although most of its articles pertaining to the movie were brief reports on the reactions in the United States, the remaining comments revealed anti-Semitic tendencies. This was especially the case with an article that basically attempted to nullify the allegations that *The Passion* conveyed anti-Jewish views. Paradoxically, however, the author argued that according to the Bible, it was the leaders of the Jewish people who expressed "lethal hatred" against Jesus,[11] implying that the movie could not be anti-Semitic since the Gospels were not sympathetic to the Jews either.

Except for *Die Kronen Zeitung*, Austrian newspapers did not approach the issue of anti-Semitism. The *Salzburger Nachrichten*, for instance, set *The Passion* in a wider context, comparing the movie and its public impact to the Passion plays in former centuries.[12] The *Kleine Zeitung* repudiated Gibson's movie outright, mainly because of its uncritical relationship to the Gospels.[13]

There was one newspaper that was different from the others. Although not a daily, the weekly *Zur Zeit* is included in this discussion because its editor is a politician of the FPÖ. *Zur Zeit* consistently represents a very nationalist, extreme right-wing point of view. It promoted the *Passion* rather emphatically. In mid-April, for instance, it published an article by Michael Dinhobl, secretary of the ultra conservative bishop of the diocese of St. Pölten, Kurt Krenn. Dinhobl explains the excitement accompanying the release of the movie, in the words of the Apostle Paul, who held that the Christians' efforts to promulgate the crucifixion of Jesus represented a source of irritation to the Jews.[14] According to Dinhobl, it is the death of Jesus that provokes the allegation that Gibson's movie was anti-Semitic, and not the images of the Jews in the film.

Some References to the Reception of *The Passion* in German Newspapers

German newspapers differed from Austrian ones by emphasizing more the anti-Semitism in the movie. Since the German Catholic and Protestant churches as well as the German Jewish community publicly condemned the anti-Jewish tendencies of the film, this issue played a greater role in the various discourses on *The Passion* than it did in Austria. The conservative *Frankfurter Allgemeine Zeitung,* for example, writes that at first it did not seem that *The Passion* was more anti-Semitic than the Gospels. At second view, however, and due to the simplicity of the staging of the movie, it could not be denied that Jews were depicted as bloodthirsty, whereas Pontius Pilate was portrayed as a "hesitating cosmopolitan." In *Die Welt*, Alan Posener focuses especially on the simplicity of the film's staging. He doubts that the movie could be called anti-Semitic, but it definitely was anti-Jewish. According to him, this could not be avoided because the film was based on the Gospels.[15] The Swiss *Neue Züricher Zeitung*, to mention just one more newspaper, refrains from calling the film anti-Semitic, but does consider it dispensable, historically false, and to a large extent problematic.[16]

In general, a review of the coverage of Gibson's movie by Austria's two quality newspapers concludes that the film was not well received. Both newspapers were highly critical of the film. The only favorable viewpoint in *Die Presse* did not lavish praise on it. *Die Kronen Zeitung*, on the other hand, took the movie as an opportunity to put forward anti-Semitic views. By and large, the newspapers' prime interest in *The Passion* was to compare the different European and American reactions to it.

Discussion Questions

1. Why did *The Passion* find only little resonance among Austrian people?
2. Austrians and Americans reacted differently to the movie. Was this due to the fact that the former are less sensitive to anti-Semitic issues touched upon in the film, or might this difference be accounted for by the fact that Austrians are widely indifferent to religious anti-Semitism, since, as everywhere in Western and Central Europe, religion plays only a very restricted role in society?
3. Hollywood contributes to the dissemination of American culture in non-American countries. Could it be that *The Passion* spreads a kind of (religious) anti-Semitism that was no longer of significance in various non-American societies, but might now gain a new lease of life?

Notes

1. http://derstandarddigital.at/standard.asp?page=archivsuchesec&action=ergebnis&artik (March 20, 2004).
2. See Werner Bergmann, Juliane Wetzel, "Manifestations of anti-Semitism in European Union." First Semester 2002, Synthesis Report on behalf of the EUMC, Vienna, March 2003, pp. 84–89.
3. http://www.kleinezeitung.at/freizeit/kino/aktuell/artikel/_592498/index.jsp (March 24, 2004). The (religiously grounded) traditionality of this view is further revealed by the fact that the Pope allegedly said the same about the movie.
4. There is, as a matter of fact, no single "Austrian perspective." Still, with respect to its Nazi past or the topic of anti-Semitism, the overwhelming majority of Austrians still endorse the view of "us" versus "them." This was especially obvious during the "Waldheim Affair," as most Austrian newspapers and Austrians rallied behind Waldheim and purportedly against the "rest of the world," which did not have a proper understanding of the whole issue—or so they thought.
5. http://derstandard.at/?id=1641142 (May 3, 2004).
6. See Klaus Hödl and Gerald Lamprecht, "Zwischen Kontinuität und Transformation. Anti-Semitismus im gegenwärtigen medialen Diskurs Österreichs," *Tel Aviver Jahrbuch für deutsche Geschichte* 33 (2005) (in print).

7. Michael Prüller, "Dieser Film ist eine Meditation," *Die Presse. Feuilleton* (March 13, 2004), p. 36, and Christoph Huber, "Die Leiden Christi als brutaler Fantasy-Blockbuster," *Die Presse. Feuilleton* (March 13, 2004), p. 36.
8. Huber, "Leiden," pp. 35–36.
9. Bert Rebhandl, "Der perforierte Jesus," *Der Standard. Album* (March 13, 2004), pp. A1–A2.
10. Rebhandl, "Der perforierte Jesus," p. A2.
11. http://dev01.krone.at/cgi-bin/search.cgi?next=18&last=16.../40321_im_heftigen_wid.htm.
12. *Salzburger Nachrichten* (March 18, 2004), p. 7.
13. www.kleinezeitung.at/freizeit/kino/aktuell/artikel/_597215/index.jsp.
14. Michael Dinhobl, " Warum die Aufregung?" *Zur Zeit*, vol. 15 (April 16, 2004), p. 26.
15. Alan Posener, "Nur Schrecken, keine Reinigung" in www.welt.de/data/2004/03/17/252161.html?prx=1 (March 17, 2004).
16. Gerhard Bodendorfer, "So viel Blut hat kein Mensch" in www.nzz.ch/2004/03/17/fe/page-article9H1E7.html (March 17, 2004).

Mel Gibson's *The Passion of the Christ* and the "Via Media"

Richard Holdredge

References to Mel Gibson's *The Passion of the Christ* are plenteous on the World Wide Web and can provide college instructors from a variety of disciplines a wide range of responses suitable for classroom presentation and discussion. This range of responses can be considered a sociological phenomenon in and of itself. Particular commentaries and position papers can be used most certainly in Religious Studies and Cinema, as well as Sociology, History and Mass Media.

Reporting data on the World Wide Web is like trying to hit a moving target, as materials on the Web are always in flux. Most articles reported here are now archived at their respective newsletter sites but may still be reached by entering the given URL (Universal Resource Locator) or address. Materials no longer available may be mentioned as part of the whole story of the presence of reactions to Mel Gibson's film on the Web.

After preliminary web searches it appears that there are three main types of resources addressing *The Passion of the Christ*:

1. **Adoration Sites**: The official movie site, "support," and fan sites exhibit a reverence for the film as "life-changing," "powerfully moving," and, as at least one site would lead a visitor to believe, "the greatest outreach opportunity in 2,000 years." One can say that such sites fall into a whole category of adoration. It seems that the producers as well as the film's fans view the film as the foremost representation of this Gospel story to the rest of the world for decades to come, bringing multitudes of converts to Christianity. These sites are unabashedly enthusiastic and supportive of Gibson's genius.

2. **Condemnation Commentaries**: The evangelical fervor of the adoration sites can certainly justify the pre-release concern of many Jewish and Jewish-Christian groups about the content of the film. These groups began airing the

deepest concerns about possible reactions of regenerated anti-Semitism attributed to the presentation of Christ's Passion in Mel Gibson's film. This group maintains a basic condemnation of the film, citing the danger in renewed but misplaced violence and antagonism against Jewry, which the Church for several centuries had incited by the presentation of Passion plays. There do not seem to be whole sites dedicated to this issue, but commentary is usually part of sites dealing with broader perspectives. Commentaries with this view see Gibson as a sensationalist who is insensitive to the work of Jewish-Christian relations groups working for Vatican II-based reconciliation after the Holocaust.

3. Analytic Commentaries: The patient web-searching educator can find more balanced critical reviews weighing the pros and cons of various issues related to the film production and its blend of theology, biblical authority, and art. Such commentaries provide ample material for debate and study, as they offer an opportunity for addressing the anxieties of the condemnation responses, and place the Gibson cinematic interpretation in sociological and theological perspective. Not all are successful however. Several rest on the fact that since Jesus was Jewish, the film cannot be thought anti-semitic. More balanced pieces will be found to maintain the credence of the alarm while endeavoring to inform an audience engaged in critical thinking. Anglican theologians and clergy generally take a middle road approach, so institutionalized in their culture that it is called the "Via Media," as they discuss an issue while respecting multiple viewpoints. Likewise, modern theologians from many religious perspectives often demonstrate a similar middle road approach.

Adoration Sites: It is important to look first at the official site for the film to get an idea about how the film's producers would like the production to be regarded. The official site for the movie is http://www.thepassionofthechrist.com. It is done in a very slick and professional style such as you would expect for a website of a major motion picture. The Flash animation for the introductory splash screen is very cinematic, enhanced by sound effects and music score from the theatrical release. Although elements on the official movie website change over time, exploring its internal and external links can show how the marketing and related sites all endeavor to place *The Passion of the Christ* as the foremost vehicle for exposure to "the story of Jesus Christ." The home page of The Passion Outreach (http:// www.thepassionoutreach.com) declares Gibson's film as "PERHAPS THE BEST OUTREACH OPPORTUNITY IN 2,000 YEARS." It is perhaps all the more reason for leaders in Jewish communities and theologians from Jewish-Christian relations groups to issue warnings and concerns about the historical and current threats to Jews as more neophyte Christians are exposed to this version of the Passion story, un-tempered by any indicators of the reconciliations of Vatican II.

Condemnation Commentaries: At the other end of the spectrum are commentaries raised, often before the film was released, by Christian-Jewish theological and scholarly communities who have been working ecumenically since Vatican II, some focusing on the need for reconciliation especially in the post-Holocaust, or Shoah, era.

On *The Jewish Week* website, June 13, 2003, the headline read: "Interfaith scholars say Jesus film could reignite deicide charge." In it, award-winning New York investigative reporter Eric Greenberg reports,

> An 18-page report sponsored by the U.S. Conference of Catholic Bishops and the Anti-Defamation League warned that the film, slated for release next year, could trigger increased anti-Semitism by reinvigorating the ancient Christian charge of deicide—that Jews were responsible for killing Jesus—which is believed to have caused the persecution and killing of Jews for two millennia. (http://www.ncsj.org/AuxPages/061303JWeek_MGibson_Passion. shtml)

From the Christian side of condemnation we have a web-based newsletter called the *Passionists Compassion* presenting an article by Lynn Ballas (http://www.cptryon.org/compassion/74/ballas.html) entitled, "*The Passion* a Forthcoming Movie," from the *Passionists Compassion,* no. 74, Autumn, 2003. The site is a Catholic website based on *Compassion* magazine, self-described as a "quarterly journal [that] explores peace, justice, mission, and much more." Ballas's article is a helpful start in exploring reactions to Mel Gibson's film. It is, however, also possible to "backtrack" the URL to reach the main page of the Autumn 2003 issue. There one can find valuable links to resources on Mel Gibson's film:

- Commercial site(s) for the movie
- Resources for the Mel Gibson Movie
- Center for Christian-Jewish Learning at Boston College
- The Anti-Defamation League—statement
- on the Mel Gibson movie
- Jews and Christians are watching different
- films—Dennis Prager
- Review by the Catholic Academy of Communications Arts Professionals (www.cptryon.org/compassion/74/act.html).

As indicated above, the Center for Christian-Jewish Learning at Boston College has an excellent resource page (http://www.bc.edu/research/cjl/meta-elements/texts/education/PASSION_resources.htm) on articles related to Mel Gibson's *The Passion of the Christ.* No less than fifty links offer connections to further lists of commentaries. One of the central statements to the whole story of the controversy is contained in an article entitled "Dramatizing the Death of Jesus: Issues that Have Surfaced in Media Reports about the Upcoming Film, The Passion." In this statement four Catholic professors, Mary C. Boys, Phillip A.

Cunningham, Lawrence E. Frizell, and John T. Pawlikowski (http://www.bc.edu/research/cjl/metaelments/texts/news/dramatizing_the_death_of_jesus.htm), allude to their review of an advance copy of the film script. Not wanting to air their review publicly, as it was intended only for Gibson's enlightenment, they present criteria which they used in their evaluation of the script, criteria "that must be considered when assessing any dramatic presentation of the death of Jesus, whether on film or on the stage." Since it deals with aspects inherent in any passion presentation, this critique is insightful and even-handed and likely to promote dialogue.

Ingrid Shafer publishes a website called "Ecumene.org," which includes a wide range of theological and environmental discussions. In an article titled "Mel Gibson's Passion: The Nun, the Priest, and the Poet," Dr. Shafer, one of the scholars on the Oberammergau 2000 Jewish-Christian advisory panel, states the following:

> There appears to be a widespread assumption that Mel Gibson's *Passion* tells the "truth" about the crucifixion. I find it fascinating that many components of this "truth" were generated in the combined imaginations of one woman and two men who lived two centuries ago and had suffered profound psychic injuries and rejections. Now, in the form of this film, their imaginative visions, augmented by Gibson's, have yet another opportunity to affect new generations of people wherever the film is shown. . . . One of the main extra-scriptural sources for Mel Gibson's film is The Dolorous Passion of Our Lord Jesus Christ by the Romantic poet and writer of fairy tales Clemens Maria Brentano. The book was inspired by the visions and meditations of Anna Katharina Emmerick (1774–1824) and first published anonymously in 1833. (http://ecumene.org/SHOAH/Mel_Gibson%s27s_Passion_Shafer2. html)

On the same website, Dr. Shafer reprints an article from the *Los Angeles Times* by James Shapiro, a professor of English and comparative literature at Columbia University, entitled "Mel Gibson's Passion: James Shapiro's Reflections," in which Shapiro reviews first some of the history of Passion plays in general and how the politics of different eras have shifted the blame to the Jews. Regarding Passion plays, he contends that

> These stories were compiled at a time when Jews were regularly accused of poisoning wells and committing ritual murder, so it's no surprise they demonized Jews. But the Passion plays that the stories inspired didn't at first make Jews Jesus' main antagonist. Through the late medieval and Renaissance periods, and as late as the 18th century, Satan was the enemy. But by the 19th century, with the rise of realism (and the Catholic Church's growing displeasure with seeing ribald devils onstage), bloodthirsty and money-grubbing Jews took over in the role, with Pontius Pilate, in this streamlined

> version, becoming something of a hero. (http://ecumene.org/SHOAH/Mel_Gibson%27s_Passion_Shapiro.html)

Moreover, Ingrid Shafer's website has an excellent resource page of its own, providing a wealth of critical articles concerning *The Passion of the Christ*, at http://ecumene.org/SHOAH/Mel_Gibson's_Passion.htm.

There are several responses from the Canadian Council of Christians and Jews that also provide insight into Gibson's film. One statement from this group warns of possible cause for concern:

> There is widely documented concern that the release of Mel Gibson's The Passion of the Christ may cause a setback to Christian-Jewish relations. There is also anxiety that Mr. Gibson's graphic film may ignite anti-Jewish feelings among some Christians at a time when a new and virulent wave of anti-Semitism is on the rise worldwide and when Jews in many parts of the world are feeling vulnerable and uneasy. (http://www.cccj-ab.iccj.org/ passion-statements.htm)

Analytical Commentaries: Responding to the concerns raised about the film, several Christian leaders have taken detailed looks at the many issues discussed relative to *The Passion of the Christ*, and many of them commonly describe the pre-release concerns as an over-reaction, and act as would-be apologists for the film. It seems that generally, the more fundamental the theology, the kinder the resulting analysis.

American Anglicans (Episcopalians) often pride themselves on taking the informed middle road referred to as the Via Media, by thoughtfully exploring several viewpoints on critical issues; however even this group has both conservative and liberal scholars.

One searching for a middle road in *The Passion of the Christ* dialogue at Anglican Mainstream (http://www.anglican-mainstream.net/default.asp) will find the comments of its conservative Anglican/Episcopal writers below less than satisfying:

> It is my intention to argue that much of the criticism leveled at the film misses the point, is overstated, and arises not from a critical assessment of the film as a whole but on an instinctive reaction to anything that we do not consider to be completely and unreservedly true to the gospel as revealed in Holy Scripture . . . (http://www.anglican-mainstream.net/news109. asp)

There are more ecumenical theological responses, mostly coming from less conservative seminarians or seminary scholars who also espouse the "Via Media," that analyze the details of the Gospel and historic accuracy reflected in

Gibson's film. This group acknowledges the need to honor post-Vatican II absolutions of Jews as killers of Christ, and its analysis is far less polarizing.

The General Theological Seminary in New York City addresses the issues of the film in several ways. Specifically the Seminary has a Center for Jewish-Christian Studies and Relations, which held a public forum in March 2004, with an address by Union Theological Seminary Professor Mary Boys, one of the authors of the aforementioned "Dramatizing the Death of Jesus." The entire lecture, "The Passion and Death of Jesus Christ and Relations Between Jews and Christians Today," was at one point available for listening on the GTS website (http://media.gts.edu/boys.mov), but is not currently available in its streaming audio format. Professor Boys gives the kind of balanced and concerned theological viewpoint that one searching for the "Via Media" would hope to find. Note that she is a Roman Catholic woman lecturing in the Episcopal Seminary.

The General Theological Seminary site also has a page devoted to the questions raised by the film, and the page headline reads, "Mel Gibson's Passion: The Gospel for Our Time?" The following bulleted subtitles are delineated:

- Will Mel Gibson's movie *The Passion* replace accounts of the suffering and death of Jesus in the Gospels of the New Testament and become the Gospel for our time?"
- Is the accusation of anti-Semitism leveled by early viewers of the movie accurate?
- Why has *The Passion* appeared at this moment? (http://www.gts.edu/academic/passion.shtml).

There is a valuable link on the GTS resource page at http://gts.edu/academic/passionweb.shtml that includes links to statements from the Consultative Panel on Lutheran-Jewish Relations, the Anti-Defamation League, and the American Jewish Committee. These several links provide a wide range of responses relative to the film.

Probably the richest listing of web-based resources regarding *The Passion of the Christ* is at TextWeek.com entitled "The Text This Week—Lectionary, Scripture Study, and Worship Links and Resources." This resource is presented by self-described amateur scholar and former seminarian Jenee Woodard. Woodard's site lists resources for any denomination of Christian clergy in search of sermon resources for the traditional Gospel lessons of the week. Her main *The Passion of the Christ* listing at http://www. textweek.com/response/ passion_movie.htm, with 150-plus links to "Articles, Study Guides, & Opinions," covers a very broad spectrum, including a link to 200 Gibson film reviews found at Rotten Tomatoes.com. There are some personal Web logs, commonly referred to as blogs, listed here, but that should not deter the inquisitive academic from discovering intelligent and learned responses among them.

From a historical perspective, a helpful analysis of the depiction of Pontius Pilate in Mel Gibson's film is found at a site of the Religious Studies Department of the University of North Carolina at Charlotte. At this site James D. Tabor, chair of the Department of Religious Studies, provides insights into the historical context:

> In the film we get a sympathetic even kind Pilate, weak under pressure to be sure, but wholly positive in overall portrayal. This is really inexcusable I think for a filmmaker, and I do not think the Gospel picture has to be taken as contradictory to the historical record. Once again we are left with the impression that it was the Jews who really wanted this, and the noble Roman leadership would have tolerated a Messianic claimant to operate freely at Passover. This is contrary to everything we know about Roman policy in Palestine in this period where dozens of such "Messiahs" were regularly hunted down and slaughtered by Roman officials. (http://www.religiousstudies. uncc.edu/jdtabor/passion.html).

A Global Witness (http://thewitness.org/agw/0interfaithecumenical.html) is a web version of a magazine from the Episcopal/Anglican viewpoint that includes articles on peace and justice issues and ecumenical matters. On the page for Religious Studies and Interfaith Issues there are several articles on Gibson's film, including one from Mark Stanger of Grace Cathedral in San Francisco entitled "Walking the Via Dolorosa with Mel Gibson" (http:// thewitness.org/agw/stanger021104.html). At this posting Stanger provides his response to a post-screening talk by Gibson:

> Gibson further trashed the idea that the four Gospel writers had "agendas," a concept that puts him firmly outside official Catholic teaching and the mainstream of most Christian biblical interpretation. That wholesome tradition, stretching back not to 1900 but to the earliest interpreters of the texts, recognized the very real and intentional theological, pastoral, and spiritual agendas of writing the Gospels, not as eyewitness factual accounts, but as theological works (spiritual screenplays, if you will) to answer questions and express divine truths in a particular time and place. The late Fr. Raymond Brown, S.S., in his masterful two-volume meditative study, *The Death of the Messiah*, or his succinct and profound little booklet *A Crucified Christ in Holy Week*, far outshines this $30 million piece of truncated and lurid propaganda.

Probably the most helpful sites are those that present guides for preparation for seeing the film for the first time, designed to engage critical thinking and to acknowledge what is Scripture portrayed in the film and what is not. The Boston College site offers a study guide for preparation that states:

> This guide is intended for anyone who sees or hears a portrayal of Jesus' Passion—the suffering Jesus underwent in the final hours of his life, when he was arrested, condemned, and crucified. To understand the Passion, you do not need special training or advanced learning; nor will you need them for this guide. We offer you some background on the challenges of telling the Passion story, as well as some hints for how to hear or watch it. (http://www. bc.edu/research/cjl/metaelements/partners/CSG/passion_guide.htm)

The website of the Episcopal church at Princeton University offers "Preparing to see Mel Gibson's *The Passion of the Christ*," with several links to other resources on the main page, including a PDF downloadable study guide:

> Mel Gibson's new film on the passion and death of Jesus Christ has stirred a great deal of controversy. There are many who applaud its appearance as a factual and uplifting depiction of the last hours of Jesus' life while others have expressed concern about its accuracy and about explicit or implicit anti-Semitic content. We strongly urge you to review the resources in the following links to prepare for seeing the movie. Then we urge you to discuss the film critically and prayerfully with your friends and fellow Christians to identify its key features. (http://www.princeton.edu/~ecp/ Mel% 20Gibson.htm)

The links presented here are but a sample of the numerous commentaries available on the World Wide Web concerning Mel Gibson's *The Passion of the Christ*. College faculty will have no problem finding many other valuable resources. To be exposed to just a few commentaries can be an excellent learning experience, since it cannot help but engage critical thinking on many levels.

From their website, The Canadian Council of Christians and Jews summarize the story well enough and provide a thoughtful, insightful, and balanced view of the film:

> It is Mr. Gibson's contention that this film is as true to the story as possible, that his sources are impeccable and his motives pure. Theologians and historians have weighed in on the accuracy of *The Passion of the Christ* even in advance of its release and their reflections are forming the basis for a welcome dialogue between people who seek mutual respect, understanding and reconciliation. Mr. Gibson has stated that: "My intention for this film was to create a lasting work of art and to stimulate serious thought and reflection among diverse audiences of all backgrounds." It would be wise for us to remember that this is indeed a work of art, not of history or theology, and that it represents Mel Gibson's personal interpretation of the last 12 hours of Jesus. Significant an achievement as this may be, it is not the whole story. (http://www.cccj-ab.iccj.org/passion-statement.htm)

For academic purposes all views of the film need research and discussion and provide a springboard for analysis and discourse. Even the most one-sided approaches provide valuable insights for classroom presentations and analysis.

Discussion Questions

1. Compare and contrast the three kinds of web commentaries the author details in this article and cite at least one example of each not quoted in the article.

2. Analyze how historical, religious, and sociological contexts converge by using a "Via Media" type approach to criticism of this film.

3. Critique Mel Gibson's Passion film and explain where your criticism falls on the continuum of adoration, condemnation, and analytical commentaries.

Section 2

Scriptural Jesus and Gibson's *Passion*

The Quest of the Historical Jesus Revisited

Gibson's The Passion of the Christ

Peter Haas

In the first chapter ("The Problem") of his famous book, *The Quest of the Historical Jesus: A Critical Study of its Progress from Reimarus to Wrede*, Albert Schweitzer notes, "It is no doubt interesting to trace how modern thoughts have found their way into the ancient dogmatic system, there to combine with eternal ideas to form new constructions; it is interesting to penetrate into the mind of the thinker in which this process is at work; but the real truth of that which here meets us as history we experience within ourselves." Despite his affirmation of the "eternal truth" of the Christian faith, the point Schweitzer is trying to make in his book is that in every work on Jesus, the way his life is portrayed reflects the mind of the portrayer. In fact, the content of the book pushes this thesis even further. What Schweitzer has shown us is that any depiction of Jesus is really much more a reflection of the time and place of the person constructing the depiction than of the subject itself.

Although Schweitzer was talking about nineteenth-century German Christian theological scholarship, what he has to say is true as well of any attempt to convey the life and teaching of Jesus—even those of popular culture such as the stage or cinema. The twentieth century has seen an impressively wide range of works, scholarly and popular, which attempt to convey the message of Jesus to a contemporary audience. The number of films based on Jesus, or at least the times of Jesus, are legion. Two of the most successful were Cecil B. DeMille's *King of Kings* and George Steven's *The Greatest Story Ever Told*. There are also counter-cultural interpretations such as *Black Jesus* of 1968 and *Greaser's Palace* in 1972, and of course Terry Jones's *Life of Brian* in 1979. The mid-seventies also saw the two musicals *Godspell* and *Jesus Christ Superstar*. Finally deserving of mention are Jean-Luc Godard's *Hail, Mary* and Martin

Scorsese's 1988 controversial *Last Temptation of Christ.* To this list we must now add Mel Gibson's *The Passion of the Christ.*

When seen in the context of its predecessors on stage and screen, Gibson's rendering of the Gospel of John stands out as starkly different. It is not about the life of Jesus—the whole story covers no more than the last twenty-four hours of Jesus' life—nor is it about the Christ in the sense of how faith in him motivates others. Rather it is about a single trope and its theological interpretation, namely the Passion. My contention in what follows is that this is truly a film reflective of our time. Such a film, I submit, could not have been made, let alone been shown, for a popular movie-going audience twenty or thirty years ago. The question this essay will address is what the character of this film has to say about the popular audience for religious films in North America in the early twenty-first century. What does the success of this film, at least among certain audiences, tell us not only about religion, but about the cinematic culture of our day?

Several features stand out in this filmic portrayal that distinguish it from its predecessors, and I think mark it as a product of its time and place. First, one has to remember that this film claims to be the most accurate historical film ever. It in fact presents itself as a sort of documentary, to the point of recording the words of the actors in the Latin and Aramaic languages of the time. Beyond this technique, itself an extremely unusual but interesting choice for a popular film, there is of course the film's relentless brutality. The film is to a significant extent one long study in how the human body can be tortured. It is also unusual in that the film focuses almost exclusively on the last day of Jesus' life, with only the briefest and most cryptic references to his earlier activity of preaching and ministry (these being relegated to short vignettes and flashbacks). Finally I want to mention the overdrawn characterizations, caricatures really, of the main characters: the indecisive Pilate, the overly masochistic Roman soldiers, the über-sybaritic Herod, and of course the muscular (one is tempted to say "buff") Jesus. In what ways do these characteristics of the film reflect the tastes, interests and aesthetics of its (intended) American (and European?) viewers? Why could this film be made now, but not a generation or more ago?

Before proceeding I want to stress that my interest here is not in the theological controversy within the Catholic Church which the film allegedly addresses, nor am I interested here in Mel Gibson's own theological orientation, although obviously both these points have played a huge role in the conception and production of the film. My interest here is the context of popular culture in which the film as an entertainment phenomenon proposes to find its audience.

Let me turn first to the "reality" and brutality of the film. There is no doubt that crucifixion was a terribly cruel and horribly painful mode of execution. Its true horror has never been so effectively portrayed in film (as far as I am aware) as in this one. Yet even here, the actual crucifixion is not the focus.

In fact, the death on the cross as we witness it through Gibson's eyes, is relatively quick, almost a post-script. What is emphasized in its full and awful detail is the pre-crucifixion torture of the condemned body. In the brutal flogging in the courtyard, in the endless violence of the Roman guards along the Via Dolorosa, in the elaborate ritual of nailing Jesus to the cross, we are confronted with a real sense of human suffering, pain and endurance. The actual hanging on the cross is remarkably staid. The three victims even engage in conversation. So as the title notes, it is the Passion, not the actual death, that is the subject of Gibson's gaze.

It is hard to separate this unsparing dwelling on realism and the pushing of the individual beyond the bounds of normal endurance from what Americans now watch any night on television. Reality TV has become part of the common vocabulary of our popular culture. In some cases this takes a more benign posture: redecorating a home, building a machine out of scrap metal, re-doing one's wardrobe. But in many cases, this has taken on a brutal, sado-masochistic tone: acrophobics forced to jump out of airplanes, young women pressured to eat live insects or worms, people putting themselves through long-term stress, pain and humiliation for the slim chance of winning an award or gaining a bride or not getting fired. What the proliferation of these reality shows illustrates is that the public now expects realism. If the personal struggle on the screen is not real, or seemingly real, then our need to be entertained is not met. In other words, extreme suffering and humiliation have now become part of our daily entertainment diet. We are, as it were, being fed Roman gladiatorial fights with commercial breaks. My contention is that it is precisely in this context that the relentless suffering of Jesus in Gibson's film makes sense. If we watch ordinary people overcome their fears and limitations every night on television, then to portray the true and redemptive *Passion of the Christ* one has to go beyond what has now become ordinary. The suffering has to be real and yet super-human. That is why a film, any film, with this level of almost pornographic brutality can be a box office hit nowadays, and why a film about the Passion has to be.

But what does this film say about American religion? There is also, I think, a cultural component to the focus on the Passion alone. Again, looking beyond the internal theological struggles of the Catholic Church, or Gibson's own place and stake in that struggle, the popularity of the film in certain religious communities is not, I submit, just accidental. In a number of ways, more conservative communities of faith in this country feel themselves in a stage of siege. The advance of a secular globalized culture has rendered individual religious foundation myths less and less believable. There is a sense in which every religion's claim to authority and truth is under assault by science, critical scholarship, and growing secularization. This has all led to a general post-modern tolerance, or even indifference, to any exclusivist claims to Truth. For growing numbers of Moderns, it is more important that one be "a good person" who is moral and caring, than that one believe in a set of doctrines or subscribe to a creed. Surveys on my own campus, for example, show that students are much more likely to define themselves as "spiritual" rather than "religious" (in the sense of identifying with a specific organized religion or creed). It is almost a commonplace, for example, to claim with full sincerity that Jews, Christians and Muslims all believe ultimately in the same God and share the same morality.

To counter this, conservative believers have to point out not only what makes their religion different, but also what makes it ontologically unique and true. In Christianity, this uniqueness and Truth has sprung historically precisely from the Passion and Resurrection. Modern scholarship has shown beyond a doubt that nothing Jesus said was new or unprecedented. This realization has sunk deep into the popular mind. It is now common knowledge among all but the most isolated and conservative Christians that as a person and teacher Jesus fits fully and without remainder into the Judaic community of his time. So for Gibson to show Jesus as a preacher and healer would only serve to emphasize his humanity and his (so-to-speak) ordinariness. What makes Jesus stand out for Gibson is the Passion, his taking on the punishment of our sins. It is thus this in particular, in Gibson's view, that has to be underscored for the Christian audience today. Not the Jewish rabbi/teacher who taught a broad morality, but the suffering Christ who died for our sins. It is this move back to what is perceived as the irreducible and horrific core of Christianity that makes this film stand apart from its predecessors. And to make its point in the broader marketplace of ideas, this Passion has to be portrayed with a realism and savageness that goes beyond what is already commonplace in popular culture.

The rather "laissez-faire" attitude on the part of the West to religion in general, and to Christianity in particular, has sparked another reaction as well. The West has become, as it were, flabby, about its religion. This flabbiness has been brought into especially sharp focus by our recent up-close encounters with the Muslim East. It has been a shock for most Americans to find a Muslim religious community (or, more accurately, a segment of the Muslim community) that is deeply committed to the absolute truth of its own religious story in a way that excludes any concession at all to Judaism or Christianity. For many religious Americans, the fervor, conviction and faith that they see displayed in the Muslim world only shows how far the Christian West has drifted into agnosticism, atheism, hedonism, and materialism. What Gibson and his audience are looking for is an equally hard-hitting statement on the part of believing conservative Christians about the potency of their foundation, and the profoundly and ontologically grounded salvific power of their own Prophet and Savior. In a sense, we might see the endless flagellation scenes in *The Passion* as a Christian reflection to counter, and maybe overtrump, the scenes we see of militant Islam on the news, especially of masses of devout Muslims ready to give up comfort and even life for their faith. Insofar as these images have become part of the popular imagination as to what true religious belief and commitment look like, then *The Passion* becomes the West's adoption of this ritual to its own ends.

This brings me then to that aspect of the film that seems most "unreal" or "Hollywood-like" and that is the over-caricaturization of many of the other leading personalities in the film: Pilate, Herod, and the Judean high priest, to take the most obvious examples. There are a number of ways these directorial decisions on the part of Gibson can be explained. One reason may be to provide a bit of comic relief to the otherwise unrelenting horror unfolding before our eyes. I think this is most clearly the case with the depiction of Herod. Another may be a kind of coded message to the audience. In many ways one of the characters most easy to identify with in the film, in my view, is Pontius Pilate. Regardless of the historical accuracy of his portrayal, I think many viewers could understand his dilemma and even sympathize with the situation in which he finds himself. He was caught, like many of us often are, between doing what he feels is right and what his duty to superiors demands. He has to navigate a course between his conscience and his political and social responsibilities. Pilate is unsure of what to do, but then most of us face that existential situation at some point or another; he is troubled by what he has to do, but many of us have had to deal with similar feelings. And also, like many of us, Pilate tries to forge a compromise and do the right thing, but then finds it going terribly wrong. True, he orders the flogging of Jesus, but then is appalled at how ferociously his subordinates carry it out; he hopes that by presenting Jesus to the crowd, they will let him go, but they perversely shout otherwise. So in a way Pilate becomes Everyman, caught in his own moral unclarity. This is of course in sharp contrast to Jesus, who suffers his fate with unwavering acceptance. So in an age when our popular culture stresses ambiguity, acceptance of other points of view, and moral complexity, the film makes a clear and uncompromising stance. There is a clear right and wrong and it is only Jesus (and his disciples in the audience) who see this and know what is to be done at whatever cost. Everyone else is to some extent clueless or just plain evil.

My point is that the film, whatever its finer theological points, is also a cultural phenomenon that intends to speak to a particular popular audience in a particular way at a particular time in the history of the West. In this regard the film has been a signal success. It has galvanized a certain segment of the Christian population by drawing on popular cultural modes of discourse ("reality TV"); by adopting what many see as the worse parts of modern culture (its tolerance of brutality as entertainment) to religious ends; by adopting for its own use popular images of other religions, especially Islam; and by presenting a certain interpretation of the meaning of Jesus' story in a way that speaks directly to the needs of that community. The film "works" for its intended audience because it talks to their deepest needs in a visual rhetoric that draws on common assumptions and images of the popular culture of its day. It is a product of its time and place; it could not have been made this way (or maybe not even conceived of in this way) a few years ago, and in a few years hence it will likely seem as "dated" as so many of the other, prior, Jesus films. But for right now, it appears to have been the right film at the right time for its intended audience.

Discussion Questions

1. Gibson's film is focused almost exclusively on the Passion. What elements or periods of life do other modern depictions of Jesus see as central? For example, what is the main focus of some of the other films mentioned in the essay and why did they choose that focus?
2. Do you agree with the assertion that our encounter today with (militant) Islam has influenced how Christians (and Jews) have come to think of their own religion? Has the struggle in the Middle East led Americans to look more to the militant elements of their religious traditions?
3. The decision to have the actors speak in "authentic" Latin and Aramaic was a very unusual one. What effect did this choice have on your own experience of the film? Did the foreignness of the language make the movie more real or did you find it alienating? In either case, what do you think Gibson's intention was, and do you think he was successful in achieving it?

The Jewish Jesus

A Partisan's Imagination

Zev Garber

My own approach to finding the historical Jesus in the text of the New Testament may appear to some as extreme. It seems to me that Mark, the earliest Gospel version on the life of Jesus compiled shortly after the destruction of the Second Jewish Temple by the Romans in 70 C.E., contains authentic traces of the historical Jesus shrouded in repeated motifs of secrecy which are intended to obscure the role of Jesus as a political revolutionary sympathizer involved in the Jewish national struggle against Rome. When the Gospel of Mark is analyzed in its own light, without recourse to the special status which canonical tradition confers, it is less history and biography and more historiosophy and parable. It also features an astute polemic against the Jewish Christian believers in Jerusalem, whose influence diminished considerably following the fall of Jerusalem in 70 C.E., and a clever apology to make early Christianity palatable for Rome by not identifying Jesus with the national aspirations of the Jews. The Markan account of the trial of Jesus and his execution, along with the portrait of a pacifistic Christ, are for the most part historically questioned by S. G. F. Brandon, who sees in these narratives attempts by the Gentile Church to win Roman favor by exculpating Pontius Pilate from his share in the crucifixion of Jesus.[1]

I agree. Regarding the Synoptic Gospels' (Matthew, Mark, Luke) account of Jesus before the Sanhedrin,[2] the trial before Pilate,[3] and the sentence of death,[4] the question of historical fairness intrudes into these accounts. Jesus is tried three times (the Sanhedrin night-trial which found him guilty of blasphemy, the trial before Herod Antipas, and the dawn-trial before Pilate), and so which court decisively condemned Jesus?[5] Where in the biblical-talmudic tradition is blasphemy defined by claiming that one is the "Messiah the Son of the Blessed?"[6] Leviticus 24:13–23 and Sanhedrin 7.5 proclaim that whoever curses God is guilty of blasphemy.[7] Rarely recorded are malediction and impious profanity by one who claims to be a messianic figure. True, Josephus reported many messianic pretenders between 6 and 70 C.E., but we have no record of any put to death. Bar-Kochba was called Messiah by Akiba, but tradition does not speak ill of either second-century hero. And no less a personality than Maimonides relegated the messianic doctrine to a secondary position among the articles of faith rendered in his name. Also, one guilty of blasphemy was stoned to death and not killed by crucifixion as recorded by Mark.[8]

That Jesus was sympathetic to the Zealot cause may explain why the charges of sedition were not overtly denied by Jesus when asked, "Are you the King of the Jews?"[9] Other references support this view. One of the trusted disciples was Simon the Zealot.[10] The Zealot Movement, rooted in the tradition of being "zealous for the Lord,"[11] arose in the Galilee in the first decade of the first century. It may be assumed that the child Jesus raised in Nazareth would have listened often to tales of Zealot exploits against the hated Romans and how many of the former died martyrs' deaths in a futile attempt to replace the bondage of Rome with the yoke of the "kingdom of heaven."[12]

These childhood experiences listened to in earnest and awe caused the adult Jesus to sympathize with the anti-Roman feelings of his people. Thus, the "cleansing of the Temple" pericope is not to be read as anti-Temple but rather as a critique of the Temple functionaries who collaborated with Rome.[13] This episode appears to have coincided with an insurrection in Jerusalem during the period of Gaius Caligula (37–41), in which the Zealots appear to have been involved.[14] The famous question concerning tribute to Caesar has Jesus saying, "Render to Caesar the things that are Caesar's and to God the things that are God's,"[15] thereby implying Jewish support of Roman fiscal and political policy. This is an assimilable position and it is very doubtful that the historical Jesus identified with it. Better to say the Rome-based school of Mark coined Jesus' answer, for it guaranteed that Jesus and his fellowship were loyal to Rome and opposed to Jewish nationalism, a necessary survivor mandate for Gentile Christians living in Rome during and after the Zealot-inspired Jewish war against Rome.

The *ipsissima verba* of Jesus, recorded in Matt 10:34, namely, "I have not come to bring peace but a sword," supports the militancy in the Jesus party mentioned in the Gethsemane tradition: Luke 22:35–38 portrays Jesus asking his disciples if they are armed and they reply that they are doubly armed. The size and arming of the arresting party "from the chief priests and the scribes, and the elders,"[16] can be cited as evidence of nationalist loyalty by Jesus. The unknown disciple who draws a sword and cuts off the ear of the High Priest's slave is identified in John's Gospel as Peter.[17]

Others say the question of Jesus, "Have you come out against a robber with swords and clubs to capture me?"[18] separates him from the Zealots. But can the parochial Jewish nationalism of Jesus be hidden in the image of the universal image of the Christ of Peace? I think not. Yet Mark's anti-Jewish bias and pro-Roman sentiments inspired him to lay the guilt of Jesus in the hands of Jewish authorities. According to the Synoptic Gospels, Jesus was not an insurrectionist, nor did he commit a crime deserving death by Roman law.[19] Later Church narrative accepts this view without serious emendation and further presents Jesus as the "Prince of Peace." An early source of this tradition is the editorial note in Matt 26:52. Here a post-70 C.E. Jewish Christian evaluating the ill-fated Jewish War declared in Jesus' name: "Put your sword back into its place; for all who take the sword will perish by the sword."[20]

A constant motif is the silence of the apostolic writings on matters pertaining to the political situation of the time. The Zealots of the period are essentially overlooked; episodes in which they are involved, as reported by Josephus and others, are not reported. Luke-Acts is silent about the identity and antecedents of James, Peter, and the other leaders of Jewish Christianity. Mark's theology prejudices the historical situation and declares that Jesus could not have involved himself in political nationalism and other contemporary issues. Later apostolic writers submissively follow the Markan line. How far theology distorts history is further shown by denigrating the Pharisees as the bitter opponents of Jesus.[21]

The received Gospel tradition appears to suggest that the catastrophe of 70 C.E. and its aftermath was brought about by Jewish leaders who plotted Jesus' death, the Jewish mob who had demanded it, and the stiff-necked Jews who refused to follow the Jesus way. Also, the Jewish disciples do not know Jesus,[22] and it is the Roman centurion at the crucifixion who recognizes Jesus as the Son of God.[23]

Our thesis suggests that the New Testament belief about "Who do the people say that I am?"[24] is more belief narrative than historicity. In my opinion, the genre of Christian Scriptures on the historical Jesus is expressed in the idiom of Midrash. By Midrash, I mean an existential understanding by man of his environment, history, and being. Its purpose is not to provide objective description of the world nor to relate objective facts, but to convey a particular cultural worldview rooted in a specific setting in the life of the people in a given historical moment (*Sitz im Leben*). Its content is doctrinal and ethical and its form is mythic. The very nature of Midrash is an invitation to "demidrashize," i.e., to decode the original form and make the content more meaningful for different time and clime. Indeed the New Testament shows evidence of this. For example:

> Given: Jesus returns in the clouds of Heaven.
>
> Pauline: Shifts the emphasis of the failure of Jesus' return to the believer's present life.
>
> Johanine: Achieves the same Pauline goal with its conception of eternal life here and now present to the faith, and of judgment as already accomplished in the world which Jesus brings.

My *Jewish* reading of Jesus in the Synoptic Gospels puts him in history and not in divinity. The Jesus of different Christologies could never find support in Judaism, since the God-man of the "hypostatic union" is foreign to Judaism's teaching on absolute monotheism. As the promised Messiah,[25] he did not meet the conditions which the prophetic-rabbinic tradition associated with the coming of the Messiah. Indeed, there was no harmony, freedom, peace, and unity in the Land of Israel—signs of the Messianic Age—and enmity and strife abounded everywhere. Not a false but failed Redeemer of the Jews, as witnessed by the words of the "King of the Jews" at the cross: *Eli, Eli, lama sabachthani* ("My God, my God, why have You *forsaken* [italics added] me")?[26] Notwithstanding, he was a loyal son of Israel, whose commitment to the Torah[27]—albeit radical and reformist—and his remarks about the great commandment[28] were steadfast and comparable to Pharisaic Judaism of the day.

Arguably, the great flaw in pre-Vatican II Catholic traditionalism (as depicted in Mel Gibson's movie *The Passion of the Christ*) and Protestant fundamentalism in the teaching of the Easter Faith is the heinous role played by the crowd/people/Jews in the execution of Jesus. The cornerstone of supersessionist Christology is the belief that Israel was spurned by divine fiat for first rejecting and then killing Jesus. This permitted the apostolic and patristic writers and Protestant Reformers to attribute to Israel the mark of Cain and the evil of the Sodomites, and more, to assign the worst dire punishment on judgment day. These are not words, just words, but they are links in an uninterrupted chain of anti-Semitic diatribes that contributed to the murder of the Jews in the heartland of Christianity and still exists in a number of Christian circles today. How to mend the cycle of pain and the legacy of shame? The key is to separate the crucifixion of Jesus from the *contra Iudaeos* tradition by demystifying the composite Passion narrative as taught and preached in ecclesiastical Christianity.

An illustration is in order. The nefarious words, "His blood be on us and on our children,"[29] seen by many as the scriptural flash point to the charge that Gibson's film is anti-Semitic, were composed in the 90s, a generation *after* the death of Jesus. And if the words are credible, then may they not be seen as composed by an anti-Zealot Jewish Christian writer who opposed the Jewish revolt against Rome and reflected on the havoc wreaked on the Jewish people because of it? Similarly, to portray Pilate as meek, gentle, kind—a Jesus alter ego—who cannot resist the aggressive demands of the Jewish mob to crucify Christ, is historically unfounded and not true.[30]

Finally, why the obsessive passion in Mel Gibson to portray endlessly the bloodied body of Jesus? May it not be this traditionalist Catholic's rejection of reforms advocated by Vatican Council II to present tolerantly the Passion of Jesus Christ? Whether conscientious or not, co-writer, director, and producer Gibson revises scriptural anti-Judaism in visual media. He does so by portraying overtly a corrupt Jewish priesthood, and especially the high priest, Caiaphas, a ferocious blood-thirsty Jewish mob, an effeminate Satan who hovers only among

Jews, satanic-like Jewish children, and a complacent Roman leadership that does the bidding of Jews. The subliminal message: the destruction of Jerusalem and the Second Temple (the film's climactic and penultimate scene) is sufficient proof for believers in Christ that God has pronounced dire punishment upon Old Israel and that He now dispenses his countenance to the New Israel, who accepts unhesitatingly Jesus as Lord and Savior. Hence, "Christ is the end of the Law,[31] in [whose] *flesh* [italics added] the law with its commandments and regulations"[32] are abolished. Thus, to flagellate unceasingly the body of Jesus is to rid Judaism unmercifully from the Body of Christ and provide salvation through the blood of Christ.[33] On Gibson's cross, replacement theology is reborn. And Satan/Mammon laughs aloud, a bitter laugh.

Discussion Questions

1. Explain the role of biblical criticism in understanding the historical Jesus.
2. In what way and to what degree does the claim that Jesus was a Jewish revolutionary ("Think not that I came to bring peace on the earth: I came not to bring peace, but a sword," Matt 10:34) advance or impede the ecclesiastical belief that he is the "Prince of Peace"?
3. How does the scriptural Jewish Jesus counter Mel Gibson's misguided cinematic crucified Christ?

Notes

1. The writings of S. G. F. Brandon, the late professor of comparative religion at the University of Manchester, have influenced my thinking on Jesus as a nationalist sympathizer and a political revolutionary. See, in particular, his *Jesus and the Zealots* (New York: Charles Scribner's Sons, 1967). Also influential is Hyam Maccoby, *Revolution in Judaea: Jesus and the Jewish Resistance* (New York: Taplinger Publishing Company, 1981).
2. Matt 26:57–75; Mark 14:53–72; Luke 22:54–71.
3. Matt 27:11–14; Mark 15:2–5; Luke 2:3–5.
4. Matt 27:15–26; Mark 15:6–15; Luke 23:17–25.
5. Cf. "The Trial of Jesus in Light of History: A Symposium," in *Judaism* 20.1 (Winter 1971).
6. Matt 26:63–65; Mark 14:61–65; Luke 22:67–70.
7. Cf. Acts 6 where Christian tradition records that Stephen was deserving of death since he spoke "blasphemous words against Moses and against God" (Acts 6:7). See too Ex 22:27; I Kgs 21:10, 13 ("you have reviled God and king").
8. A brief description of the crucifixion is found in Matt 27:33–44; Mark 15:22–32; Luke 23: 33–43.
9. Matt 27:11; Mark 15:2; Luke 23:3. Cf., also, Mark 15:9, 12 and the charge against Jesus inscribed on the cross (Matt 27:37; Mark 15:26; John 19:19).
10. Cf. Matt 10:14; Mark 3:18; Luke 6:15; Acts 1:3. In Matthew and Mark it is written, "Simon the Cananaean" (Zealot). Matthew's Jewish audience can understand the Aramaism, but Mark, who normally translates Aramaisms (e.g., Mark 7:34) into Greek, purposely does

not here. The writer of Luke-Acts, writing a generation after Mark, no longer sees the taint of political sedition about Jesus or is simply unaware of Mark's dilemma and unashamedly identifies Simon as a Zealot.

11. Cf. the roles of Phineas (Num 25:7–10), Matthias (I Macc 2:15ff.), and Elijah (I Kgs 19:19ff) as zealot types.

12. "Blessed be His Name, whose glorious kingdom is forever and ever," recited in the Temple during the Day of Atonement services, was added by the Rabbis to accompany the opening verse of the *Shema* (Deut 6:4). Since the period of Gaius Caligula (37–41), Roman emperors demanded from their subjects divine respect. The loyalist Jew (religious, nationalist) who refused did so on penalty of death. He submitted to the rule of God alone, whom he proclaimed in "Hear O Israel, the Lord is our God, the Lord alone," and followed by the above doxology.

13. Mark 11:15–19; Matt 21:21; Luke 19:45–48.

14. A reference to Pilate's ruthless suppression of the rebellion may be found in Luke 13:1.

15. Mark 12:17; Matt 22:21; Luke 20:25.

16. The episode of Jesus taken captive is found in Mark 14:43–52; Matt 26:47–56; Luke 22:47–53.

17. Mark 14:46; Matt 26:51; Luke 22:50; John 18:10.

18. Mark 14:48; Matt 26:55; Luke 22:52.

19. Matt 27:23; Mark 15:14; Luke 23:22.

20. Also Luke 22:50. A similar message is associated with national restoration and rebuilding the Second Temple (515 B.C.E.) in Zech 4:6, which is later linked to the synagogue service of Chanukkah by the Rabbis in order to play down the militancy of the Maccabean victory and state imitated by the ill-fated revolt against Rome.

21. The word "Pharisees" occurs over a hundred times in the New Testament (29 times in Matthew; 12 times in Mark; 27 times in Luke; 19 times in John; 9 times in Acts; and one time in Philippians). There is ample fodder in these references to portray Pharisaism as sanctimonious, self-righteous, hypocritical petrified formalism, and a degraded religious system corroded by casuistry. The bitterest tirade against the Pharisees is found in Matt 23.

22 Cf. Mark 8:27–33; Matt 16:13–23; Luke 9:18–22. The Petrine blessing found in Matt 16: 17–19 was added by a Jewish Christian to offset Mark's rebuke of Peter (The Jerusalem Church) as Satan by Jesus (Mark 8:33).

23. Matt 27:54; Mark 15:39; Luke 23:47.

24. Matt 16:13; Mark 8:27; Luke 9:18.

25. Cf., among others, Matt 26:62–64; Mark 14:60–62; Luke 22:66–70.

26. Matt 27:46; Mark 15:34.

27. Matt 5:17–20.

28. Matt 22:37 = Mark 12:30 = Luke 10:27 – Deut 6:5; Mark 12:29 – Deut 6:4; Matt 23:39 = Mark 12:31 = Luke 10:27b – Lev 19:18; Mark 12:33 – cf. I Sam 15:22.

29. Matt 27:25. In *The Passion,* these words are heard in the original Aramaic but deleted in the English subtitles.

30. Philo Judaeus wrote about Pilate's "endless and intolerable cruelties"; this was no doubt why he was recalled to Rome in 37 C.E.

31. Rom 10:4a.

32. Eph 2:15.

33. Conversely, blood fixation by Jews is not associated with suffering, torture, and death but with birth, hope, and life. Consider the Ezekielian verse recited at the Circumcision rite linking the birth of a Jewish male child (potential Messiah) with the birth of Jerusalem ; "I (Lord God) said to you: 'In your blood, live.' Yea, I said to you, 'in your blood, live'" (Ezek 16:6).

History, Archaeology, and Mel Gibson's *Passion*

Gordon D. Young

Whatever else *The Passion of the Christ* is about, it is about history. Thus, it is important to examine the film from the perspective of history, and see how, and *if*, the film incorporates what we have come to know about that era. A great deal of progress has been made into the recovery of the first century C.E. in the last several decades, and much of it has been done by archaeologists. In my few pages in this section, I propose to examine the film's depiction of the last few hours of the life of Jesus in the larger context of the world in which his crucifixion took place. It must be admitted that our sources are not very good. What passes for most of our written sources were written well after the death of Jesus, many by followers who did not witness the crucifixion and who were anxious to demonstrate how the world had changed because of his life and death.

The early 30s C.E. were relatively quiet ones in Roman history—as far as hot wars were concerned. There were no major conflicts. Domestically, however, they were years full of turmoil. Tiberius, the *princeps*, now in his 70s, was living a comfortable semi-retirement on the island of Capri, but in Rome the furor over the removal from power and execution of Sejanus, his notorious Praetorian Prefect, raged on. One might have suspected that high treason and domestic politics might have overshadowed Roman foreign policy concerns, but such was not the case. There was a state that had been at the center of Roman planning since 64 B.C.E.—Parthia.

Located in what is now Iraq, parts of eastern Syria, Iran, and Afghanistan, Parthia was rich and powerful. It sat astride profitable trade routes connecting East and West, and had obliterated a Roman army in 53 B.C.E. at Carrhae in Syria, where over 30,000 men were lost. Ever since, various Roman leaders, including Julius Caesar, had considered plans for retaliation. Bruised egos, profits, and worries about Parthia's plans for its western neighbor kept Roman planners busy over the years, but other events got in the way of a Parthian campaign. While Augustus may have eased the tension with Parthia a bit, taking advantage of an "unstable political situation in Parthia and forcing [the Parthians] to withdraw from Armenia,"[1] the eastern frontier of the empire remained a concern. A result of all this was that there were four full Roman divisions based in the Syro-Palestinian Levant. Most of the troops were billeted in the north, a convenient placement because of the converging highways and trade routes leading east-west, and a good spot for watching events in Anatolia and Armenia farther north and east.

In the south, however, Judea was not so heavily guarded. The nearly impassable desert to its east made it unlikely that a Parthian attack would come from that direction, or that it would be a good jumping off point for a Roman invasion. At the time, Judea had a puppet king—Herod Antipas (who has only a bit part in the film)—but the real authority was the Roman procurator, Pontius Pilate, who governed from 26 to 36 C.E. By the way, we have his name on an inscription from Caesarea which reads [Pon]tius [P]ilatus—one of the few direct contemporary witnesses to this story. Roman sources also confirm his presence.

As procurator, Pilate was under the authority of the curator based in Damascus. Curator and procurator are the titles of those men who governed imperial provinces—that is, provinces under the direct control of the *princeps* and not the Roman Senate. They were provinces that were either rich—Egypt, for example—or where there were serious military concerns. For Pilate, however, the military concerns were not so important. He had more serious domestic problems.

His world comprised the small entities of Judea proper, Idumea (biblical Edom) to the east, Samaria in the hilly country to the north, and Ituria (the Galilee region farther north and east). Relations between these small entities were often violent, and banditry was common. In several areas, what we would call warlords maintained their own forces and controlled and contested small areas. Nor were things much quieter in Judea proper.

The population Pilate governed was an explosive mixture, divided variously on ethnic, religious, social, and economic grounds. There were Samaritans, Idumaeans, Roman veterans who had settled there, foreign businessmen, Greek descendants from Alexander's veterans, and various kinds of Jews.

There was the political, social and economic elite, the Sadducees. Under the leadership of Caiaphas, they dominated Jewish governance, controlled activities in the temple, and mediated for all Jews with the Romans. They were not very popular with rank-and-file Judeans, but they had power. It might be said that their necessary collaboration with the Romans, coupled with their wealth and control of the temple, doomed them to unpopularity, and their frustrations clearly played a part in their rage at Jesus and his followers. (This part of the story is not made clear in the film.)

Then there were Pharisees—Judeans who practiced a Bible-centered faith, and who were followers of what may be termed rabbinic authorities who were in the process of creating what has been called the Oral Torah—interpretations of Bible portions that would ultimately be codified in the famous works known as the Mishnah and Talmud. (Pharisees would have been enormously influential in religious affairs, but are absent from the film.)

Still other Judeans, dissatisfied with the world in which they lived, opted for Essenism—a sort of drop-out, plague-on-all-your-houses faith. They were deeply attached to the Bible, hostile to the temple authorities, but not to the temple itself. Their most famous location was at Qumran near the northern end of the Dead Sea, and very remote.[2] Essenes could also be found living in communities in the towns and cities of Judea. At Qumran, Essenes lived what can only be described as a monastic style of life—highly regimented and practicing a life of cleanliness, both spiritual and physical. (These, too, are absent from the film.)

Then there were those who advocated confrontation with Rome—who would eventually precipitate the Jewish War of 66–70 C.E.

Finally, there were those who followed a young Galilean by the name of Jesus. They were not well organized and came mostly from rank-and-file Judeans not wealthy enough to be either Pharisees, whose life required time for serious study (time unavailable to those who had to work day and night to make ends meet), or Sadducees, the wealthy elite. The message of Jesus was neither confrontational nor pro-Roman. He could compete with Pharisees on biblical interpretation; he could offer an alternative to life as an Essene, and he didn't need the Temple of the Sadducees. In short, he offered an alternative to most everything the establishments had to offer. Further, he ridiculed them: Pharisaic legalists who "strain at a gnat and swallow a camel," for example, or the comment about the eye of the needle and the rich man's chance of gaining heaven (read Sadducees). He was, then, a serious threat to the existing order. (This, too, is not well developed in the film.)

Here, then, is a major point of criticism of the film. It does not provide any context for the last hours of Jesus' life. It does not show why Caiaphas and his supporters were so angry with Jesus, nor does it show why Pilate acted as he did—why it was so important for Pilate to side with Caiaphas. In this, as Gordon Mork demonstrates in the next section, the film chose to echo the themes of medieval Passion plays rather than attempt to understand the event historically. It is a very medieval conception. Even the excessive use of violence in the film echoes the medieval fixation with the horror that was Jesus' death, concentrating as it does on the savagery of the scourging and crucifixion. These, by the way, were not images popular among early Christians.

And now some specifics:[3]

1. Language: We have many inscriptions from this time in Judean history. They have been analyzed many ways. Back in the '60s a simple count was made. Overwhelmingly, the inscriptions are written in two languages: Greek

and Aramaic. There is hardly any Latin, and where it occurs, Roman troops were stationed. There isn't even much Hebrew, and that primarily in funereal, hence ceremonial, circumstances. To have a simple Galilean speak Greek is very unlikely. To have Jesus speak Latin, as he does on occasion in the film, is simply absurd. Rome governed the East Mediterranean in Greek, and not Latin.

2. Crucifixion: This was a common Roman punishment for a variety of crimes (and was also used by other states), but was used exclusively for slaves, non-Roman citizens, traitors, and the like. (By the way, the reason Paul was not crucified was that he was a Roman citizen and entitled to a trial by a jury of his peers in Rome.) Two things are wrong in Gibson's portrayal: In antiquity, the condemned carried only the cross beam of the cross, not the whole thing. Further, ropes were generally used to tie people to the cross, and when nails were used, they were nailed through the wrist. In the film, Gibson is following centuries of art-historical tradition in which Jesus' crucifixion is depicted showing him carrying the entire cross, and being nailed through the palms of his hands. One final thing: Only Romans could order a crucifixion. Hence, Caiaphas needed Pilate's cooperation.

3. Torture: Scourging was commonplace. The only weapon attested so far is the reed, and not the horrendous implement used in the film. Surely the Gospel writers would have included this in their accounts had these implements been so used. Nor were armed Jewish soldiers a part of the story. Rome would not have tolerated Jewish (or anybody else's) soldiers. The Bible simply speaks of a mob with swords and clubs.

4. Finally, as Mork points out, Gibson has chosen to include the visions of Anna Katharina Emmerich in his film. There is no biblical evidence to support the throwing of Jesus off the bridge, the gender-unspecific Satan, or the handing of cloth to Mary by Claudia, the wife of Pilate. This is pure fantasy, but is quite indicative of the sort of medieval attitude that pervades his film.

In conclusion, let me say that the film does not do justice to either history or Jesus. The failure to place the last hours of Jesus in the larger context of his time is unforgivable. People who do not know the story well will not learn it from the film. Worse, people who do not know the story at all can gain exactly the opposite of what Gibson professes his intentions were—that he did not intend to make an anti-Semitic film, and that anti-Semites will not take comfort from the film.

Fortunately, I don't believe that Christians in America will form mobs after viewing the film and go looking for Jews to beat up or kill—as often happened following the older Passion plays, but here is a revealing clip from the Sunday, March 28, 2004 *Journal and Courier* of Lafayette, Indiana:

> A top Shiite cleric on Saturday urged Kuwait to let Mel Gibson's film *The Passion of the Christ* be shown in this conservative state because it "reveals crimes committed by Jews against Christ."[4]

Finally, I would like to make one last point. The film is correct in showing that there were just two kinds of people involved in this story—Romans and Jews. Notice, I did not say THE Jews, merely Jews. The key word here is THE. Did THE Jews kill Jesus, or was it simply that some Jews were complicit in Jesus' death? This was a struggle involving Jews of Judea, of whom Jesus was definitely one. There were no Christians yet.

Nor did Jews living in other parts of the world participate. None of our sources implicate the Jews of Rome (and there were many), Anatolia, Greece, Macedonia, Egypt, even Parthia in the crucifixion of Jesus. It was simply a local Judean affair. If Christians and Jews are ever to get together, it is fundamental that the word THE be removed from this question of Jewish culpability.

Further, what lay in the future when there were Christians has no place in this film, or this story, and we shouldn't read any of that back into it.

In sum, Mel Gibson's *Passion* does justice neither to the Bible, nor to history, archaeology, and decades of research by scholars from a wide range of disciplines. That it passed muster from its scholarly technical consultants, and that so many people have reacted so positively to it is an appalling circumstance. One hopes that the extensive efforts of the past few years to build bridges between Jews and Christians will not suffer because of it. Wounds that are healed should not be reopened.

Discussion Questions

1. Why does blaming "the Jews" for the death of Jesus serve no useful purpose other than fueling the fires of anti-Semitism? Does this film teach us anything about Jew-hatred at the time of Jesus?
2. What conditions on the eastern frontier of the Roman Empire made the "Jesus problem" so acute for Pontius Pilate?
3. If you knew absolutely nothing about the story of the crucifixion and resurrection of the Christ, and only had *The Passion of the Christ* to guide you, what might you learn from this film?
4. Does placing the story of the crucifixion and the resurrection in the larger context of Roman, Mediterranean, and Near Eastern history serve any useful purpose? If so, what?

Notes

This paper is a slightly revised version of my remarks at the symposium "Mel Gibson's *Passion*: The Film, the Controversy, and Its Implications," held at Purdue University on March 30, 2004. Space limitations prohibit expansion of specific points.

1. Edward Dabrowa, "The Frontier in Syria in the First Century AD," in Philip Freeman and David Kennedy, eds., *The Defence of the Roman and Byzantine East: Proceedings of a Collo-*

quium Held at the University of Sheffield in April 1986, Part 1. British Institute of Archaeology in Ankara monograph No. 8, BAR International Series 297 (i) (Oxford, 1986), p. 96.

2. The controversy over the relationship of Qumran to the Essenes needn't bother us here. A preponderance of modern scholars feel that Qumran was an Essene settlement and something akin to a monastery. The presence of Essenes in first-century Judea is well documented whether in a "monastery" or not.
3. These and other specific problems of historicity and archaeological inaccuracy are nicely developed in Andrea Merlin and Jodi Magness, "Movie Commentary: Two Archaeologists Comment on the Passion of the Christ, http://www.archaeological.org/webinfo.php?page=10243&source=ereport."
4. "Passion in Kuwait," *Journal and Courier* (Lafayette, IN), March 28, 2004, p. 3.

Where Is the History in Mel Gibson's *The Passion of the Christ*?

S. Scott Bartchy

Why has this film, which is claimed by many to be the most historically reliable presentation ever made in a movie about Jesus of Nazareth, become so controversial, so potentially dangerous in arousing anti-Jewish sentiment, and in my judgment such a betrayal of the memory of the historical Jesus?

More than twenty feature-length commercial films have dealt with the life and death of Jesus of Nazareth, beginning in 1898 with Alice Guy's French film, *Jesus devant Pilate.* Among the best known that followed are Cecil B. DeMille's *The King of Kings* (1927), George Stevens's *The Greatest Story Ever Told* (1965), Pier Paolo Pasolini's *The Gospel According to St. Matthew* (1966), Franco Zeffirelli's *Jesus of Nazareth* (1977), and then Martin Scorsese's very controversial *The Last Temptation of Christ* (1988), based on the novel by Nicos Kazantzakis—a film that told us about Scorsese's sexual fantasies rather than anything about those of the historical Jesus.[1]

These films have portrayed Jesus through widely diverse characterizations, ranging from that of a dreamy-eyed utopian to a self-doubting revolutionary, with many intermediate images. They have ranged from the solemnly reverent to the wonderfully satiric *Life of Brian* by the Monty Python group, from musical to grand epic. Gibson's *The Passion of the Christ* outdoes them all with its stunning aesthetic values and amazing applications of cinematic technology. Has, then, Mel Gibson improved on the efforts of previous writers and directors who have made Jesus of Nazareth the subject of their movies? Has he made the most biblically accurate presentation of Jesus' last hours in Jerusalem ever filmed, as he has repeatedly claimed? For example, Gibson has stated: "I think that my first duty is to be as faithful as possible in telling the story so that it doesn't contradict the Scriptures."[2] And in an interview with Raymond Arroyo broadcast by the Eternal Word Television Network on January 23, 2004, Gibson asked rhetorically about the difference between the biblical Jesus and the historical Jesus, "Please, tell me what's the difference? John was an eyewitness—is that not history? Matthew was there—is that not history?"

Although Gibson has said that this film "is not meant as a historical documentary,"[3] from the very first frame he encourages his viewers to think that this will be the most historically accurate film ever made about Jesus, a perception emphasized by his use of Aramaic and Latin, with American English subtitles for most of the dialogue. Thus it cannot be surprising that the president of the National Association of Evangelicals, Ted Haggard, has commented: "This film is probably the most accurate film historically—more than anything that's ever been made in the English world. . . . We were watching it for biblical accuracy, and we thought it was as close as you can get."[4]

This film is undoubtedly the most ambitious and most commercially successful exploitation of the Christian Scriptures to date. It has become a major cultural event. So what's there not to like? Plenty!

Gibson's claim for the accuracy of this film inevitably raises the question: Where's the history here? To answer this question I comment in this essay on Gibson's presentation of

- a complete absence of context for understanding what happens to Jesus in this film
- a very limited respect for historical research
- his reliance on medieval speculations and nineteenth-century visions
- the Roman prefect Pontius Pilate and his wife
- the Jewish leaders, in particular Caiaphas and Herod Antipas
- Mary, Jesus' mother
- his severely truncated presentation of the historical Jesus' radical actions and his total ignoring of Jesus' prophetic social critique.

Crucifixion

Before going into those details, it may be helpful for me to make some preliminary comments about the manner of the execution of Jesus of Nazareth—crucifixion.

In our attempts as post-Enlightenment, analytical historians to sort out the facts from faith's interpretations of the facts, and both facts and faith from fantasies of many kinds, there is no more secure fact in the case of Jesus of Nazareth than the statement that this Jesus was tortured and executed by crucifixion at the order of the then-authorized provincial representative of the Roman Empire. The Romans had dominated and exploited the Land of Israel as the humiliated province they called Palestine for more than ninety years before Jesus of Nazareth became a public figure there. Although the Romans had not invented death by nailing or binding condemned persons to a simple wood structure shaped like a "T" [the *crux commissa*] or with the horizontal cross-beam [the *patibulum*] attached below the top of the upright [the *crux immissa*], they perfected its use on non-citizens of the Empire to extend imperial terror.

Herodotus notes that Persians used crucifixion for executions, and in turn Alexander the Great repeatedly resorted to crucifixion, at one point ordering this very humiliating death for at least 2,000 survivors of his siege of Tyre in Syria. Among Alexander's Hellenistic successors, Antiochus IV, ruler of Syria, in 167 B.C.E ordered the crucifixion of many Israelite males who remained faithful to Jewish Law, thereby adding to the humiliation that provoked the Maccabean revolt. Almost a century later, the Hellenized Judean Sadducee and high priest Alexander Janneus experimented with crucifixion by ordering this form of torture and execution for 800 Pharisees, his Jewish opposition, before whose eyes their wives and children were slaughtered as the men hung there dying. Note: This is the only Judean use of crucifixion known to me; in the House of Israel, stoning was the traditional and preferred means of capital punishment.

But it was the Romans who perfected this form of torture and capital punishment as a major means of social control and shaming of non-Roman citizens, perhaps having first observed its power as a deterrent to rebellion as practiced by the North African Carthaginians. From the time the Romans began to control affairs in Palestine in 63 B.C.E., they insisted that they alone had the authority to execute, and their favored mode was crucifixion. It combined excruciating torture with an exceedingly humiliating, public death. And it was efficient in the sense that following the binding and nailing of the condemned, it took only a guard or two to stand watch over a large number of them. The great Roman Cicero called crucifixion the *summum supplicum,* or most extreme form of punishment. A century later, the Stoic philosopher Seneca argued that suicide was greatly preferable to facing the extreme and drawn-out suffering created by crucifixion. And another first-century writer, the Jewish historian Josephus, after witnessing as many as five hundred crucifixions each day during the Roman army's siege of Jerusalem, called it "the most wretched of deaths." As the great New Testament historian Martin Hengel observes, "crucifixion was a punishment in which the caprice and sadism of the executioners were given full rein."[5]

That said, how plausible are the reports that Jesus of Nazareth was tortured and executed by crucifixion, including the conclusion that this form of death was ordered by the local representative of Roman authority, Pontius Pilate? Do our sources lead us to conclude that we are dealing with fact or with fantasy? Let's begin our analysis by noting and comparing the comments made by two disinterested (i.e., non-Christian), early historians who mention Jesus of Nazareth. From the early-second-century Roman historian Tacitus and the late-first-century Jewish historian Josephus we read four points on which they agree: A person called Jesus of Nazareth was active in Roman Palestine as a public figure during the rule of Pontius Pilate; second, his activity created a movement of some sort; third, the governing authorities (Tacitus mentions only the Romans; Josephus involves both the leaders of the Jews in Jerusalem and the Romans) crucified Jesus, thinking that would stop the movement. Fourth, this effort failed, and the movement continued to spread among both Jews and Gentiles. Tacitus calls this movement a "pernicious superstition" and observes that it had made its way to Rome, "where all things horrible or shameful in the world collect and find a vogue" (*Annals* 15.44, Loeb edition, vol. 4).

Turning then to an analysis of the first-century Christian sources, the widely-reported execution of Jesus by crucifixion satisfies two of the most demanding criteria that historians have developed to sort out the facts from faith and from fantasy. A high degree of historical probability is found in reports that caused embarrassment to the followers of Jesus and in multiple attestations of Jesus' sayings and deeds in ancient sources that were written independently of each other.

The criterion of embarrassment is satisfied here because speaking of a crucified Messiah was an unacceptable oxymoron (the "messiah" who was anticipated by many would be victorious and certainly never be executed—see Deuteronomy 21:23). And the criterion of multiple attestations in independent sources is met earliest by the letters of Paul of Tarsus, then by the Gospel according to Mark, then by Matthew's unique material, by Luke's unique material, and finally by the apparently independent narrative in the Gospel according to John. To be sure, there is no question that devout reflection on the meaning of Jesus' death and the desire to find prophetic anticipations of it colored these narratives. But there can be no serious historical question about whether Jesus of Nazareth existed as a public figure in Roman Palestine or whether he was crucified by order of Pontius Pilate. In this Gibson is true to history, apart from his distortion of some of the mechanics of crucifixion and his thorough whitewashing of Pilate's role.

Among Gibson's distortions is having Jesus drag a fully assembled cross, both cross-beam and vertical post, as has been imagined by those who had never observed a real crucifixion. Together those two large pieces of wood were prohibitively heavy for one person to carry, even before having been brutally beaten. Thus, in fact, the historical Jesus would have carried only the *patibulum* lashed across his shoulders, as the two rebels crucified with Jesus do in this film. And depicting later tradition but not historical plausibility, Gibson's soldiers pound the nails into Jesus' palms, which would fairly quickly have torn away from the cross, rather than through the wrist bones as required to bear the weight of the body. Further, the jarring dislocation of Jesus' shoulders to make his hands reach to holes pre-drilled for the nails is another visual detail taken not from the New Testament but from fourteenth-century Passion plays.[6]

No "Back Story"

So what is the fundamental historical problem with this movie, not the only problem to be sure, but the fundamental one? Simply this: there is no back story, no historical context. The viewer is given no clue why anyone respected, loved and followed Jesus of Nazareth—or why anyone had come to hate, fear, and desire to kill him.

This script cries out for a "prequel," a film that would present the historical Jesus in a narrative that would make sense of both the hostility and the adulation that he generated. A real estate agent will tell you that the most important factor regarding a piece of property is location. And the second most important factor is location. And, if you want to know, the third most important factor is, of course, location. Likewise, in history the most important thing to know to make adequate judgments about any person, event, document, etc., is context. And the second most important factor is more context. Then, of course, the third most important consideration is even more context. Much of the needed back story is indeed supplied by the writers of the New Testament Gospels. As John Dominic Crossan points out, Matthew, Mark, Luke, and John all have a certain ratio of chapters for the Public Life / Passion / Resurrection of Jesus. "Mark has 13/2/1, Matthew has 25/2/1, Luke has 21/2/1, and John has 17/2/1."[7] More on the needed back story in a few minutes. First consider the consequences of Gibson's practically context-less presentation of this crucifixion.

Since Gibson provides no back story, no serious illumination of the context, every viewer views this film in his or her own context, providing that context from his or her own conceptual "bucket" shaped by specific and prior expectations. A good education challenges students to trade in the inevitably limiting intellectual and emotional buckets they bring to a history course for buckets that can more adequately contain the truth of the subject being studied. But this film is not a classroom, and Gibson seems only to have one kind of bucket in mind—that of pious Roman Catholics, fundamentalist Christians, and some who prefer to call themselves "evangelical" Christians—and they have flocked to this film, with their leaders buying blocks of tickets for entire congregations.

In this case, those who regard Jesus as the first *Christian* will see unreasonably angry *Jewish* leaders encouraging the brutalizing of their Lord. Visually this impression is strongly reinforced by the appearance of the actor who plays Jesus, an attractive Italian-American man, Jim Caviezel, a "hunk" complete with a finely sculptured Roman nose, who is captured, tortured, and handed over to the Roman governor by Jewish leaders made up with stereotypical hooked noses and ugly visages and voices. As Alan F. Segal observes, "the costuming and make-up of this film make clear that the Jesus and the disciples of this film are not Jews."[8] While I think that it surely is a graphic improvement over certain medieval portrayals of a wimpy-looking Jesus finally to have a Jesus with "abs," who looks as if he could have created violent resistance if he had chosen to do so, it is very misleading and potentially dangerous to present a Jesus who looks so much different from his own people.

When Albert Schweitzer published his watershed treatment of *The Quest for the Historical Jesus* in 1906, the most far-reaching of his conclusions was that any future scholarship about Jesus of Nazareth had to begin with the fact that Jesus was a Jew and that most if not all of the first generation of his followers were Judeans. In addition, Schweitzer observed that all the "lives of Jesus" known to him revealed much more about the writers than about Jesus himself. In response to Schweitzer's critique, during the twentieth century, historians developed methods to help avoid this solipsistic trap. But Gibson apparently has ignored their hard and productive work and presents a Jesus who reveals more about Gibson than about Jesus in his context. Gibson has made it possible for viewers to forget that Jesus was born and raised as a son of the House of Israel. Even having a Jesus speak his native language, Aramaic, will most likely not anchor him firmly as a Jew among Jews for most viewers of his Roman nose.

What This Film Is Not—It Is Neither True to History Nor to the Writings in the Christian New Testament

Although most viewers of this film probably have not noticed, Gibson signals his lack of respect for historical scholarship in the very first frame. Printed in that opening frame is a famous quotation from the great Israelite Prophet Isaiah, chapter 53, including the phrase "by his stripes we shall be healed." Under the quotation Gibson provides a date, namely, 700 B.C.E., a pre-scholarly dating that is based on the assumption of an original unity of all 66 chapters of this edited book. So what? For most of the twentieth century the consensus among ancient historians has been that this part of the Book of Isaiah (sometimes referred to as "Second Isaiah") was not written until about 540 B.C.E.—a good 160 years later than Gibson acknowledges. I cannot take space here to detail what difference those 160 years make for the context of that part of Isaiah. Here my point is simply that Gibson could have presented this quotation without any date at all. But by putting the year "700 BC" under the quotation, Gibson thumbs his nose at historical analysis before any human being appears on the screen.

I would be glad to say that the remainder of the film shows that this initial ignoring or rejecting of historical scholarship was a momentary slip. But I cannot, for this unhistorical claim foreshadows many historical errors yet to come. Indeed, Gibson's film presents so many historical and linguistic errors that the overall effect must distress anyone who has studied the Mediterranean world of the first century of our era. For example, Gibson clearly intends for the use of Aramaic and Latin to convince the viewer that his presentation is true to history—not a documentary, perhaps, but certainly not a historical novel either. Yet, except for the exchanges in Latin between Pilate and the soldiers under his command, Greek would have been heard as the dominant second language in Roman Palestine after Aramaic. But here even the Latin is not historical—for both the grammar and the soft pronunciation are medieval, not the hard-consonant Latin pronunciation most likely used in the first century of our era. Note, for example, the Italian-sounding *facia* ("do it") with a soft "c" rather than *fac* or *facias* with a hard "c." Gibson did retain Professor William Fulco, a priest-scholar and medievalist at Loyola Marymount University, as consultant about the Latin, but apparently he did not consult with New Testament scholars or classicists who could have saved him from a lot of unnecessary errors.

This anachronistic use of language is a tip-off to something much more important: The plot of this film is not based directly on any New Testament narrative but on the traditions associated with the fourteen stations of the cross in medieval Roman Catholic piety. I say "medieval piety" rather than just Roman Catholic piety as such because the Second Vatican Council of the Roman Catholic Church eliminated from the stations of the cross two legendary traditions, namely, Veronica's mopping the blood from Jesus' face and Jesus falling three times while carrying the cross up the hill to Golgotha. That is, in accord with Gibson's own rejection of the reforms made by the Second Vatican Council, his story follows pre-Vatican II liturgies—and certainly not the New Testament writers.

The heavy emphasis in this film on the instruments of torture is also taken from the stations of the cross. In the New Testament only a crown of thorns and the cross itself are mentioned. A flogging is mentioned, to be sure, but the means for doing this are never described in the New Testament documents. Indeed, Gibson found much of the storyline not in the New Testament but in the meditations of a nineteenth-century nun named Anna Katharina Emmerich (1774–1824), a German Augustinian nun and mystic who dictated her visions during the last year of her life, later printed as *The Dolorous Passion of Our Lord Jesus Christ.* John Dominic Crossan, a specialist in research on the historical Jesus, drolly suggests that if *The Passion* receives an Oscar for its screenplay, the Oscar should be awarded posthumously to Sister Anna Katharina! He observes that about 80 percent of the outline and sequence of events is taken from Emmerich, 15 percent from Gibson's imagination, and only 5 percent from the New Testament (Corley and Webb, p. 12).

Here, then, are some of the details provided by Emmerich's visions, and I quote an English translation:

> After the flagellation, I saw Claudia Procles, the wife of Pilate, send some large pieces of linen to the Mother of God. I know not whether she thought that Jesus would be set free, and that his Mother would then require linen to dress his wounds, or whether this compassionate lady was aware of the use which would be made of her present . . . I soon after saw Mary and Magdalen approach the pillar where Jesus had been scourged . . . they knelt down on the ground near the pillar, and wiped up the sacred blood with the linen which Claudia Procles had sent.[9]

To be sure, Gibson does not follow Emmerich's narrative in every detail in this film, but in this case he does, suggesting that Pilate's wife had become very sympathetic to Jesus, if not a secret believer herself. The scene in which Mary receives the gift of linens sent by Claudia Procles provides as well a natural segue to pulling the camera back for a dramatic shot of the bloody pavement. This scene is crucial, since this is a film focused on blood, physical violence, and much more blood—implying sanguinary magic.

Within six minutes of the opening scene in the Garden of Gethsemane, Jewish authorities begin beating Jesus and binding him with chains already while still on the Mount of Olives; and this brutal treatment is continued for a full two hours without significant interruption. On a personal note, I confess that although I thought that I knew the story well enough to be ready for whatever would appear on the screen, my back muscles jerked straight when suddenly, shortly after his capture, Jesus was tossed over a bridge leading back to Jerusalem—followed by a loud "thunk," as the chains cut into his flesh! The film critic Roger Ebert has said that *The Passion* is the most violent film he's ever seen. It certainly is the most violent film I've ever seen—and in the end I felt emotionally abused and alienated from the story line.[10]

How the Romans Are Presented: Indecisive and Rather Clueless

Gibson completely whitewashes Pontius Pilate. In this film Pilate is pensive, philosophical, indecisive, almost winsome in his ways. To be sure, already in the Gospel according to Matthew he is depicted as washing his hands of this case (27:24). But Gibson takes that image of Pilate and pushes it way over the top.

The simple fact is that without the Roman governor's order no public capital punishment could be undertaken, as Josephus's report about the stoning of James, Jesus' brother, demonstrates (*Jewish Antiquities*, Bk. 20.9.1). So how are we to imagine the response of the historical Pilate to the historical Jesus? In my own analysis I've concluded that the historical Pilate sought, as usual, to do everything it took to blend keeping order with keeping people alive—for neither rebellious people nor dead people pay their taxes on time. "How could Jesus from Galilee be truly dangerous?" he must have asked himself. Jesus was apparently captured alone. "If he was a dangerous leader, where were his followers?" If his words and actions had created a disturbance among the milling crowds swelling Jerusalem to ten times its usual population during the politically delicate time of the Passover, the Liberation Feast of the Israelites, then shut him down and warn his followers by scourging him. Under the circumstances, Pilate must have thought: "Don't make this a bigger deal than it needs to be. Why turn him into a martyr in the eyes of anyone inclined to be sympathetic with his pathetic intentions?"

At the other end of the spectrum from Gibson's presentation of Pilate, treatments of Pilate not infrequently stress the ruthlessness and cultural insensitivity of his rule in Palestine. These negative judgments are based on the descriptions found in the writings of the Alexandrian Judean philosopher and leader Philo and the later Judean historian and Roman freedman Josephus. To be sure, there was no Roman school for diplomats or military leaders in which Pilate had been prepared for his work as prefect of Palestine. So the reports of his clashes with Jewish culture are certainly plausible. But it seems frequently to be ignored that both Philo and Josephus had their own respective reasons for presenting Pilate in an exaggerated and sharply negative manner. Had Pilate been as provocative and cruel as is often portrayed by scholars, he would have had great difficulty remaining the governor of Palestine for more than ten years. According to Josephus, when Pilate did seriously mishandle the Roman rule over the Samaritans, the Emperor Vitellius removed him from office. Up until then, Pilate had apparently done an acceptable job of looking after the empire's interests.

Integral to Pilate's success was the ongoing support of the Jewish elite who acted as middlemen in keeping the peace. Caiaphas, the high priest, had been in that office throughout Pilate's tenure serving at Pilate's pleasure, and Caiaphas had proven himself to be a reliable servant of Rome's interests in Palestine even before Pilate was sent there to become the governor. So why should Pilate question Caiaphas's judgment in this case? Pilate's earlier actions as the representative of Rome had always been pragmatic, and in my judgment they continued to be in the case of Jesus of Nazareth. Pilate's probable thoughts: "An innocent man? Who knows? Who cares? Better safe than sorry. Better to crucify one man and nip in the bud any potential uprising." Pilate must have been aware that Herod Antipas, who ruled to the north in the Galilee, had already sought to avoid an uprising of the people when he beheaded John the Baptist. So Pilate had at hand an attractive example of how to deal with such pesky prophets. And he ordered Jesus' crucifixion.

Not only Pilate but also Pilate's wife is played much too positively in this film. And as I've mentioned, the scene in which she brings cloths to Jesus' mother and Mary Magdalene to use in mopping up the pools of Jesus' blood on the floor of the flogging room is excessively dramatic. In a later story circulated in Egypt and North Africa (reported by the late-second-century Christian writer Tertullian), Pilate eventually became a Christian. Likewise, in Gibson's film, Pilate's wife already seems to be a not-so-secret follower of Jesus, opposed to his being crucified, as indeed she is presented in late medieval Passion plays, where she is given the name Claudia Procles.

How the Jews are Presented: Irrationally Angry and Hateful

None of the Jewish authorities are given any lines that would explain their determination to have Jesus killed. Although there are indeed a few Jewish leaders who protest the manner of the proceedings against Jesus, they are quickly forgotten as the charge of "blasphemy" is so strongly, angrily, and repeatedly thrown into Jesus' face. Yet, in sharp contract to the way I have heard the matter presented in sermons by many Christians, the "blasphemy" was not in a human being's being called a "messiah"—nor even for claiming to be a "son of

God" (as David was called in a widely respected tradition, see 2 Samuel 7:14; Psalm 2:7). Rather the blasphemy was found in the connections Jesus of Nazareth had made between the future destruction of the temple (in the spirit of the great prophet Jeremiah) and the undermining of the Pharisaic purity system on the one hand, and his claim to speak for the God of Israel on behalf of the poor, the marginalized, the sick and the mentally ill on the other. The blasphemy was seen in his directly forgiving people in God's name, making Temple sacrifice irrelevant and encouraging non-violent but aggressive resistance to exploitation of the poor by the elite. No wonder so many came to regard him as a prophet—like Elijah in his outreach even to non-Judeans (see Luke 4:25–26) and like Jeremiah in his sharp critique of temple religion (see Jeremiah, chapters 7 and 26). *That* was the blasphemy. And Pilate would have had no trouble regarding this behavior as *maiestas*—treason against the empire.

The high priest Caiaphas had learned well how to get along with the Roman occupation forces. Indeed, he apparently had made himself seem indispensable. For when the Roman authorities were appointing new Jewish high priests on the average of every 16 months (17 high priests in 22 years), they retained Caiaphas in power for 18 years. After the prefect Valerius Gratus appointed Caiaphas to be high priest around 18 C.E., Valerius's successor, Pontius Pilate, reappointed Caiaphas and kept him in that office throughout the entire period of Pilate's rule. Caiaphas clearly understood how to "play the game" to preserve Jewish privileges and his own power under the Roman occupying force. The temple authorities under Caiaphas cooperated with a very oppressive system of taxation. So, it can be no surprise that shortly after the first Jewish revolt against the Roman Empire began in 66 C.E., the peasants stormed specific buildings in the Temple courts in order to burn the debt records that the elite landowners had archived there.

Nevertheless, in this film the brutality at the hands of the Jewish authorities is excessive beyond historical plausibility. Nothing in the New Testament suggests that the flogging of Jesus was non-stop before he was brought to Pilate. But in the film, Jesus is already in such bad shape when presented to Pilate, that Pilate asks the Jewish leaders, "Do you always punish your prisoners before they are judged?"

Here I remind you of who directed and produced this film: *Braveheart*, with *Lethal Weapons*—that is, Mel Gibson, in roles in which he takes everything anyone has to throw at him. Gibson's Jesus can take beating, flogging, flaying, even filleting, and finally crucifying—with the result for me that this no longer looks like sacrifice but like macho masochism. In his *Christian Century* review, screenwriter John Petrakis ends with this sentence: "To reduce Jesus Christ to a tough dude who can take a licking and keep on ticking is not exactly a feat that calls for hosannas" (March 23, 2004, p. 40). Yet it is apparently the sheer physical endurance of Gibson's Jesus, rather than the appeal of his life and words, that converts Simon of Cyrene and the Roman centurion.

For anyone who already knows something about the story, the violence is so excessive and extensive, it is highly probable that the film bludgeons rather than evokes the imagination, as great art typically does. In the end, the non-stop violence and brutality became unconvincing for me, both historically and emotionally. Yet it is clear that not everyone has this negative reaction. During the winter quarter of 2004, one of my teaching assistants was a man from Mexico City. He commented to me that the film was "going gangbusters" back home, for such an intense focus on the immense suffering of Jesus is a perfect fit with typical Latin American piety. He observed that for these believers it is the bleeding, suffering, and grotesquely disfigured Jesus on the cross that is more important than anything else about him.

Another contribution of Sister Anna Katharina to the film is the black-hooded figure who incarnates evil. In Emmerich's visions, during Jesus' agonizing decision-making in the Garden of Gethsemane, the Evil One tempted Jesus to give up his redemptive vision by addressing such words as these to him: "Takest thou even this sin upon thyself" (i.e., all the sins of the human race). "Art thou willing to bear its penalty? Art thou prepared to satisfy for all these sins?" Gibson takes this motif and has a sexually ambiguous figure whisper just such words, suggesting that bearing the sins of the world is simply too much for anyone, including Jesus. Then an ominous-looking snake (is there any other kind?) slithers from under the Tempter's robe, and Jesus dramatically crushes the serpent's head beneath his sandaled heel, making vivid the metaphorical image and prediction in Genesis 3:15. In that passage, set in the Garden of Eden, God tells the serpent: "He (the offspring of woman) will strike your head and you will strike his heel."

In the memory of Jewish friends of mine who have seen this film, this black-hooded figure appears among the high priests and then in the crowd scenes solely among the Jews, suggesting that he/she was especially welcome or effective among them. This impression prevails even though the Evil One also glides among the Roman soldiers as Jesus is scourged with barbed whips.[11]

The historically questionable scene with Herod Antipas and his entourage in Jerusalem is also worth a brief comment. Gibson presents Antipas as a gender-ambiguous, naked-to-the-waist, licentious figure whose debauchery is interrupted by the arrival of Jesus in chains. To be sure, Antipas was irreligious and had no doubt come to Jerusalem first of all to keep an eye on things rather than simply to celebrate the Passover. Yet there is nothing in Gibson's film to suggest that Antipas was a sensible and clever politician, who ruled Galilee and Peraea successfully (i.e., without direct Roman interference) for forty-three years! To the contrary, Gibson has created an effete and ineffectual figure who can hardly be taken seriously as a ruler.

How the Historical Jesus Is Betrayed and Christians Are Misled

Although there are a few flashbacks to Jesus' life before his Passion, in none of them does Gibson present the evidence for Jesus as a strong advocate for the poor, the marginalized, the physically and mentally ill. None of the few flashbacks stresses the socially revolutionary character of his aggressive nonviolence and his filtering and focusing of the traditions of Israel. And perhaps the most misleading of these scenes presents Jesus showing his mother Mary the high table and chairs that he had crafted, implying that he was pleased to serve an elite clientele.

As mentioned above, a viewer of this film would have no awareness of Jesus' challenge to Temple religion: Rejecting the idea of sacred space (Matthew 18:20 asserts that Jesus' spirit will be *anywhere* two or three are gathered in Jesus' name), of a brokered relation to the God of Israel via priests (human beings can directly forgive each other as Jesus did), and of the value of ritual sacrifice ("sacrifice" is now to be made in terms of treating others with justice and mercy). In Jesus' massive critique of the then-current religious establishment, we hear vigorous echoes of the voices of the great prophets Amos, Jeremiah, and Isaiah. The opposition of the Jewish elite to Jesus' activity was not at all irrational as suggested by the film (echoing, to be sure, the way the situation has been portrayed in too many sermons for centuries).

There is nothing in this film about the historical Jesus' challenge in God's name to patriarchal authority, to the demands of blood kinship, to the male honor code with its violent agenda, or to the related female code of avoiding shame at all costs. Jesus taught that only God is to be called "father" (Matthew 23:9), and one's true brothers and sisters are those who do the will of God (Mark 3:31–35 and parallels in Matthew and Luke). And even the apparently promiscuous and shameless "woman at the well" in John 4 is portrayed as the first Samaritan to testify publicly to Jesus' authority.

Nothing in the film suggests that Jesus proclaimed God's ruling in a redeemed society that rejected intimidation, dominance, shaming and violence, and in which brother and sister values characterized all human relationships. "The most honored among you will be the one who serves" (Mark 10:35–45, verse 43).

By ignoring the points that I have just made, persons on the so-called religious right have concluded that Gibson initially had so much difficulty getting this film distributed because of "liberal" American culture's hostility to "real Christianity." As one person said: "Boy, it's just getting harder and harder to be a Christian anymore. Here's Mel Gibson being persecuted for making a Christian film. The last days are upon us."[12] It is profoundly disturbing to me how a violent and obsessive, pre-Vatican II Roman Catholic film becomes a touchstone for many American Protestants. Apparently, the egregious violence in this film plugs into the so-called "culture war" between right-wing Christians and those Christians who are not. And this "war" is fed by right-wing claims that those Christians who are not part of the nationalistic right wing are not patriotic, for example, if they oppose the war in Iraq or oppose other attempts to solve the world's problems by overwhelming violence. I must ask: Which God do they worship?

This question becomes particularly acute in the amazing scene in which a large black bird flies down and ominously perches on the top of the cross of the rebel who mocked Jesus. In horror the viewer anticipates and then sees this hideous bird peck out this helpless rebel's eyes. Is Gibson inviting the viewer to regard this as payback for unbelief in Jesus? Is this supposed to be understood as an act of God? If so, who is this God?—certainly not the God who loves his enemies, as proclaimed and demonstrated by the historical Jesus. This scene is made all the more questionable by the next one in which a tiny drop of water reflects a satellite photo of Jesus on the cross and is morphed into a tear from God's eye. When this tear hits the ground, an earthquake hits![13] Who *is* this God?

Who, Then, Was Responsible for the Death of Jesus of Nazareth?

Prior to the Second Vatican Council of the Roman Catholic Church, it was common to hear in the churches that "Jews are Christ-killers" (stated also by my high school civics teacher, of all people, in a classroom discussion).[14] On the other hand, according to Charlotte Allen, writing in the *Los Angeles Times* (February 29, 2004), Professor Paula Fredriksen, my colleague at Boston University, asserted in a truly puzzling response to pre-release rumors about Gibson's film that not a single Jew, not even the corrupt high priest and collaborator, Caiaphas, had anything material to do with the crucifixion of Jesus of Nazareth.

Will this film generate anti-Jewish attitudes and actions? According to a survey of 1,703 Americans released in early April 2004 by the prestigious Pew Research Center for the People and the Press, "a growing minority of Americans believe that Jews were responsible for Christ's death. Roughly a quarter of the public (26%) now expresses that view." The effect of seeing Gibson's film is indicated by the fact that a significantly larger proportion of people who have seen the film feel that the Jews were responsible for Jesus' death, namely, 36 percent, an increase of a full 10 percent. The percentage is even higher among those aged 18–34 (426 of those surveyed) who have seen the film, namely, 42 percent![15] Such high numbers do not bode well for our culture and our life together in the United States. And the potentially anti-Jewish effect of the worldwide distribution of this film must be watched very carefully. As a result both of Gibson's relatively positive portrayal of Pilate and his presentation of the Jewish leaders as irrational and hateful, "one definitely comes away from the film with the understanding that it was primarily the Jews who are responsible for the crucifixion of Jesus" (Corley and Webb, 2004:173). Yes, there is a great need for good historical education regarding Jesus and his social/economic/political/religious context.

Now, asking "*who* was responsible for Jesus' death?" is in my judgment the wrong question. A much better question would be: "*What* was responsible for Jesus' death?" By asking the question this way, I agree with Ellis Rivkin of Hebrew Union College in Cincinnati, who has published a book with this question as its title (*What Crucified Jesus?* 1984), and with an increasing number of New Testament scholars. The blame must be placed on a ruthless military dictatorship, on imperial politics, on colonial corruption of local elites, and on a Roman culture that thrived on brutality. In my judgment, it would be helpful to consider that Jesus died *because of*, as a result of, humanity's sins and not just *on behalf of* humanity's sins.

Mary and the Problem with Passion Plays

As in all Passion plays known to me, as the plot unfolds other characters prove to be more interesting than Jesus himself. Often it is Judas, because of the character development. Even a negative change is more interesting than none at all. And so it is in this film. Also, Peter's role is well developed and is wonderfully acted in this film. In terms of human interest, however, I think it is Mary, the mother of Jesus, who is the center of this film. In striking contrast to her limited portrayal in the New Testament, Mary is omnipresent; there is hardly a scene without her. Her confusion and growing agony are powerfully portrayed by a superb actress, Maia Morgenstern. And then, toward the end of the film, her tender concern for her son is mocked by the incarnation of Evil and the deformed monster baby or imp cradled in his/her arms whom we see on the way to Golgotha, the striking counter-image of an evil Pieta.[16]

This "baby," or rather this *homunculus* (miniature fully formed human), seems to follow the imagination of the eleventh-century medieval demonologist Michael Psellos (1018–1078), who suggested that the entire earth was governed by a host of small, impish, sub-demon classes. According to Psellos, the Anti-Christ will be such an imp who eventually grows into an even more dangerous adult.[17]

The Presentation of the Resurrection of Jesus

In light of the strong emphasis in the early Christian movement on the God of Israel's having honored and confirmed Jesus' actions and message by raising him into a new dimension of life, as the "first fruits of those who have died" (1 Corinthians 15:20), I found myself wondering how Gibson would choose to end this film, especially since he had ignored so much of Jesus' life prior to the Passion.

As dark patches move quickly across the screen, the viewer becomes gradually aware that these are the shifting shadows cast by the apparently self-activated rolling of a huge stone. At first, with a certain relief, I thought that Gibson had chosen to end his film as the earliest manuscripts of the Gospel according to Mark end (at 16:8), with an empty tomb and a young man's message to meet Jesus, who has been raised by God, in "Galilee" in the future.[18] But no, next the camera enters the tomb and focuses on an apparently occupied shroud. Then the viewer is shown a deflating of the shroud—a hokey touch, in my judgment. Note: These details are not to be found in any New Testament document. The film ends by showing a beautifully cleaned-up Jesus in profile—and, if I am not mistaken, this scene is supported by martial-sounding music.

In any case, the impression left with me—as a continuation of that horrible raven's eye-pecking—was: Now it's payback time. John Petrakis comments in *The Christian Century* that the scene showing Jesus after the resurrection "suggests an angry man with a hangover who is going to take it out on someone" (March 23, 2004, p. 40). My mind raced to the fourth century and the post-Constantinian establishment of Christianity by Theodosius the Great as the only legal religion in the Roman Empire. This act, in 391 C.E., effectively outlawed Judaism as well as all forms of paganism and opened the door to brutal persecution of Jews by people calling themselves Christians. This co-opting of Christianity by Rome's military dictatorship was not the first or the last betrayal of the historical Jesus, but in my judgment it may well be the ultimate betrayal of Jesus of Nazareth's mission and of his vision of God's ruling in the here and now: "Your kingdom come, Your will be done, on earth as it is in heaven."

Discussion Questions

1. According to this article, what verbal and graphic clues did Gibson provide that would lead the reader to conclude that Jesus of Nazareth was a first-century Jew—or that he was not really a Jew but the "first Christian"? If you've seen this film, do you remember any additional clues?
2. This article has stressed the importance of the historical context for understanding the execution of Jesus of Nazareth. In your judgment, what is the minimum that a person must know to prevent serious misunderstanding of this event?
3. What is gained or lost in the various attempts to blame "the Jews" or "the Romans" as such for Jesus' death?

Notes

1. Reprinted with permission of the *Journal of Pastoral Psychology*. For a fascinating review of films made about Jesus of Nazareth, see W. Graham Tatum, *Jesus at the Movies: A Guide to the First Hundred Years* (Santa Rosa, CA: Polebridge Press, 1997).
2. Stated in "Dude That Was Graphic: An Interview of Mel Gibson" by David Neff and Jane Johnson Strunk, posted February 23, 2004; available from www.christianitytoday.com/movies/interviews/melgibson.html.
3. Mel Gibson, "Foreword" in Jim Bolton et al. (eds.), *The Passion: Photography from the Movie "The Passion of the Christ"* (Wheaton, IL: Tyndale House, 2004), p. v.

4. Stated in Steve Little's interview of Haggard for CBN.com, " 'The Passion of the Christ' Is Historically Accurate, Not Anti-Semitic," no date. Available from www.cbn.com/CBNNews/CWN/080803tedhaggard.asp.
5. Martin Hengel, *Crucifixion* (Philadelphia: Fortress Press, 1977), p. 25.
6. See, for example, the Passion sequence in the "Wakefield" play of Corpus Christi, the medieval festival that followed Easter by about six weeks, at which—over time—a variety of Passion plays were performed.
7. John Dominic Crossan, "Hymn to a Savage God." in Kathleen E. Corley and Robert L. Webb (eds.), *Jesus and Mel Gibson's "The Passion of the Christ": The Film, the Gospels and the Claims of History* (New York: Continuum, 2004), pp. 8–27.
8. Alan Segal, "The Jewish Leaders," In Corley and Webb, *Jesus and Mel Gibson's The Passion of the Christ*, p. 93. Furthermore, as Gary Gilbert observes: "Male Jews who oppose Jesus are often seen wearing prayer shawls over their heads. By contrast, the good Jews, the disciples, and Simon of Cyrene go bareheaded." "Anti-Semitism without Erasure." In J. Shawn Landres and Michael Berenbaum (eds.), *After the Passion Is Gone: American Religious Consequences* (New York: AltaMira Press, 2004), p. 128.
9. This book is published in several editions, e.g., A. C. Emmerich, *The Dolorous Passion of Our Lord Jesus Christ* (ed. Clemens Maria Brentano. El Sobranta, CA: North Bay Books, 2003).
10. Mark Juergensmeyer observes: "It almost would be the stuff of a horror movie if it were not couched in such a religious setting. In many ways, though, it *is* a horror movie, an orgy of bloodshed that goes far beyond the Christian tradition's norm for portraying the agony and sacrifice of Jesus." "Afterword: The Passion of War," in Landres and Berenbaum, p. 280.
11. Mark Allan Powell observes: "The portrayal of Satan as an observer of Christ's suffering—or, specifically, of his scourging and procession to Calvary—appears to be completely without biblical parallel." "Satan and the Demons," in Corley and Webb, p. 75.
12. Reported by Eric R. Samuelson, "Unremitting Passion," *Sunstone*, vol. 13, p. 70.
13. And as Jeffrey Siker observes: "Pilate's palace shakes, but nothing is destroyed; by contrast, not only does the Jewish Temple suffer the familiar torn curtain, but the foundation of the Temple itself suffers a devastating fissure—apparently Gibson's commentary on the status of Judaism after the death of Jesus." "Theologizing the Death of Jesus," In Landres and Berenbaum, p. 145.
14. Richard L. Rubenstein comments: "The accusation of deicide made against Jews places *unbelieving* Jews squarely in the camp of Satan, as does Gibson's film. To make his point, Gibson inserts into the narrative a perhaps hermaphroditic Satan and seven demonic young Jewish boys. The Gospels offer no warrant for either insertion." "The Exposed Fault Line," in Landres and Berenbaum, p. 207.
15. Pew Research Center for the People and the Press. "Belief that Jews were Responsible for Christ's Death Increases. Survey Reports." Released April 2, 2004. Available from http://people-press.org.
16. Mark Allan Powell concludes that Gibson presents Satan as an "anti-mother," noting that Mary the mother of Jesus moves through the crowd on Jesus' right while Satan is doing the same but on Jesus' left. "Thus Satan's interest in Jesus is portrayed as being like that of his mother, only perverse." In Corley and Webb, p. 73.
17. For a fascinating discussion of medieval demonology, see Jeffrey Russell, *Lucifer: The Devil in the Middle Ages* (New York: Cornell University Press, 1991).

18. The women who have come to the tomb to anoint Jesus' body are told "Go, tell his disciples and Peter that he is going ahead of you to Galilee; there you will see him, just as he told you." Later readers of Mark were dissatisfied with the absence of a resurrection appearance as such and added as many as twelve additional verses, in different manuscript traditions, to incorporate appearances modeled on those reported in the other Gospel accounts.

Reflections on Mel Gibson's *The Passion of the Christ*

Louis H. Feldman

As Elie Wiesel has said, the world is willing to forget the slaughter of six million innocent Jews sixty years ago, but it will never forget the execution of that one Jew two thousand years ago.

What we have in the film *The Passion* is a Passion play of the sort that used to be put on in Oberammergau and that was always an occasion not merely for the production of the play, but also for raising the population against the Jews. And I believe that the danger of such a film is tremendous, precisely because it is of the Passion play type; and this will be the most watched Passion play in history. Billy Graham has remarked that *The Passion* is a lifetime of sermons in one movie. Michael Novak, Professor of Philosophy and Religion at the American Enterprise Institute in Washington, D.C., writes, "This drama . . . is situated in the soul of each of us, where a war is being fought out. . . . It brings one to one's knees. Silence is what one craves at the end."[1] Nevertheless, a measured, yet critical response to the film, *The Passion of the Christ*, must also be stated.[2]

The film opened to packed houses in Jordan, Syria, and Lebanon.[3] According to Hamze Mansoor, secretary-general of the Islamic Action Front of Jordan, "The Jews are most upset because it reveals their crimes against the prophets, reformers, and whoever contradicts their opinions." Mel Gibson himself has said that the film stems from a personal crisis about twelve years ago that found him on the verge of suicide, forcing him to re-examine his faith, and, in particular, to meditate upon the nature of suffering, pain, forgiveness, and redemption.

Furthermore, Gibson has been quoted as saying that he was particularly inspired by the visions of an early-nineteenth-century German mystic and stigmatic nun, Anna Katharina Emmerich, as recorded by Clemens Brentano, the nineteenth-century German romantic poet.[4] Sister Anna Katharina claimed to receive visitations from Jesus, as a result of which she describes the scourging of Jesus in gruesome and brutal detail. This is the nun who reports that an old Jewish woman told her that the Jews in former times, both in Germany and elsewhere, had strangled many Christians, principally children, and used their blood for all sorts of diabolical practices. She asserts that the Jews still follow such practices in Germany and elsewhere but do so very secretly because of commercial ties with Christians. Her world-view of a cosmic battle between demonic powers, joined with Jews, against the believers in Jesus pervades Gibson's film. This is the nun who has already attained the title of "venerable," indicating that she had lived a life of heroic virtue and who has, at various times, been considered for possible sainthood.

What has Mel Gibson done in this movie? He himself has said that his intention was to make "a responsible, historically accurate movie." Indeed, *The Passion* is presented as a documentary. He has been quoted as saying that this is what he wanted critics to consider, whether it is historically accurate, whether it is a responsible movie. The fact that he chose to have the movie in two languages that most people do not know—the Jews speak Aramaic and the Romans speak Latin (the rumor is that Gibson originally planned not to include subtitles)—would seem to be a key to his intention. Indeed, the original reaction of Pope John Paul II to the film is reported to have been precisely this, "It is as it was," although Vatican officials later denied this. Gibson wanted to have people think that this is the way it really was—this is what really was said by both the Jews and by the Romans.

The fact that he chose Latin is a very significant point because at that particular time, in that particular place in Judea, Latin was not the prevalent language, although, in all fairness, it must be stated that, as Matthew Dillon has noted,[5] it was the official language of the law courts and the army, the two major contexts where it occurs in the film; and an inscription with the name of Pontius Pilate inscribed in Latin has been found in Caesarea in Judea. The soldiers in the Roman army apparently came predominantly from the immediate area, and most of them, we may assume, spoke Greek. Moreover, there is no reason to believe that Jesus knew Latin, and so it is most likely that conversations between Jesus and Pilate occurred in Greek. So why should Gibson have chosen to have the Roman soldiers speak Latin? The answer, it would seem, is that he, a conservative Catholic, was very much upset by Vatican II forty years ago, which permitted the mass, which had been recited for hundreds of years in Latin in the West, to be recited in any language; and he wanted to turn the clock back. And the Latin in the film, it should be noted, is not the Latin that was spoken by Caesar and Cicero. It is Church Latin. He wanted to have this film as a religious experience and as an emotional experience, not as an intellectual experience. As to the Aramaic spoken by the Jews in the film, there is a real question whether the subtitles, which are in English, accurately correspond to the spoken words. Thus, at one point the high priest Caiaphas turns to his cohorts and says something in Aramaic. The subtitle says: "You take care of it." In point of fact, he is saying, "Take care of my laundry."

Anyone watching the film would have wondered how much difficulty the actors must have had in memorizing their lines in a foreign language. They did not know Aramaic; they did not know Latin. Then I realized, as I watched the film, why it was not really so difficult, namely because the film actually has very few spoken lines, very little dialogue. It is basically an attempt to present these people as having faces; and there is a tremendous number of shots of individuals, particularly the high priest. The film is, in effect, much more than the words. It is really a panorama.

The film, of course, claims to be accurate in the sense that from Mel Gibson's point of view it is a correct representation of the account of the last hours in the life of Jesus according to the Gospels. However, the fact that it depends upon the Gospels immediately raises a number of questions because, after all, there are four different accounts in the Gospels, and they do not agree with one another in a number of respects. For example, there are different genealogies of Jesus. They have different accounts of the trial of Jesus. And there are other discrepancies.

In addition to these four accounts, there are a number of accounts that never made it into the canon of the New Testament. So, therefore, to speak of something that will be dependent upon the Gospels, we should ask "Which Gospel?" And as we shall see, Gibson picks and chooses whichever he wants.

Secondly, how can you depend upon the Gospels when, after all, the Gospels were not composed in Galilee, where Jesus came from. They were not composed in Jerusalem, where Jesus died. They were not composed in Aramaic, the language that Jesus spoke, but in Greek. They were written by people who never knew Jesus in person. One of them, Luke, was not a Jew. And they were written at least forty years after the death of Jesus. Now, coming from such sources, would evidence be admitted in a court today, let alone be ready to convict somebody?

To be sure, in the first century we hear that there appeared at the eastern end of the Mediterranean a remarkable religious leader who taught the worship of the true G-d and declared that religion meant not the sacrifice of beasts but the practice of charity and piety and the shunning of hatred and enmity. He was said to have worked miracles and goodness, casting out demons, healing the sick, raising the dead. His exemplary life led some of his followers to claim that he was the son of G-d, though he himself called himself the son of a man. Accused of sedition against Rome, he was arrested. After his death his disciples claimed he had risen from the dead. Who was this teacher and wonder worker? He was born about 4 B.C.E., the year in which much of scholarship believes Jesus was born. His name, however, was Apollonius of Tyana. His story may be read in Philostratus's *Life of Apollonius of Tyana*. It would seem that Jesus was not unique. And a case can be made for the view that Jesus was not the founder but the foundling of Christianity and that Christianity is a religion not of Jesus but about Jesus.

Moreover, the Koran (23.51) has a very different account of the death of Jesus. There we read that Jesus was put on the cross but was taken down before he died and was resurrected, that he thereafter departed from Judea to carry his message to the lost tribes of Israel and eventually died at a good old age on a pleasant plateau with springs of running water.

Mel Gibson's movie intends to create a mood. One sees it at the very beginning of the movie and throughout. Jews are depicted as being in the company of devils. One is reminded of the words of the fourth-century Church Father John Chrysostom, that the Jews are possessed by the devil, that they murder their offspring and immolate them to the devil, and that the synagogue is the domicile of the devil, who is the veritable soul of the Jews. In the film it is Satan, who, in the form of an androgynous hooded figure—an addition to the Gospel account—tempts Jesus in the garden of Gethsemane. He asks Jesus, "Who is your father? Who are you?" What is the connection of the devils with the events that the movie tries to present? What Gibson is trying to do is based upon the New Testament and the church fathers, who look upon the Jews as possessed by the devil, who murder their offspring. Thus John Chrysostom—his name Chrysostom indicates that he was a great, golden-mouthed orator—in the fourth century declares: "They murder their offspring, they immolate them to the devil."[6] "The synagogue is the domicile of the devil, a cavern of devils."[7]

And having the Jews associated with devils creates a certain mood, and that mood prevails through the movie as a whole. One sees Jewish children, for example, in the movie taunting Judas. And they turn into demons. And that particular scene is not in the Gospels at all but is part of the mood that Gibson is trying to create.

The result of Vatican II was that the Roman Catholic Church decided that something had to be done to prevent the mass attacks upon Jews that had prevailed through the centuries. And they suggested, in particular, two things, which, as we shall see, Gibson does not do. One of them was to drop the scenes of large, chanting Jewish crowds. Of course, there were some large Jewish crowds. Maybe they did chant. But the fact that there are large crowds in the movie constantly chanting creates mass hysteria, which the Roman Catholic Church itself has advised its adherents to drop.

And secondly, the church urged dropping the device of the Sanhedrin trial. To be sure, that is in the Gospels. But the fact is that it has served to create quite a number of attacks upon the Jews that are unwarranted.

In 1988 the United States Bishops' Committee for Ecumenical and Interreligious Affairs issued "Criteria for the Evaluation of Dramatizations of the Passion." In particular, they recommended that such dramatizations should present the diversity of Jewish communities in Jesus' time, that Jews should not be portrayed as avaricious or bloodthirsty, that any crowd scenes should reflect the fact that some in the crowd and among the Jewish leaders supported Jesus and that the rest were manipulated by his opponents, that Jesus' opponents should not be made to look sinister while his friends are depicted in lighter tones, that if a particular Gospel is offensive to Jews it should not be used, and that Pontius Pilate should be presented as a ruthless figure. The film violates each of these recommendations.

In particular, what Gibson did was to take these mass-crowd scenes and to give all the ingredients for an outbreak against the Jews. Certainly the most vicious anti-Jewish remark in the Gospels is one in Matthew (27:25) where the Jews say, "His blood be upon us and on our children." In other words, that not only they themselves but also their children, presumably forever, take this curse upon themselves. And that it is upon present-day Jews, too. That statement has often been said to be more responsible for attacks upon Jews than any other single statement in the whole New Testament.

Now, Gibson was made aware of this. He had a council of advisers when he made the movie, consisting of people who were experts in the field of New Testament study and the whole Hellenistic period. And they advised him to remove that from the film. He finally decided on a compromise. What he did was to remove it from the subtitles, but he did not remove it from the original language. So, therefore, if you happen to know Aramaic, you will hear it. That, it would seem, is again an indication of where he stands.

In regard to the Sanhedrin, the Roman Catholic Church itself, as noted above, realized the danger in presenting the scene where Jesus is questioned before the Sanhedrin. There are a number of problems that the Roman Catholic Church itself understood. First of all, the word that is used in the Greek is Synedron, which is the same word as our *Sanhedrin*. There are some people who claim that it's not really *the* Sanhedrin; it is just a meeting, the kind of meeting of people who get together, a conference.

But the fact is that it is called the Sanhedrin; and that is the way it is presented in the movie as well. Once it is identified with the Sanhedrin, there are a number of differences between the way in which that particular group met and the way in which the Sanhedrin conducted itself. For example, the Sanhedrin had a presiding officer who was a Pharisaic scholar. In the movie, as in the Gospels (Matthew 26:59 ff., Mark 14:53 ff., Luke 22:66 ff.), it is the high priest himself. What Gibson has done is to focus on the two figures who are the main figures in the whole story, aside from Jesus himself, and they are the high priest, on the one hand, who represents the Jews, and Pontius Pilate, who represents the Romans. The high priest is presiding over the Sanhedrin. That is not the way in which the Sanhedrin conducted itself so far as we can see in Mishnah and the Gemara and, so far as we can tell, throughout the time that the Sanhedrin was functioning.

Secondly, the place where the Sanhedrin met is not, as in the Gospels

(Matthew 26:57–58, Mark 14:53–54, Luke 22:54, John 18:15, 24) and in the film, the house of the high priest, but rather in the particular hall known as the Chamber of Hewn Stone. The time when the Sanhedrin met is not, as it is in the New Testament and in the movie, at night (Mark 14:53–54, Matthew 26:57 ff.) or on a festival (Luke 22:66) or both (Mark 15:1, Matthew 26:57 ff., 27:1–2). They did not meet that way so far as the Mishnah (*Sanhedrin* 4:1) is concerned.

Again, according to the procedure of the *Sanhedrin*, the trial must begin with the reasons for acquittal. That is not the procedure according to the Gospels and according to the film. Moreover, according to the procedure mentioned by the rabbis (*Sanhedrin* 8b, 80b), no person may be convicted of a capital offense unless two lawfully qualified witnesses testify that they had first warned him of the criminality of the act and of the penalty prescribed for it. That is not the way in which this procedure is presented in the Gospels or in the film itself. Witnesses must be warned before they give evidence that they are doing something very important, very serious (Mishnah, *Sanhedrin* 4:5). They are not warned in the Gospels or in the film. And most important, in the procedure the person who is on trial is not permitted to incriminate himself (Tosefta *Sanhedrin* 11:1, *Shavuot* 3:8). The idea of self-incrimination is completely foreign to the procedure, whereas in the film Jesus is asked to incriminate himself. And in one of the Gospels (Mark 14:62) he does incriminate himself.

Then a verdict of guilt may not be given on the same day (Mishnah, *Sanhedrin* 5:5). The committee or the Sanhedrin has to sleep on it, so to speak. Some people say that that is the reason why Jews have two days of Rosh Hashanah, because Rosh Hashanah is a day of judgment, and one should not have the verdict on the same day. One last point: the Sanhedrin is a Jewish organization. According to the rules of the Sanhedrin, if there was a unanimous vote then the defendant was automatically freed (*Sanhedrin* 17a; Maimonides, *Mishneh Torah, Sanhedrin* 7.1). Apparently, the feeling was that if one could get a large group to agree on something, they were in cahoots or something like that.

In short, the procedure that was followed in the trial of Jesus, as depicted in the Gospels and in the film, was not the procedure with which we are familiar in the Talmud. Moreover, we have a statement that a Sanhedrin that condemned one person to death in seventy years is called a bloody Sanhedrin *Makkot* 7a). It was not very common, to put it mildly.

Now, what were the charges in this particular case before the high priest in the movie before the Sanhedrin? Here we have a matter of great importance. Jesus is told, "Tell us if you are the Christ, the son of G-d" (Matthew 26:60–64, Mark 14:61–64, Luke 22:66–71). Now, the word *Christos* in Greek means "anointed one" and is the word that is the translation of Messiah. And in one of the Gospels, Mark (14:62), he actually says, "I am." In the others he is equivocal about it.

The high priest then says, "He has uttered blasphemy" (Matthew 26:65, Mark 14:64). Now blasphemy means that one has uttered the name of G-d, the

Tetragrammaton, in vain. There is no indication, so far as we can tell in the Gospels or in the movie for that matter, that Jesus ever did commit blasphemy in that particular sense, because it is a very technical sense. Then the high priest says, "Do we still need witnesses?" (Matthew 26:65, Mark 14:63). Of course, from a Jewish point of view, "the matter rests upon two witnesses" (Deuteronomy 17:6, 19:15). And yet, the high priest in the Gospels says that witnesses are not needed because he has incriminated himself.

Moreover, the assumption of the title *Mashiach*, "Messiah," (Mark 14:62) is not in itself blasphemous. As a matter of fact, there have been quite a number of people in Jewish history who have claimed to be a Messiah. Not long after Jesus, for example, Bar Kochba was so declared. And there were others as well.

With regard to the charge concerning the temple, Jesus says, "I am able to destroy the Temple of G-d and to build it in three days" (Matthew 26:61; cf. Mark 14:58). Moreover, we are told (Mark 14:56, 59) that the witnesses did not agree. But if their testimony did not agree that particular charge should have been thrown out. Furthermore, to say that the temple would be destroyed is not a ground for conviction. According to Jewish law, a person is convicted not because of words but because of deed. We find that the same kind of talk, predicting that the temple will be destroyed, is found in the prophet Jeremiah and the prophet Ezekiel, for example, and is not a ground for conviction.

Another one of the charges is in the film but not in the New Testament itself. Witnesses tell the Sanhedrin that Jesus worked magic with the devil. That is part of the mood that is created by the film, that the Jews are connected with the devil. That is much more than the charge that a man claimed to be the Messiah or even claimed to be G-d. Moreover, in the film, in Jesus' encounter with the council of the Jews, he is, in an addition to the Gospels, physically assaulted by a crowd of dozens of Jews, many of whom are visibly identified as Jews since they are wearing prayer shawls.

Someone then says, "He said that if we don't eat his flesh and blood that we will not inherit eternal life." That is not in the Gospels; that is in the film. And again, it is part and parcel of the agenda of the person who made the film.

Another charge made in the film but not in the New Testament account of the cross-examination of Jesus by the Sanhedrin is that Jesus violated the Sabbath. That is a very serious charge, of course. Moreover, in the film witnesses tell the Sanhedrin that Jesus worked magic with the devil. That is not in the Gospels.

The Gospels sometimes disagree with one another. What Mel Gibson has done is to pick and choose from the various Gospels those things that he wanted to emphasize. It may very well be that this interrogation of Jesus was not before the Sanhedrin but rather was before a kind of grand jury proceeding, of the sort that Haim Cohn, for example, has described.[8]

Furthermore, what is extremely vital in understanding what Mel Gibson has done is that he has taken the character of the high priest and made him into a major figure. Now, at one time the high priest was really a major figure. At the time of the Hasmoneans, the high priest was the king and indeed had tremendous power. But when the Hasmoneans were overthrown and the Romans then took over, King Herod was for many years a kind of puppet of the Romans; and when he died, he was succeeded by his son. There was great dissatisfaction with his son, Archelaus, and then the procurators took over.

By the beginning or toward the beginning of the first century B.C.E., the procurators were the ones in control. They were the ones who, in effect, appointed the high priest. That is very important to bear in mind, because in the film what we find is that the high priest has tremendous power and tremendous influence, and that Pontius Pilate, the procurator, is afraid to go against his advice. But, as noted above, the high priest was an appointee of the procurator; and we hear, for example, that a high priest, Ananus, served only three months (Josephus, *Antiquities* 20.203) and that his successor, Jesus the son of Damnaeus, served not much longer (*Antiquities* 20.213).

That is not the sort of person who would exercise the kind of control that one would expect from the film. Consider the fact that the high priest is given his clothes by the procurator—imagine, in order to get the clothes he had to turn to the procurator. As we know, there is a very elaborate set of clothes that the high priest had to wear on Yom Kippur. He had to go to the procurator to get those clothes.

Again, that is not the sort of thing that you would get from the movie at all. But what you do get in the movie is the power of the high priest, Caiaphas. He is constantly on the screen, especially during the time when Jesus is tortured. We have a statement in the Gospel of John (18:14) that it was Caiaphas who had given counsel to the Jews that it was expedient that one man should die for the people, in other words, that one person should be handed over to the Romans and in that way should presumably save the Jewish people. Otherwise, they would suffer terribly.

We can, however, see from rabbinic literature that Jews would recoil from doing such a thing, especially when the person who was handed over would be subjected to a punishment that was not acceptable and without proper procedure. There is one case in rabbinic literature where Joshua ben Levi persuaded Ulla to give himself up because the Romans demanded it, and they threatened to destroy the city of Lydda unless Ulla was surrendered to them. We are told that the prophet Elijah had been accustomed to reveal himself to Joshua ben Levi, but not after this incident. Finally, Elijah appeared to him, and when Joshua asked him why he had not appeared to him, he replied that it was because of what Joshua had done (Jerusalem Talmud, *Terumot* 8.46b).

There is one account outside the Gospels, namely by Josephus (*Antiquities* 18.63–64), which, if it is authentic, does deal with the matter of the crucifixion of Jesus. It states specifically that Jesus was the Messiah (*Christos*) and that

Pilate, upon hearing him accused by Jews of the highest standing, condemned him to be crucified. The question is whether Josephus really wrote it. I myself have concluded[9] that he could not have written it, certainly in the form that we have it, largely because the Christian church father Origen (*Against Celsus* 1.47 and *Commentary on Matthew* 13.55) says that Josephus did not recognize that Jesus was the *Christos*.

But the fact is that it is there in our Greek text. Now, it so happens that in the tenth century an Arab Christian named Agapius wrote an account closely paraphrasing Josephus.[10] This particular passage in Josephus, as we have it in the Greek, says that Jesus was turned over by the Jewish leaders to Pilate. In Agapius's very close paraphrase he says that Jesus was crucified but he does not indicate on whose recommendation he was crucified. So it may very well be that the original version of Josephus, which was used by Christians for a long time as evidence that the Jews also recognized what Jesus had done, did not contain the statement that he was turned over by the Jewish leaders to Pilate.

There is one other thing that we have to realize as we watch the film. We find that in the Gospels the word "Romans" appears only once, namely in the Gospel of John (11:48). Now, why is it that the Gospels should have said so little about the Romans, hardly mentioning them by name? The answer would seem to be, and this is part and parcel of what Gibson then develops in his film, that the Romans really are not the culprits. They are not really responsible.

One might ask why the Christians did not give a more prominent place to the Romans. It may well be that they were afraid that if they did so, they would not be getting the kind of treatment or acceptance that they wanted, such as the Jews had, and that they would, in effect, be regarded as people who were trying to overthrow Rome.

One thing that we have to understand is that in the parables that Jesus gives, at least as recorded in the Gospels, the name of king is prominent. Jesus is presented as, in effect, a king. When the Romans heard that, they assumed that this particular person was trying to establish an independent state. Independent state means that they were going to overthrow the Romans. Therefore, the Christians were very sensitive on that score, and so they did not want to give that impression. Consequently, they cut the role of the Romans considerably.

One sees in the film, and this happens to be in the New Testament, that Pontius Pilate says that there is a custom that on the occasion of the three pilgrimage festivals—Passover, Pentecost, and Tabernacles—the person who is in charge, that is, the procurator, frees a prisoner. Outside of the Gospels we know of no such practice. We know a good deal about Roman history. We know a good deal about the practices of the Romans, the way in which they administered their provinces. Nowhere else do we find this particular custom ever mentioned, let alone put into practice.

It seems very unlikely that the Romans would do a thing like that because they were always afraid that they would be overthrown. There were so many revolts in the Roman Empire. They would not be likely to yield to the demands of the provincials.

One thing that certainly emerges from the Gospels and is emphasized even more by Gibson in the film is the character of Pontius Pilate. There are really only two authors who deal with Pontius Pilate at any length, namely, Philo, the Jewish philosopher, who was a leader of the Jewish community of Alexandria, and Josephus. Josephus mentions Pontius Pilate in both the *Jewish War* (2.169–177) and the *Antiquities* (18.35, 55–64, 87–89, 177). The major difference between the two accounts of Josephus is that the version in the *Jewish War*, which is almost as long as the one in the *Antiquities*, does not mention the passage about Jesus; and that, indeed, is one of the reasons why we are suspicious about the authenticity of the account about Jesus in the *Antiquities*. Pilate, according to Josephus, we may add, was the procurator who actually took money from the Temple and built aqueducts in Jerusalem.

Philo (*Embassy to Gaius* 299–305) mentions Pilate in connection with the way in which he put down the masses of the people when they rose up against him when he tried to introduce the standards of the Roman emperor into the Temple in Jerusalem. Pilate, he says, was "inflexible, stubborn, and of cruel disposition. He executed troublemakers without a trial." He refers to Pilate's "venality, violence, thefts, assaults, abusive behavior, endless executions, endless savage ferocity." And this is a quotation.

Now, Philo is a good source in the sense that he was not actually there. He was certainly a scholar. He certainly had good information. One can see that he tries his best to be fair towards the Romans. He got along with the Romans. He was the head of a delegation to the Roman Emperor Gaius Caligula. And this is the way Josephus (*Antiquities* 18.67) speaks about Pontius Pilate: "When the Samaritans arose to make a pilgrimage to Mount Gerizim, Pilate sent his soldiers dressed to kill actually, and they slaughtered the people. Eventually, he was deposed. The Roman governor of Syria, who was in charge of the procurators, actually forced him out of office."

In the film Pilate is rehabilitated even beyond the Gospels. Thus, when Jesus is handed over to Pilate by the Jews, Pilate asks: "Do you always punish your prisoners before they are judged?" Such a statement is not to be found in the Gospels.

In the film Jesus tells Pilate that the high priest, Caiaphas, bore the greater sin for delivering him over to the Roman authority. That is not in the New Testament. It is intended to put the emphasis upon the high priest, Caiaphas, and on the practice that the Jews hand over people who are wanted by the Roman government. That is something which, as noted previously, we have no reason to believe the Jews did.

There is one point in the film where Mary Magdalene tries to get help from Roman soldiers when Jesus is taken by the Jewish priests, the implication being that she would get further with the Roman soldiers than with the Jews.

That is not in the New Testament. The fact is that this was intended to show the Jewish culpability and Jewish control.

At one point Pilate says to his wife that if he does not condemn Jesus Caiaphas would start a rebellion. This is not in the Gospels. And Caiaphas was in no position to start a rebellion. He was powerless. He was appointed by the procurator, and he would have been deposed if he ever tried anything at all independently.

The clear impression that Gibson is trying to create is that Pilate was unable to resist the tremendous pressure from a powerful Caiaphas. As for the charges that were brought before Pilate against Jesus, all four of the Gospels agree that Jesus was asked whether he was King of the Jews. That is the first charge. The only way that we can understand the question is that Jesus is being asked whether he is trying to create an independent state, because one of the functions of the messiah is to create an independent state.

Maimonides, in his codification of Jewish law, the *Mishneh Torah* (Book 14, *Judges*, chapters 11–12), gives guidelines as to how the Messiah will be recognized when he comes. One major thing that he will do is to establish an independent state, that is, a state that is not going to be subservient even to a major power, but is, rather, a truly independent state. Moreover, he will gather the Jews from all four corners of the earth; and all of them are going to come to Israel.

The fact is that the Messiah is known by what he does. Once the question is asked, "Are you king of the Jews," meaning, are you going to establish an independent state, the implication is that we have reason to think that that is your intention. Now, Jesus gives answers that are sort of in-between or he is silent. But the fact of the matter is that the charge is made.

In one of the Gospels, Luke (23:2), we read: "We have found this man perverting our nation and forbidding us to give tribute to Caesar, saying that he is Christ," meaning, *mashiach,* a king. He stirs people up, forbidding to give tribute to Caesar, rendering to Caesar the things that are Caesar's (Luke 20:25). Remember the coin that is given to him (Luke 20:24). The implication is that if one does not pay the Romans what is due to the Romans, then one is revolting against the Romans. We recall the famous line in Virgil: "Parcere subjectis et debellare superbos," "to spare those who are giving in to you and to humble those who are haughty" (*Aeneid* 6.853). But that is the way the Romans did it.

What emerges is that Jesus was a political rebel; and that is why he is crucified. And that is why the inscription on the cross—the wording is a little different in all four Gospels (Matthew 27:37, Mark 15:26, Luke 23:38, John 19:19)—reads "Jesus of Nazareth, King of the Jews." He tried to establish an independent state as Messiah.

At one point, we hear of a band of soldiers and their captain and the officers of the Jews who seize him with weapons (John 18:12). Why would a band of soldiers be needed to seize Jesus? It sounds as if the Romans suspected that there was somebody who was trying to promote a revolution, like the Fourth Philosophy that Josephus mentions. Therefore, they had to seize him before he actually carried it out. We note that the other two who are crucified with Jesus are crucified as *leistai* (Matthew 27:38, Mark 15:27, Luke 23:32-33, John 19:18). In the Talmud this word is used with reference to robbers, but these people are not robbers. They are revolutionaries. Jesus was a revolutionary. One can see that he was a political figure from the fact that he says to his disciples, "Whoever has no sword, let him sell his mantle and buy one" (Luke 22:36).

Why do they have to buy swords? Matthew 10:34: "I bring you not peace but the sword." Why? It sounds again as if he had political ambitions to establish an independent state after the terrible years under Herod and under the procurators. The fact that he is linked with Barabbas may well be a duplicate of Jesus: Bar Abbas means "the son of the father," and Barabbas led a recent insurrection against the Romans, according to Mark (15:7). So Jesus is coupled with revolutionaries.

One of his followers is Simon the Zealot. Now the word "Zealot" there is Zealot with a capital "Z." There was a revolutionary party called the Zealots, who tried to overthrow the Romans and establish an independent state. One of Jesus' followers is Judas Iscariot. Iscariot is probably "Ish Sicarius," "a man of the Sicarii," that is, a member of the sect known as the Sicarii, the group that took over Masada, for example. These were revolutionaries who wanted to establish an independent state.

In the Book of Acts, depicting the period immediately after the crucifixion when his followers came to see Jesus risen, the disciples ask the allegedly resurrected Jesus, "Lord, will you at this time restore the kingdom to Israel?" (Acts 1:6). What kind of question is that? Restore the kingdom to Israel means to establish an independent state, such as the Jews had under Saul and David and Solomon and under the Hasmoneans.

It is significant that one of the authorities who refers to Jesus is Tacitus, the Roman historian who lived at the end of the first and the beginning of the second centuries. This is probably the most important source for establishing the historicity of Jesus, because it is well known that there are people who claim that Jesus never lived. A whole book was written about that by David Strauss in 1835.[11] Tacitus, no great friend of the Jews and no great friend of the Christians also, mentions "Christos, from whom the name had its origin, suffered the extreme penalty during the reign of Tiberius at the hands of one of our procurators, Pontius Pilate. And the most mischievous superstition, thus checked for the moment, again broke out not only in Judea, the first source of the evil, but even in Rome, where all things hideous and shameful from every part of the world find their center and become popular" (*Annals* 15.44). It is significant that Tacitus mentions Tiberius, the emperor, as well as Pontius Pilate, the procurator, and says nothing about the Jews, whom he despised, as we see from the first thirteen sections of Tacitus's *Histories*, book 5, which is the most extensive account by a non-Jew of the Jewish religion and Jewish history that has come down to us from antiquity.

Moreover, as we have noted, the version of the *Testimonium Flavianum* in Josephus's *Antiquities* (18.63–64) by Agapius, a Christian Arab of the tenth century, does not say that it was the Jewish leaders, let alone the high priest, who had anything to do with what happened to Jesus.

The film emphasizes the scourging, where Jesus is mercilessly beaten, blow by blow. One can understand why someone would want to mention it, but why go into it at such length? Here again there is a major difference between Mel Gibson and the New Testament in what he does with the scourging, which is the central feature of the film. Surely those who go to see the film will never forget this part of the film. This certainly has tremendous potential for trouble for the Jewish people.

What do the Gospels say about this preparation for the crucifixion known as scourging, this merciless whipping? Matthew 17:26: "When Pilate had scourged Jesus, he delivered him to be crucified." He says nothing about the details of the scourging at all. Mark 15:15: ditto. He mentions that Jesus was scourged but says nothing about the details. Luke 23:26 mentions nothing at all. He simply mentions the crucifixion. And John, the most anti-Jewish of all the Gospels, 19:1–3, simply states that Pilate had him flogged and that his soldiers struck him on the face.

It is significant that none of the church fathers, who are so numerous and write in such detail through the twelfth century, has a treatise on the sufferings of Jesus. In the Christ cycle in the Sistine Chapel there is no scene from the Passion and no panel depicting the crucifixion. Moreover, Vatican II apparently felt that undue attention to the Passion of Jesus would lead to neglect of the Resurrection.

Yet, here is Mel Gibson, who has given a blow-by-blow account—terrible, bloody, and brutal—of what happened. One sees endless blood, flesh, bones, teeth, eyes, eye sockets, limbs. Jesus' arm is dislocated by the crucifix in order to line him up with the pre-drilled holes in the cross. The flogging, indeed, approaches the pornographic. And who is the master of ceremonies of this account? The high priest, who is watching over all of it. His face is constantly shown. One can see the vicious bitterness in that face. So that the high priest and his wicked associates may be clearly identified as Jews, they wear prayer shawls and are bedecked with precious metals. Moreover, whereas Jesus in the film is portrayed as a light-featured Gentile, the Jews in contrast are portrayed as dark, ugly, and scheming. Pilate's discomfort in the film while viewing the scourging of Jesus is not recorded in the Gospels and is contrasted with the cruelty of the Jews. That is what Mel Gibson is trying to convey.

Furthermore, again unrecorded in the Gospels, Pilate attempts but fails to quiet the crowd and asks, "Isn't this enough?" Eventually, lifting his hands, he proclaims, "It is you who want him crucified, not I." On the other hand, the high priest sarcastically asks, to appreciative laughter, whether they have no respect for Pilate.

To be sure, there are certain things in the film that do present positive things about the Jews. Simon is actually forced to carry the cross, but he is identified as a Jew. Veronica brings a cloth to wipe the face of Jesus when he is beaten. The Jews in the crowd cry out to stop the torture. And the truth is that even though the Romans are treated rather lightly, the Romans also are laughing at the scourging and at the crucifixion too.

If one looks at the film as a whole, what Gibson has done is to cover himself by saying, in effect, that there are a couple of Jews, here or there, who are doing something positive. And there are a couple of Romans who are presented negatively. But the overall impression, especially the visual impression of the Jews, is negative; look, incidentally, at the teeth of the Jews. Gibson goes to great length to present the vicious side of the Jews.

Of course, if the Jews had anything to do with it, why should all the Jews of today be responsible for it, any more than all the Athenians are responsible for what the Athenians did to Socrates. Or the Italians because of what Pontius Pilate, a Roman from Italy, did to Jesus?

Again, at the beginning of the film one sees devils. The little boys who pursue Judas Iscariot are transformed into little demons, the metaphoric progeny of Satan himself, who flits among the Jewish crowds. At the end of the film we see the destruction of the Temple in Jerusalem. Now, the destruction of the Temple is Gibson's way of saying that G-d has finally given the Jews what was coming to them. Of course, the Temple was not destroyed until considerably later, the year 68 according to the rabbinic Seder Olam and the year 70 according to the usual chronology.

Now why didn't Mel Gibson, as he was advised by a number of people, put in the end of the film a statement to the effect that the Jews of today are not responsible for what Jews are alleged to have said or done two thousand years ago? Why did he not close the film with the prayer uttered by Pope John Paul II at the Kotel, the Western Wall of the Temple, on March 26, 2000, and inserted into a nook in the wall: "G-d of our fathers, you chose Abraham and his descendants to bring Your name to the nations. You are deeply saddened by the behavior of those who, in the course of history, have caused these children of Yours to suffer; and, asking Your forgiveness, we wish to commit ourselves to genuine brotherhood with the people of the Covenant."

Discussion Questions

1. In what way was Mel Gibson influenced by Anna Katharina Emmerich?
2. Why did Mel Gibson choose to have Aramaic and Latin spoken in his movie?

3. Compare the procedure of the Sanhedrin as depicted in rabbinic literature with the procedure as depicted in the Gospels and in Gibson's film.

4. How does Gibson's depiction of the scourging (flogging) of Jesus compare with the accounts in the Gospels?

Notes

1. *Jerusalem Post*, February 27, 2004.
2. Such a statement, learned and balanced, is to be found in David Berger, "Jews, Christians, and the 'The Passion.'" *Commentary* 117.5 (May 2004): 23–31.
3. Associated Press, April 3, 2004.
4. *The Dolorous Passion of Our Lord Jesus Christ According to the Meditations of Anne Catherine Emmerich*, translated and edited by Clemens Maria Brentano (reprinted by El Sobrante, CA: North Bay Books, 2003).
5. Matthew Dillon, "Ancient Languages in Mel Gibson's *The Passion of the Christ*, *Amphora* 2.2 (Fall, 2004): 14.
6. John Chrysostom, *Homilies against the Jews* 1.6.
7. John Chrysostom, *Homilies against the Jews* 6.6.
8. Haim Cohen, *The Trial and Death of Jesus* (New York: Harper, 1971).
9. Louis H. Feldman, "The *Testimonium Flavianum*: The State of the Question," in *Christological Perspectives: Essays in Honor of Harvey K. McArthur*, ed. Robert F. Berkey and Sarah A. Edwards (New York: Pilgrim, 1982), pp. 179–199, 288–293. The literature on Josephus's passage concerning Jesus is enormous. See also Alice Whealey, *Josephus on Jesus: The Testimonium Flavianum Controversy from Late Antiquity to Modern Times* (New York: Peter Lang, 2003), who carefully avoids taking sides in the controversy. For a very fair, dispassionate, scholarly approach, see John P. Meier, *A Marginal Jew: Rethinking the Historical Jesus*, vol. 1: *The Roots of the Problem and the Person* (New York: Doubleday, 1991), pp. 56-88.
10. See Shlomo Pines, *An Arabic Version of the Testimonium Flavianum and Its Implications* (Jerusalem: Israel Academy of Sciences and Humanities, 1971).
11. David F. Strauss, *Das Leben Jesus, kritisch bearbeitet*, 2 vols. (Tübingen, 1835–36).

Crucifixion in Rabbinic Context

Juridical or Theological?

Jacob Neusner

A Secular, Juridical, versus a Sacred, Theological Reading of the Passion Narratives: What Is the Difference?

How people view the death penalty governs their reading of the Passion narratives. The prevailing picture is simple and secular. Execution after trial and conviction represents a legal punishment after an unjust trial—pure and simple. Jesus was tried for a crime, found guilty, and executed. Reading the execution as penalty for a crime does not accommodate the next chapter in the story. The resurrection disrupts that narrative rather than completing it and forming its climax. Within that framework, Good Friday alone—the trial, conviction, sentence, and execution—registers. Within the teleology of the juridical narrative there is no accounting for Easter Sunday. That destroys the juridical transaction.

That juridical perspective on the Passion narratives, secular at its heart, governs in the prevailing culture and stresses a secular reading of the matter. It draws attention away from those components of the narratives that underscore an other-than-punitive evaluation, an other-than-juridical approach to the story. There is no compelling logic, from that perspective, that requires the climactic chapter of resurrection.

Accordingly, the culture in which we live affords no space for an other-than-secular perspective, accords short shrift to a final chapter of resurrection and eternal life. So the representation of the Passion narratives is truncated, with its emphasis on trial and execution, and it is unable to explain the resurrection except as a contradiction. That is why the culture, defying the continuity and logic of the narrative as a whole, dwells on Good Friday, not on Easter Sunday, to speak liturgically: the death of Jesus the man, not the resurrection of

Christ, atoning for humanity's sins. That secular reading of the Passion with its emphasis on the horror of the trial and the gruesome penalty inflicted necessarily rather than on the sublime conception realized in the narrative treats as an epilogue what is and theologically is meant to be the climax.

And it is not how the Gospels present the matter. But how else, and in what context, if not the juridical one, are we to read the Passion narratives? A perspective on the death penalty formed within the theology of monotheism restores the correct emphasis of the Passion narrative, that is, within monotheism we see the climactic place of the resurrection and the realization of eternal life. What I wish to show is how the model of the rabbinic framing of the monotheist narrative allows us to read the Passion narratives in all their proper proportion and perspective: how the crucifixion fits into the salvific narrative. And that, we shall see, not only accommodates all of the details in a governing theory of the transaction, but imposes the focus on the Passion narratives that the punitive, juridical model distorts.

The Monotheist Narrative

To understand the centrality of resurrection in monotheism, and therefore the trial and punishment of the felon as an act of mercy, we have to stand back and ask, Why is resurrection, whether of Christ on Easter Sunday or of holy Israel at the end of days, critical to the monotheist system, whether that system is expressed in philosophical or mythic categories?

Monotheism resolves the problem of evil, which so troubled Ecclesiastes and Job, by a narrative. Specifically, God ultimately will restore that perfection that embodied his plan for creation. In the work of restoration death that comes about by reason of sin will die, the dead will be raised and judged for their deeds in this life, and most of them, having been justified, will go on to eternal life in the world to come. The paradigm of man restored to Eden is realized in Israel's return to the Land of Israel. In that world or age to come, however, that sector of humanity that through the Torah knows God will encompass all of humanity. Idolaters will perish, and humanity that comprises Israel at the end will know the one, true God and spend eternity in his light.

The importance of resurrection in the realization of the logic of monotheism is now self-evident. The narrative requires that justice ultimately prevail, God's mercy ultimately come to full expression. Life cannot end at the grave, death cannot mark the last chapter, for there is no ultimate justice prior to a final judgment and a restoration of humanity, cleared of sin, to Eden. In that systemic context, the death penalty constitutes an act of mercy, as I shall now show.

The Death Penalty as an Act of Mercy

The Mishnah's laws governing the death penalty, which are set forth in the tractates *Sanhedrin* and *Makkot,* define a theological and narrative, not a juridical, context in which the Passion narratives may be read. The law, Halakhah, forms Judaism's principal medium of theology and translates details of law into a theological system expressed in patterns of deeds.

Given the rabbinic conviction that all Israel possesses a share in the world to come—meaning, nearly everybody will rise from the grave—the sages took as their task a very particular one. It was the specification of how, in this world, criminals—sinners—would receive appropriate punishment in a proper procedure, so expiating sin or crime that, in the world to come, they would take their place along with everyone else in the resurrection and eternal life.

It follows that the religious principle that comes to expression in the double tractate *Sanhedrin-Makkot* concerns the meaning of man's being in God's image. That means, as God lives forever, so it is in man's nature to surpass the grave. And how, God being just, does the sinner or criminal survive his sin or crime? It is by atonement, specifically, paying with his life in the here and now, so that at the resurrection, he may regain life, along with all Israel. That is why the climactic moment in the Halakhah comes at the end of the long catalogue of those sins and crimes penalized with capital punishment. It is with ample reason that the Bavli places at the conclusion and climax of its version the ringing declaration, "all Israel has a portion in the world to come, except . . ." And the exceptions pointedly do not include any of those listed in the long catalogues of persons executed for sins or crimes.

When, accordingly, we come to the heart of the matter, the criminal justice system, we take up an entirely abstract theological problem, the fate of man after death. Here we move to the limits of Eden, viewed as a situation and a story, focusing upon what is explicit in Eden, the governing simile for man. And that is God, which is to say, man is in God's image, after God's likeness, possessed of an autonomous, and free, will. That is what accounts for man's fall from the paradise of repose by reason of rebellion. In the setting of the civil order, then, the issue of man's rebellion plays itself out, for in the criminal justice system we turn to the outcome of it all. Now we consider what happens to the sinful or criminal Israelite, the one who willfully does what God forbids, or deliberately refrains from doing what God commands, the fate of the sinner or criminal who acts in the manner of Adam and Eve. If we broaden the matter, we see that the most profound question facing Israelite thinkers concerns the fate of the Israelite at the hands of the perfectly just and merciful God. Since essential to their thought is the conviction that all creatures are answerable to their Creator, and absolutely critical to their system is the fact that at the end of days the dead are raised for eternal life, the criminal justice system encompasses deep thought on the interplay of God's justice and God's mercy: How are these reconciled in the case of the sinner or criminal?

Within Israel's social order the Halakhah addresses from a theological perspective the profound question of social justice: What shall we make of the Israelite sinner or criminal? Specifically, does the sin or crime, which has estranged him from God, close the door to life eternal? If it does, then justice is implacable and perfect. If it does not, then God shows his mercy—but what of justice? We can understand the answer only if we keep in mind that the Halakhah takes for granted the resurrection of the dead, the final judgment, and the life of the world to come beyond the grave. So this world's justice and consequent penalties do not complete the transaction of God with the sinner or criminal. Eden restored at the end of days awaits. From that perspective, death becomes an event in life but not the end of life. And, it must follow, the death penalty too does not mark the utter annihilation of the person of the sinner or criminal. On the contrary, because he pays for his crime or sin in this life, he situates himself with all of the rest of supernatural Israel, ready for the final judgment. Having been judged, he will "stand in judgment," meaning, he will find his way to the life of the world to come along with everyone else. Within the dialectics formed by those two facts—punishment now, eternal life later on—we identify as the two critical passages in the Halakhah of *Sanhedrin-Makkot*, Mishnah 6:2 and 10:1.

As to the former: The rite of stoning involves an admonition that explicitly declares the death penalty the means of atoning for all crimes and sins, leaving the criminal blameless and welcome into the kingdom of Heaven; I italicize the key language:

> A. [When] he was ten cubits from the place of stoning, they say to him, "Confess," for it is usual for those about to be put to death to confess.
>
> B. For whoever confesses has a share in the world to come.
>
> C. For so we find concerning Achan, to whom Joshua said, "My son, I pray you, give glory to the Lord, the God of Israel, and confess to him, [and tell me now what you have done; hide it not from me.] And Achan answered Joshua and said, Truly have I sinned against the Lord, the God of Israel, and thus and thus I have done" (Josh. 7:19). And how do we know that his confession achieved atonement for him? For it is said, "And Joshua said, Why have you troubled us? The Lord will trouble you this day" (Josh. 7:25)—*This day you will be troubled, but you will not be troubled in the world to come.*[1]

So within the very center of the Halakhic exposition comes the theological principle that the death penalty opens the way for life eternal. Achan pays the supreme penalty but secures his place in the world to come; all Israel, with only a few exceptions, is going to stand in judgment and enter the world to come, explicitly including all manner of criminals and sinners. And the latter passage states explicitly that all Israel, with specified exceptions, will inherit the world to come:

> A. All Israelites have a share in the world to come, as it is said, "your people also shall be all righteous, they shall inherit the land forever; the branch of my planting, the work of my hands, that I may be glorified" (Is. 60:21).

> B. And these are the ones who have no portion in the world to come: He who says, the resurrection of the dead is a teaching which does not derive from the Torah, and the Torah does not come from Heaven; and an Epicurean.[2]

The executed criminal does not figure among these exceptions, only those who willfully defy God in matters of eternity.

What the Halakhah wishes to explore, then, is: How is the Israelite sinner or criminal rehabilitated, through the criminal justice system, so as to rejoin Israel in all its eternity? The answer is that the criminal or sinner remains Israelite, no matter what he does—even though he sins—and the death penalty is exacted by the earthly court. So the Halakhah of Sanhedrin embodies these religious principles: (1) Israel—Man "in our image"—endures forever, encompassing (nearly) all Israelites; (2) sinners or criminals are able to retain their position within that eternal Israel by reason of the penalties that expiate the specific sins or crimes spelled out by the Halakhah; (3) it is an act of merciful justice that is done when the sinner or criminal is put to death, for at that point, he is assured of eternity along with everyone else. God's justice comes to full expression in the penalty, which is instrumental and contingent; God's mercy endures forever in the forgiveness that follows expiation of guilt through the imposition of the penalty.

That explains why the governing religious principle of Sanhedrin-Makkot is the perfect, merciful justice of God, and it accounts for the detailed exposition of the correct form of the capital penalty for each capital sin or crime. The punishment must fit the crime within the context of the Torah in particular so that, at the resurrection and the judgment, the crime will have been correctly expiated. Because the Halakhah rests on the premise that God is just and that God has made man in his image, after his likeness, the Halakhah cannot deem it sufficient that the punishment fit the crime. Rather, given its premises, the Halakhah must pursue the issue, What of the sinner once he has been punished? And the entire construction of the continuous exposition of Sanhedrin-Makkot aims at making this simple statement: The criminal, in God's image, after God's likeness, pays the penalty for his crime in this world but, like the rest of Israel, will stand in justice and, rehabilitated, will enjoy the world to come.

Conclusion

In the Halakhic context, the death penalty achieves atonement of sin, leading to the resurrection at the end of days. It is an act of mercy, atoning for the sin that otherwise traps the sinner/criminal in death. In the context of the Gospel narrative, with its stress on repentance at the end and atonement on the cross by a single unique man, representative of all of humanity, for the sins of all humanity, we deal with no juridical transaction at all. It is an eschatological realization of the resurrection of humanity through that of Jesus Christ on Easter Sunday. Read in light of Mishnah-tractate Sanhedrin and its Halakhic theology with its climax, "All Israel has a portion in the world to come," the Passion narrative coheres, each component in its right proportion and position, all details fitting together.

The Mishnah interprets the death penalty as a medium of atonement in preparation for judgment leading to resurrection, just as the theology of the Passion narratives has always maintained. For both the Mishnah and the Gospels, the death penalty is a means to an end. It does not mark the end but the beginning. The trial and crucifixion of Christ for Christianity, like the trial and execution of the Israelite criminal or sinner for Judaism, form necessary steps toward the redemption of humanity from death, as both religions have maintained, each in its own idiom.

Indeed, in the context of the law as articulated in the Mishnah, the details of the Passion narratives take on acute meaning. All that requires translation is Christ for the criminal, and the Passion narrative covers that ground in the context of the larger theology of atonement. A truly Christian film of the Passion narratives begins with a prologue of suffering on the cross, giving way to Christianity's luminous, truly sublime vision of resurrection in all its glory. The climax comes not on Friday but on Sunday.

Discussion Questions

1. What is the difference between a secular and a religious interpretation of an important event?
2. What is the problem of evil, and how does monotheism solve it?
3. How can the death penalty be interpreted as an act of mercy?
4. What is the difference between a truly Christian film of the Passion narratives and the version of Mel Gibson?

Notes

1. *Sanhedrin* 6:2.
2. *Sanhedrin* 11:1.

Section 3

Diversity and Dialogue

Dramatizing the Passion

From Oberammergau to Gibson

Gordon R. Mork

In 1633 the village of Oberammergau, in the Bavarian Alps, fell victim to the plague. It seemed to the village elders that their community would be wiped out by the sudden onslaught of the feared disease. Therefore they gathered beneath the crucifix of the parish church and prayerfully swore that if God would protect them from further depredations of the plague, they would perform the Passion play, once each decade, forever. According to local records, no one died thereafter from the plague, so the villagers put on the first of their Passion plays the next year, 1634, and have been doing so religiously ever since.

Some time in the 1990s the actor and filmmaker Mel Gibson felt himself "trapped with feelings of terrible, isolated emptiness." Through prayer and meditation, he says, he "first conceived the idea of making a film about the Passion."[1] Though compatriots in the film industry tried to discourage him, he persevered. The film opened in the United States on Ash Wednesday, February 25, 2004, and was still running in most markets a month later, a remarkable box office success.

I think it is fair to say that the major motivation behind both reenactments of Christ's Passion were pious and even lofty, rather than merely commercial or political. But in historic times, when religion can be a life and death issue—during the wars of religion during the seventeenth century or nationalist and racist struggles of the twentieth and twenty-first centuries—the political messages embedded within religious activities cannot be ignored. This is especially true when the activities are played out on stage or screen before millions of viewers. In the next few pages I will set forth four questions which I believe to be important for the critical understanding of Passion dramas, and how those dramas may be used and misused; and then I will address those questions for the traditional Oberammergau Passion Play and for *The Passion of the Christ*, the Gibson film.

Here are the questions:

1. Do the presenters claim that the Passion drama (play or film) is an authentic representation of the biblical record?
2. How do the presenters deal with key Bible verses, especially Matthew 27:25, in which the Jews assembled before Pilate are said to call out "His blood be upon us and on our children"?
3. Do the presenters make clear the Jewishness of Jesus and his followers?
4. Do the presenters show "the Jews" as collectively guilty of Jesus' suffering and death?

Let us turn first to Oberammergau. The Passion play has been performed there for nearly four centuries, and there have been many changes in the production and the script over that time period. But what I will call the "traditional" play was firmly established early in the nineteenth century with a text by two priests, Ottmar Weiss and Joseph Daisenberger; this form continued, with few significant changes, through 1984.

1. Is it authentically biblical? The town fathers of Oberammergau, who controlled the play through an elaborate system of rules and committees, claimed their Passion play was wholly biblical. The drama opened with a festive entry into Jerusalem by Jesus mounted on a donkey with choirs of children and adults waving palms and singing his praises. The drama of Christian Holy Week then unfolded, including the Last Supper, the arrest and trial, and the crucifixion, and ended with an elaborate resurrection scene. Flashbacks in the form of "living pictures" (motionless tableaux) emphasized Old Testament foreshadowing of New Testament events. With few exceptions (like the insertion of St. Veronica and a character called "Rabbi"), the scenes were based on Scripture. The presentation, however, reflected choices made by the authors and directors about what to emphasize and how to do so. The outcome was a melodrama in which a clear distinction was made between "good Christians" and "wicked Jews," with Pontius Pilate and the Romans trying to stand nobly above the fray.[2]

2. Key Bible verses: The traditional Oberammergauers' interpretive twist is very clearly shown in their use of Matt 27:25. In Matthew's Gospel, Pilate tells the Jewish crowd that he refuses to take responsibility for condemning Jesus. Then Matthew writes: "And all the people answered and said, 'His blood be upon us and on our children.'"

In the traditional Oberammergau Passion Play this verse became a major theme, repeated by the choir, by the people in the square, and by Pilate himself, time after time. The standard Christian understanding of the verse in the nineteenth century was that these words were a "blood curse," which justified the charge that Jews were "Christ-killers"—not only in biblical times, but for all time—and therefore deserved to be treated harshly.

3. The Jewishness of Jesus: The traditional play also made a clear and visual distinction between "Christians" and "Jews" on stage. Jesus, his apostles, Mary, and the other women followers were dressed in modest earth tones, humble but honorable. Jesus' opponents, whether priests, members of the high council, temple traders, or the crowd before Pilate, were dressed in "oriental" styles, with garish colors and elaborate headgear (some of which suggested the horns of the devil himself). Jewish symbols, like the menorah, were associated with the high council which condemned Jesus. A particularly nasty opponent of Jesus was named "Rabbi." There was little to suggest that the Last Supper was a meal to commemorate the Passover.[3]

4. Jewish "guilt": Both the structure and the particulars of the traditional Oberammergau Passion Play were constructed to show "the Jews" as collectively guilty for Jesus' suffering and death. This was the Passion play that Adolf Hitler knew and loved, because it matched closely with his own anti-Semitic conception of the world.

It is important to note that beginning in the 1970s there was much criticism concerning the traditional version of the Oberammergau play. Pressures both from within the town and from Christians and Jews beyond its borders called for reform. After some false starts an internal reform group, led by Christian Stückl and Otto Huber, gained leadership of the play and made major reforms. The 1990 version corrected several major problems, and the 2000 version went even further. The Matt 27:25 line is now entirely gone. Jesus is costumed as a Jew, and a menorah is present at the Last Supper. Some critics still argue that the reform was too little and too late, but most of the controversy has subsided.[4]

Now let us turn to the Gibson production:

1. Mel Gibson claims biblical authenticity for his film. "I'm telling the story as the Bible tells it," he is quoted as saying in a "discussion guide" put out by a Protestant publisher. "The Gospel is a complete script," he says, "and that's what we're filming. . . . I'm trying to make it as authentic as I possibly can."[5] In Gibson's own book on the film he is a bit more nuanced: He says he drew upon "Holy Scripture and accepted visions of the Passion. . . ."[6]

In fact the film draws very heavily on the written account of the Passion by an early-nineteenth-century German nun, Anna Katharina Emmerich. Gibson skillfully blends her visions into the film narrative, leading some viewers to conclude naively that the nun's visions are actually scriptural.[7]

Here are two examples of the visions (which do not appear in the Passion Gospels) which Gibson used in his film:

According to the Gospels, Jesus is scourged after being brought to Pilate, and on orders from Pilate. No details are given. But Sister Anna Katharina goes into vivid detail concerning the nature and effects of the whipping. "The two ruffians continued to strike our Lord with unremitting violence for a quarter of an hour, and were succeeded by two others. . . . Furious cries which issued from among the assembled Jews showed that their cruelty was far from being satiated. . . . Two fresh executioners took the places of the last mentioned, who were beginning to flag; their scourges were composed of small chains, or straps covered with iron hooks, which penetrated to the bone, and tore off large pieces of flesh at every blow. . . ."[8] The Gibson film draws heavily on these details.

According to Matthew (27:19), the wife of Pilate sends word to him that he should have nothing to do with Jesus, "that righteous man," because she had "suffered much over him in a dream." Sister Anna Katharina's account goes well beyond that one mention in the Gospels. In her vision she says, "I saw Claudia Procles, the wife of Pilate, send some large pieces of linen to the Mother of God. . . . I soon after saw Mary and Magdalen approach the pillar where Jesus had been scourged; . . . they knelt down on the ground near the pillar, and wiped up the sacred blood with the linen which Claudia Procles had sent."[9] Those who have seen the film will immediately recall this poignant but wholly non-biblical scene.

Using Sister Anna Katharina's material, Gibson is able to make his film excruciatingly vivid. He thrusts blame for brutality on the Jewish leaders and the Jewish crowd, while showing Pilate's wife, a Roman, to be kindly and sympathetic. In sum, viewers of the film should understand that much of what they see on the screen, including the brutal depiction of the scourging which has caused so much comment, is visionary rather than biblical.

2. Key Bible verses. The crucial verse in the Gospel of Matthew is 27:25, in which he quotes the Jewish crowd crying out to Pilate, "His blood be upon us and our children." These words have been used for centuries as a "blood curse" and proof text that the Jews were "Christ killers."

The Vatican II reforms of the 1960s, and Catholic teachings implementing them, cautioned that this verse must always be properly explained, so that the concept of deicide would not be justified by a literal reading of it. Therefore, it was suggested to Mr. Gibson that the line be dropped from his Passion film.[10] As late as February 10, 2004, it was unclear from the information publicly available whether or not he would do so. Apparently, some of the early versions of the film had used the line, and Mr. Gibson responded to criticisms by declaring that he would not bow to pressures to revise the film.[11] On the other hand, in his interview with Diane Sawyer on February 16, 2004, he indicated that it had been removed.[12]

When I saw the film on February 25, 2004, the first day of its public release, I learned that there had been something of a compromise. The lines were spoken in Aramaic; in the film English subtitles conveyed meaning to the great majority of American viewers. However, because Aramaic is comprehensible to speakers of Hebrew, some members of the audience with those skills reported that the "blood curse" line had indeed been spoken. But it was omitted from the English subtitles.

3. The Jewishness of Jesus and his followers. The Gibson film provides a mixed picture. Much has been made about casting a woman of Jewish heritage, Maia Morgenstern, as Mary, the mother of Jesus, and some viewers have suggested that the film emphasizes her suffering as well as that of Jesus himself. Yet the presentation of the story as being only of the last twelve hours of Jesus' life on earth eliminates all but the briefest flashbacks to his earlier life—as a child, as a carpenter, on Palm Sunday, and at the Last Supper, and virtually nothing of his teachings. Thus there is little or no opportunity to develop the theme of the Jewishness of Jesus. The Jewish high priests and the Jewish crowd are consistently shown in negative stereotypes. On the other hand, Simon of Cyrene (who, according to the Gospel accounts, carried Jesus' cross) and St. Veronica (who does not appear in the Bible) both come across as Jews sympathetic to Jesus.

Gibson himself has repeatedly denied that he has any personal antipathy toward Jews as a group, either in biblical times or today. Yet he has made much of his feeling that "dark forces" were trying to prevent him from making the film and developing a successful release.[13]

4. Does the film imply collective guilt of "the Jews" for Jesus' suffering and death? The dramatization which Gibson presents, based upon the Gospel accounts and the visions of Sister Anna Katharina, shows both Jews and Romans as brutal participants in the suffering and death of Jesus. The Jewish high priests, Caiaphas and Ananus; the Roman governor, Pontius Pilate; the anonymous crowd—Aramaic-speaking Jews—and most of the Roman soldiers who carry out the whipping and the crucifixion, all come across looking extremely ugly. If one went into the theatre seeking anti-Semitic stereotypes of people to blame, one would have no trouble finding them. As such, the negative images go well beyond the measured words of the Gospel writers.

Christian Stückl, the director who was instrumental in the reform of the Oberammergau Passion Play, believes there are too many old anti-Jewish clichés in the Gibson film. Thus, Stückl says, he has sympathy for Jewish organizations that expressed fear that the film would fuel hatred against Jews.[14]

Gibson himself argues that Jews should not be blamed for Jesus' death, because—he says—Jesus died because of the sins of all mankind. "When you look at the reasons behind why Christ came, why he was crucified, he died and suffered for all mankind, so that really anybody who transgresses has to look at their own part in his death."[15] Gibson has made much of the fact that he inserted his own hand holding a nail before the camera, so that he would personally take responsibility for nailing Jesus to the cross (though there is no way of knowing that by simply watching the film, without Gibson's personal declaration).

In interviews, Gibson has articulated his position that his portrayal of Jews in the film is not anti-Semitic, and his view that Jesus was a Jew among Jews. At times his denial that he is anti-Semitic seems petulant and defensive, but at other times he seems to be sincere, recognizing that Jews have reason for concern, and that he has made legitimate efforts to address their concerns.[16]

Clear statements about the universal nature of the culpability for Jesus' suffering and death—by Gibson and by those who favor the film—are very useful because they counteract the old charge of deicide. The tradition of Passion plays' laying explicit blame on "the Jews" needs to be counteracted. The Catholic Church and many Protestant churches have explicitly decried the charge of deicide as a response to fears that the Gibson film would revive the view of Jews as "Christ-killers." Public academic discussions and publications are important for the same reason.

Without clear statements from Christians that blaming Jews for the suffering and death of Jesus is bad history, bad theology, and disastrous in its effects through the ages, some Christians may still jump to the wrong conclusions when witnessing Passion dramas.

Discussion Questions

1. Why should Germans be especially concerned about a Bavarian play in which Jews were blamed for the suffering and death of Jesus?
2. Why should Catholics who are committed to the reforms of the Vatican II Council be especially concerned about any dramatization of Jesus' Passion which appears to show the Jews as the cause of Jesus' suffering and death?
3. Is it possible to dramatize Jesus' life and death while recognizing his essential Jewishness? How might such a portrayal contribute to understanding between Christians and Jews?

Notes

1. Mel Gibson in the Foreword to companion volume to his film, *The Passion: Photography from the Movie, The Passion of The Christ* (Icon, 2004), p. iv.
2. For details see Gordon R. Mork, "'Wicked Jews' and 'Suffering Christians' in the Oberammergau Passion Play," in *Representations of Jews through the Ages* (Creighton University Press, 1996), pp. 153–169, and "Christ's Passion on Stage: The Traditional Melodrama of Deicide," *Journal of Religion & Society* 6 (2004), online at http://www. creighton.edu/JRS/.
3. In recent years, the Oberammergau play producers have published elaborate picture books, with colorful photographs showing the costume design. The contrast between the 1984 book, which shows the last of the "traditional" design, and the 2000 book, which shows a fully reformed version, is remarkable.
4. The texts of the successive play years are regularly published, in German and in English translation, so direct comparisons are easily made. For continuing criticism from the Anti-Defamation League, see http://www.adl.org/Interfaith/Oberammergau/Intro.asp.
5. Lee Strobel and Garry Poole, *Experiencing the Passion of Jesus* (Zondervan, 2004), p. 34.
6. Gibson, p. iv.

7. Anne Catherine Emmerich (1774–1824), *The Dolorous Passion of Our Lord Jesus Christ* (Rockford, IL: Tan Books, 1983, originally published in English c. 1928).
8. Emmerich, pp. 220–221.
9. Emmerich, pp. 224–225.
10. "Report of the Ad Hoc Scholars Group Reviewing the Script of *The Passion,*" May 2, 2003. www.bc.edu/research/cjl/meta-elements/texts/education/Passion_adhoc_report_2May.pdf.
11. Interview with Raymond Arroyo on "The World Over," EWTN cable network, tape provided by EWTN, dated 2/20/04.
12. Interview with Diane Sawyer, on ABC "Primetime Live," 2/16/04, transcript on LexisNexis Academic.
13. Interviews, EWTN and ABC.
14. *Spiegel Online,* 16 March 2004.
15. Strobel and Poole, p. 21.
16. Compare the EWTN and the ABC interviews.

Deicide Déjà Vu

Mel Gibson's Film The Passion—*An Attack on Forty Years of Jewish-Christian Dialogue*

Samuel Edelman

Carol Edelman

It is now four decades after "Nostra Aetate" and a few years after both *A Sacred Obligation: Rethinking Christian Faith in Relation to Judaism and the Jewish People* and *Dabru Emet: A Jewish Statement on Christians and Christianity*. In addition, the Scholar's Conference on the Holocaust and the Churches has for more than thirty years now been a positive force for Jewish-Christian dialogues in both North America and Europe. The results of these documents and dialogues have been far-reaching, even to the parish and local church level. The results of these dialogues have even begun in a modest way to have an impact on the liturgy of some churches. There has even been a shift in the rhetoric of some in the Christian fundamentalist community regarding Jews, Judaism, Israel, and the Shoah. Would all of this progress in Christian-Jewish dialogue be wiped away with one video representation of the death of Jesus? Would the film resurrect the ancient accusation of deicide against the Jews? Would it be the precursor of a new era of Christian religious anti-Judaism akin to that already existing in the Moslem world? These are critical questions that must be addressed in any discussion of Mel Gibson's *The Passion.*

To paraphrase the warden's famous line from *Cool Hand Luke*, "What we have here is a failure of interpretation!" Mel Gibson's *The Passion* is a film based on a personal interpretation of the Gospel story of the last hours of Jesus. That specific interpretation is in part idiosyncratic to Mel Gibson and to the brand of Catholicism he and his father and others express, which rejects the changes in Catholic theology and liturgy generated out of Vatican I and II. That interpretation is also colored by the very anti-Jewish diaries of the nun Anna

Katharina Emmerich, who wrote *The Dolorous Passion of Our Lord Jesus Christ* in the early 1800s. (In what must be the height of bad taste, bad timing, and obvious pandering to the right wing of the Catholic Church, the Church leadership has begun the process of beatifying Emmerich as the first step towards sainthood.)

Gibson has said in numerous interviews that he is simply being faithful to the Gospels themselves. This is hardly true. Any rendition of the Gospel story which condenses all four works into one cannot by definition be true to the Gospel story. But Gibson also adds many images to the story not contained in the Gospels. The executive director of Boston College's Center for Christian Jewish Learning, Phillip Cunningham, offers a brilliant analysis of the film, *Gibson's The Passion of the Christ: A Challenge to Catholic Teaching,* in which he gives evidence of this in a most graphic way. Cunningham points out the numerous non-biblical references contained in the film, primarily drawn from the demented ravings of Emmerich. Gibson's artistic license, in part drawn from Emmerich, raises the level of anti-Jewish images well beyond those in the Gospels themselves and gives rise to the accusation of anti-Semitism, which Gibson denies.

However, it is not the intent of this paper to recount those anti-Jewish aspects of the film, but rather to focus on the impact of the film on Christian-Jewish dialogue. In a survey done of viewers of the film, pollster Gary Tobin reported that the film did not have the negative impact Jewish groups predicted. As reported in the JTA on March 17' 2004, according to

> . . . a random national survey of 1,003 adults conducted by Tobin's group March 5–9, nearly two weeks after the movie's premiere, 12 percent of the 146 people who had seen *The Passion* said it made them "less likely" to blame Jews today for the crucifixion, compared to 5 percent who said they were "more likely" to blame all Jews for killing Jesus.

Was Gibson correct that the film was not anti-Semitic? Were Jewish, Catholic and Protestant groups crying wolf? The doomsday predictions of immediate increased anti-Jewish attitudes and anti-Semitic violence never happened.

Gibson was not correct; religious groups were not crying wolf. The Jewish community was indeed justified in predicting dire outcomes from the film. However, something monumental in the history of Jewish-Christian relations happened as a result of the Gibson film to thwart the threat. In the months, weeks, and even days before the opening of the film and after, Jewish and Christian scholars hit the radio, the television, and the talk circuit and wrote editorials and articles to discuss the anti-Jewish aspects of the film. Christian scholars such as John Dominic Crossan, Phillip Cunningham, Father John Pawlikowski and Eugene Fisher, associate director of the Secretariat for Ecumenical and Interreligious Relations, U.S. Conference of Catholic Bishops, became the main spokespersons with their Jewish colleagues in the struggle to prepare Christians for the film. Because of that early and strong Jewish outcry against the film *coupled with* an equally strong and visible response from many respected Christian organizations, the film's potential to stimulate anti-Semitism was muted. Jewish, Catholic, and Protestant groups, based on their strong bonds developed over thirty-plus years of dialogue, were able to successfully inoculate their parishioners and church and synagogue members to this film's potential anti-Jewish impact. This inoculation process significantly lessened the potential anti-Jewish fallout.

How did the reverse of the dire predictions happen in the U.S. and globally? The growing positive relationship between Christians and Jews sponsored by Catholic, Jewish, and Protestant groups in creating a post-Shoah theological vision for both Jews and Christians immediately came to the battle lines. The Anti-Defamation League, the American Jewish Committee, the Simon Wiesenthal Center, and the World Jewish Congress all made available and distributed worldwide a host of documents in multiple languages refuting the film. The Center for Christian-Jewish Relations at Boston College, a liberal Jesuit institution, issued "Facts, Faith and Film-making: Jesus' Passion and Its Portrayal," and the U.S. Conference of Catholic Bishops issued "The Bible, the Jews and the Death of Jesus," a collection of church papers intended to "end prejudices against Jews and Judaism." The Lutheran and Methodist Churches, as well as many other denominations, issued documents as well to prepare their congregations for the potential impact of the film. Not only in the United States but in Europe and Latin America too, both Catholic and Protestant organizations issued statements—even in places where there were few Jews. The German and French churches' responses were very critical in preparing Europeans, already suffering under an onslaught of anti-Semitic incidents, from adding to them with a violent upsurge instigated by the film's release in Europe. Even in a number of Islamic countries where the film was to be released, Islamic scholars condemned the film as idolatry, without reference to the film's anti-Jewish content.

Possibly one of the reasons for the very strong Catholic response was that many scholars have begun to understand that Gibson's film is as much an attack on modern Catholic post-Shoah theology as it is an attempt to revitalize the accusation of Jewish deicide and reinstitute the teaching of contempt. Gibson's film is a direct attack on the core of Vatican I and II. It attacks the church's removal of the "perfidious Jew" prayers on Good Friday and the teaching of contempt from the Catechism. It also was an attack on the church's movement to use vernacular languages over Latin. In general it was a device to highlight Gibson's breakaway church and to support the extreme right of the Catholic Church, which has not gone in the direction of Gibson and his father but often expresses similar sentiments.

On the whole, the strength of the positive Christian-Jewish post-Shoah dialogue and the changes to Christianity in light of that dialogue from Vatican I and II to Sacred Obligation and from Pope John the XXIII to Pope John Paul II stood up to the test of this very famous and charismatic actor's film. A coalition of religious groups worked together to preempt what could have been the beginning of a horrible situation for the Jewish community worldwide. The success was not total. The Catholic Church was sending mixed signals at times, including the *Wall Street Journal*'s report that the pope's own response to the film was, "It is as it was." This, coupled with positive articles in conservative Catholic newspapers and journals and statements from more right-wing Catholic commentators, certainly gave off mixed signals at times. As a result, there were a few anti-Jewish incidents worldwide attributable to the release of the film. Yet these deviations turned out to be minor. The weight of response was clearly on the side of those in support of Christian-Jewish dialogue, and the paucity of anti-Jewish incidents following the film's release and the resulting surveys of attitudes suggest great success on the part of the supporters of dialogue.

What possibly was damaged by these events was the developing relationship between the Jewish community and the Christian fundamentalist community, whose support for Gibson's film was vociferous and uncritical. Another possible negative was that the film may impact how the positive dialogue between Jews and Christians in higher education and theology may filter down to the parish and church level. That filtering down may now find some resistance based on responses to the film. Finally, we do not know what impact the DVD release will have on those who have access to it without the benefit of the inoculation materials prepared by both the Catholic and Protestant churches and various Jewish organizations. These possible negative outcomes aside, the real winner in the controversy over Gibson's film is the strength of more than thirty years of Christian-Jewish dialogue and the positive relationship this dialogue has forged. The power of the dialogue resides in statements such as prayer about the Jews attributed to Pope John XXIII. The text, which was to be read in all Catholic churches said, "We are conscious today that many centuries of blindness have cloaked our eyes so that we can no longer see the beauty of Thy chosen people. . . . We realize that the mark of Cain stands on our foreheads. Across the centuries our Brother Able has lain in the blood which we drew, or shed tears we caused, forgetting Thy love. Forgive us for crucifying Thee a second time in their flesh. For we knew not what we did."

Discussion Questions

1. In what ways has all of this progress in Christian-Jewish dialogue been positively or negatively affected by Gibson's video representation of the death of Jesus?

2. Why did the film not succeed in resurrecting the ancient accusation of deicide against the Jews?

3. Will there be a new era of Christian religious anti-Judaism akin to that already existing in the Moslem world or will Christian-Jewish dialogue move to new levels of understanding and mutual respect?

Gibson's *Passion*

The Challenges for Catholics

John T. Pawlikowski

A contemporary film on Christian anti-Semitism terms this centuries-long disease within the church as a "shadow" on the cross. Recent Catholic documents have spoken in even stronger language. In 1989 the Pontifical Commission for Justice and Peace at the Vatican issued a major document on racism in which it clearly placed anti-Semitism high on its list of continuing manifestations of racist ideologies. In point of fact, it called anti-Semitism the most tragic example of racism to appear in the twentieth century.

Pope John Paul II provided decisive leadership in the effort to awaken the conscience of the global community regarding the fundamental sinfulness of anti-Semitism. During a visit to Hungary in 1991, John Paul spoke of the urgent need for the church to atone for its sin of anti-Semitism and to repudiate anti-Semitism as a great sin against humanity, a call he repeated in his book *Crossing the Threshold of Hope*.

Over the years I have insisted in my writings that we cannot regard Nazism as simply the final and most gruesome form of classical Christian anti-Semitism. Hitler and his collaborators elevated anti-Semitism to a new level by setting it within a biological framework that totally dehumanized Jews, making them into vermin. Unlike the Christian version, which aimed at marginalizing Jews and making them perpetually miserable as a supposed reminder of what happens to people who reject Christ, the Nazi version of anti-Semitism aimed at the total annihilation of the Jewish community worldwide. Both forms of anti-Semitism are fundamentally immoral. But a distinction needs to be maintained.

But, despite my insistence on the need to differentiate classical Christian anti-Semitism from its Nazi version, any effort to disconnect the two totally, as the 1998 Vatican document on the Shoah has, is equally in error. We must recognize that the widespread acquiescence and even collaboration with the Nazi effort to exterminate Jews were strongly influenced by the anti-Semitic legacy of Christianity. This legacy provided what I like to term "an indispensable seedbed" for the incubation of Nazism in European society. Nazi ideologues drew upon classical anti-Jewish church legislation in developing the legislation through which they dispossessed Jews of property and civil rights, and they made use of Christian-based cultural events, such as the Oberammergau Passion Play, to promote their attack on the Jewish community among the masses.

In light of the very real involvement of classical Christian anti-Semitism with the Nazi onslaught against the Jews, Catholics today have a moral obligation in the post-Holocaust era to wipe out any remaining seeds of this anti-Semitism legacy still embedded within institutional Catholicism. There is need for spiritual chemotherapy in this regard. Regrettably, Mel Gibson's *The Passion of the Christ* moves us in the opposite direction. It has become a carrier of traditional anti-Semitism even though it may not bring about immediate, direct attacks on the Jewish community. Its fundamental story line of a Jewish cabal pursuing Jesus relentlessly until its members were able to blackmail a weak-kneed Pilate into ordering his execution, the interjection of the blood libel curse from the Gospel of Matthew (27:25), arguably the most toxic New Testament text historically in terms of undergirding Christian anti-Semitism, the use of devil imagery in connection with the Jews, and the total fabrication about the complete destruction of the Temple at the time of Jesus' death are all repetitions of classical anti-Semitic themes which Mel Gibson has brought back to the forefront. This is especially troubling in view of the marketing of the film as a DVD for use in Christian education. Fortunately a recent communiqué issued from the United States Conference of Catholic Bishops and the National Council of Synagogues does warn teachers about using the DVD without incorporating into classroom presentations the official teachings of the Catholic Church on Jews and Judaism found in the several documents issued from Rome since the Second Vatican Council.

The Gibson film clearly has the possibility of undoing the more than forty years of painstaking work on revising Catholic textbooks. This possibility creates special concern at a time when the rise of anti-Semitism has been amply documented by the European Union and in a 2004 Pew Research Center survey in which the number of people attributing responsibility for Jesus' death to the Jews has risen by some 9 percent since the release of *The Passion of the Christ*. This increase is especially noticeable in people under thirty, which clearly presents a challenge for contemporary Catholic education.

Catholic leadership now faces a significant moral challenge. Clearly, institutional Christianity generally failed its membership in not making clear the return to classical Christian anti-Semitic themes in the film. There were a few notable exceptions to this record, such as the statement from the chairman of the

German Catholic Bishops Conference and the one issued in the name of the French Bishops' Conference, which was the clearest statement of the anti-Semitic potential inherent in *The Passion of the Christ.* After some discussion with members of the U.S. Catholic Bishops Advisory Committee on Catholic-Jewish Relations and the National Council of Synagogues, Cardinal William Keeler, who serves as the episcopal moderator of this committee, acknowledged that some aspects of the film might generate anti-Semitic attitudes, after first playing down its anti-Semitic dimensions. But by and large Catholic church leaders denied any anti-Semitism in the film, and some, such as Archbishop Charles Chaput of Denver and certain officials in the Vatican curia, became aggressive proponents of the film, denouncing those scholars who had originally critiqued the film. The controversy generated by the initially claimed papal support for the film, which was followed by an official denial of such support, definitely blemished Pope John Paul II's strong overall record in terms of positive Catholic-Jewish relations. In light of the experience of the Holocaust and the almost forty years of strong statements on Catholic-Jewish relations, *The Passion of the Christ* required strong critique. In not offering such critique Catholic leaders put into question the practical effectiveness of their official statements on Catholic-Jewish relations and created a measure of mistrust between themselves and Jewish leaders committed to dialogue—mistrust that still requires some healing.

A committed moral response to the Holocaust demands zero tolerance for Christian anti-Semitism (or any other manifestation of racism). Mel Gibson's reseeding of popular Christian consciousness with traditional anti-Semitic imagery must be identified for what it is—a basic violation of post-Holocaust morality. It has been disturbing to me as a person intensely involved with the discussion of the film for over a year to see how few church leaders seem aware of Christianity's anti-Semitic legacy. The only "saving" dimension of the controversy over the film was the strong critique of the film offered by many scholars and sensitive Christian laypeople. In most cases, they stood head and shoulders over institutional Christian leaders. This situation struck me as continuous vindication of the late Fr. Edward Flannery's remark that Jews know best the pages of Christian history which Christians have frequently torn out of their textbooks. If Catholic leaders are not going to apply official texts on Christian-Jewish relations to concrete situations such as the appearance of *The Passion of the Christ,* we may as well have a solemn burning of them in St. Peter's Square. It was totally inadequate for Catholic leaders to say they reissued their guidelines on Catholic-Jewish relations and on Passion plays during the controversy and not follow through on these guidelines in applying them to the film itself. In so doing they fulfilled only half of the required task.

If Christian leaders are to restore a sense of moral credibility to Christian-Jewish dialogue in light of Gibson's film, they must make it clear that the film cannot become a central educational tool within the church, as Gibson hopes it will. The film cannot replace the revised textbooks in terms of an understanding of the crucifixion of Jesus. This must be communicated in a clear and decisive manner by Christian leaders to the people in their churches responsible for educational programming if we are to return to the moral high ground after *The Passion of the Christ.*

Apart from the morally challenging issue of anti-Semitism in the Gibson film, there are other important ethical questions that arise from the traditionalist theological perspective on atonement that undergirds this film. Gibson has set his film within the framework of the oldest and grimmest understanding of Jesus' ministry in terms of human salvation. Images of devils, ravens, and other satanic symbols are frequent in the film (usually connected with Jews). These images are meant to highlight Satan's central role in the drama of salvation in Gibson's eyes. In this theological vision Jesus came to earth to suffer in order to overcome the domination Satan exercised over humanity. Only Jesus' intense sufferings mattered in the final analysis—not his public ministry of service, not his resurrection. The atonement theology that serves as the substrate for *The Passion of the Christ* generally lost its appeal in Western Christianity around 1100. It is virtually absent from the theologies of Eastern Christianity. Later Christian writers, such as Anselm of Canterbury and Peter Abelard, developed an atonement theology in which Jesus' death on Calvary was directly linked to his public ministry as the culmination of his life of loving service of humanity, a loving service that his followers were to emulate in their own lives. In this later theology moral commitment on the part of Christians remains central to the understanding of salvation in Christ. In Gibson's film it is inconsequential. Gibson's attempt to revive the patristically based theology of atonement accounts for his reliance on the visions of Anna Katharina Emmerich. Clemens Brentano, the German romantic poet who converted Emmerich's visions into a written text, believed that a restoration of the old notion of atonement was absolutely necessary for the overcoming of what he regarded as the deep-seated sinfulness of his contemporaries. In parallel fashion Gibson's inclusion of episodes from her visions serves the same goal in our time—overcoming the sinfulness he sees throughout the world today, even within the church itself.

This theological background of the Gibson film is especially critical for the issue of moral commitment after the Shoah. Ethicists such as Peter Haas and Didier Pollefeyt as well as the historian Peter Hayes have pointed to the destruction of any notion of personal commitment within the so-called "Nazi ethics." The basic theological perspective on atonement adopted by Gibson as the foundation of the film plays right into the destruction of personal commitment during the Holocaust described by scholars such as Hayes, Pollefeyt, and Haas. Such a viewpoint contradicts the basic moral thrust of the Second Vatican Council, especially its "Declaration on the Church and the Modern World" as well as subsequent central documents, such as the 1971 Bishops' Synod document "Justice in the World," where the pursuit of justice is described as integral to the authentic proclamation of the Gospel. The basic theology of *The Passion of the Christ*, whether directly intended by Gibson or not, opens the door to the marginalization of concrete human activity in terms of personal salvation: It is not what I do but what God has done for me and the rest of humanity that ultimately matters. This can create a sense of moral density that will undercut the necessary moral commitment today to fight the revival of anti-Semitism, against other forms of fascism and human-rights violations, and against economic injustice and ecological destruction.

The horrible violence in the film, which goes far beyond anything presented in the New Testament or mainstream Christian spirituality, can also contribute to the process of dehumanizing victims that was part and parcel of the Nazi perspective, as Henry Friedlander has ably demonstrated. What we see in Jesus in this film is a hunk of humanity totally torn apart. We grasp little of the soul and spirit of Jesus. A number of perceptive film critics, such as Michael Wilmington of the *Chicago Tribune,* have pointed out that Jesus is totally dehumanized by Gibson, as are the Roman soldiers directly involved in beating him to a pulp. President Susan Thistlethwaite of Chicago Theological Seminary has described this aspect of the film as sadomasochistic. If the extreme violence and human brutalization so central to the film become a centerpiece of the contemporary understanding of Jesus' ministry, suffering, and death, it can seriously undercut the challenge now facing religion to become a frontal force in the protection of human dignity worldwide, which is so much a moral imperative in light of the experience of the Holocaust.

Overall *The Passion of the Christ* remains a highly problematic film from the standpoint of contemporary Christian morality, especially when we reflect on ethical commitment through the lens of the Shoah. Christian leaders and educators have a basic decision before them. Will they allow the basic ethos of the Gibson film to dominate Christian faith, understanding, and expression in the years ahead? If they do, I believe they are failing to honor the memory of the victims of the Holocaust and neglecting its basic moral lessons.

Discussion Questions

1. How do we relate new historical understandings to traditional faith affirmations if the new understandings seem to undercut the traditional assertions?

2. What parts of Gibson's film have no basis in the New Testament?

3. Are we able to present the account of Jesus' Passion in a way that does not denigrate Jews?

Gibson's *Passion* on a Catholic Campus

Richard Libowitz

Saint Joseph's University, a Jesuit institution of higher education, occupies a 43-acre campus at the extreme western edge of Philadelphia, abutting the affluent suburban "Main Line." While offering graduate degrees in business and education, its primary student clientele consists of approximately 4,000 undergraduates, the majority of whom have matriculated from homes within one hundred miles of the campus. The student body, as might be expected, is overwhelmingly Roman Catholic in religious confession; many are products of parochial elementary and/or secondary schools. Female students outnumber their male counterparts by several percentage points. The faculty, consisting primarily of laymen and women, embodies greater diversity than the student body.

The university has experienced a sharp increase in admissions in recent years; the resultant student body has become geographically more diverse, comes from more affluent families with higher levels of formal education, and presents educational qualifications for admission superior than those of their predecessors fifteen years earlier. All students are required to complete three theology courses prior to graduation, the second of which offers courses on a variety of world religions as well as the Holocaust.

As the pre-release furor over Mel Gibson's *The Passion of the Christ* grew in late 2003–early 2004, reaction on the campus remained muted. The Catholic Church had, since the Second Vatican Council and "Nostra Aetate," attempted to improve relationships and understandings between Catholics and Jews. The phrase "perfidious Jews" had been removed from the liturgy, while dialogue had been instituted both among clergy and on the parish-synagogue level. Studies, such as those conducted by Fr. John Pawlikowski, had reviewed and revised parochial school textbook materials concerning Jews, Judaism, and the State of Israel. More recent papal statements expressing regret for past misdeeds and granting formal diplomatic recognition of *Medinat Yisrael* continued these most positive of efforts. The release of statements from the Vatican which affirmed post-"Nostra Aetate" positions contrary to the positions presented in the Gibson film was consistent with the direction the Church had taken.

Few Saint Joseph's students exhibited any special fervor about *The Passion* prior to its release. Although some faculty discussed the film and the student newspaper, *The Hawk*, published articles about its controversial scenes and language, students were far more interested in the progress of their men's basketball team, which had gained national attention as it was racing through an undefeated regular season.

Upon *The Passion*'s Lenten opening, newspapers, magazines, television, and the Internet provided the public with reviews which were generally negative and frequently scathing. The film's extreme violence, its factual errors, distortions, and depictions of Jews in all too familiar negative stereotypes were detailed by both secular and religious critics. At the same time, a fundamentalist religious fervor, fueled by Gibson, a veteran of Hollywood and master of the art of hype and publicity, was making *The Passion* financially the most successful "religious" film of all time. The product no major distributor would touch was cashing in at box offices around the country.

At Saint Joseph's, the reaction remained one of curiosity rather than fervor. A minority of students actually viewed the film. Most talked about the violence; few said they felt a personal religious resurgence. Teaching two sections of my course "Jewish and Christian Responses to the Holocaust" as well as a class on world religions, and known on campus as a rabbi as well as a professor of religion, I was being asked for my opinion of the film and questioned about particular scenes even before I had the opportunity to watch it. Viewing the film and comparing the Aramaic dialogue with the subtitles, I found my negative expectations were confirmed. I was disgusted by the gratuitous violence and dismayed by the ancient stereotyped portraits and language. I agreed to share those views with students, faculty, and other members of the Saint Joseph's community by participating on a panel devoted to the film, to be held during free period, a regular block of time in which no classes are scheduled, allowing for campus activities with university-wide participation.

The panel met on March 22, 2004, organized around presentations by four members of the faculty: Fr. Rick Malloy, SJ, a sociologist and acting university chaplain; theology department faculty Allen Kerkeslager (a specialist in religions of the ancient world); Richard Libowitz (Judaism); and Jeffrey Hyson, of the history department, an authority on American pop culture.[1] Each panelist was given approximately twelve minutes for his remarks, with several minutes set aside for questions from the audience. More questions and discussion followed the final presentation.

Kerkeslager, the opening speaker, expressed concerned with the casting of Jim Caviezel as Jesus, then focused upon the task of evaluating the film's historical accuracy. He noted Gibson's reliance on Anna Katharina Emmerich's *The Dolorous Passion,* a nineteenth-century devotional work lacking in any scholarly credibility. He was critical of the portrayal of Pontius Pilate, who was shown as sensitive to the concerns and sensibilities of the Jewish community, a characteristic not to be found in any historic Roman document. In more general remarks, he commented on the internal contradictions within the Gospels themselves and on Mel Gibson's emphasis upon violence. Cognizant of the very conservative variety of Roman Catholicism practiced by Gibson, Kerkeslager offered a rationale behind Gibson's aggressive defense of the film, which transcended the financial risk he had taken, noting "To criticize the film is to criticize Gibson's faith."

Having been given the task of evaluating the film for its alleged anti-Semitic content, I began my presentation by asking "What constitutes anti-Semitism?" Tracing the history of the term back to Wilhelm Marr, I suggested that

> Anti-Semitism is anything which negatively targets Jews—singly or as a group—because they are Jews. Acts do not have to be violent to be anti-Semitic. They can be acts of commission, such as painting swastikas on walls, knocking over headstones in cemeteries, posting neo-Nazi web sites, denying the Holocaust, or advocating the destruction of the State of Israel. They can also be acts of omission, such as penalizing Jewish school children in a public school system by scheduling major events on the Jewish New Year or Day of Atonement, refusing to sell a home to a Jew, barring Jews from country clubs, business associations or social groups, or refusing to hire or promote someone because he/she is Jewish. All of these are, at ground zero, anti-Semitic acts of hate, although some will be explained or justified in the loftiest tones.

When questioned from the audience, I rejected the contention that *The Passion of the Christ* was an anti-Semitic film *per se*, but argued that many of the images which Gibson had chosen to use—of Caiaphas, the mob, etc.—were stereotypical in nature. I added,

> I believe Gibson distorted a number of scenes, placing dramatic effect above accuracy and frankly, his research notwithstanding, there are so many historical errors in the film that it is difficult to list them all. When one adds together all of these problems you have a film that is most certainly anti-Jewish and one that can be a vehicle for anti-Semitism. Considering that European Jews are experiencing the worst outbreak of anti-Semitic acts since the Holocaust, this film has the potential of adding gasoline to the fire.

My final comment was to describe *The Passion* as "the first religious slasher film."

Rev. Malloy, the third speaker, addressed the audience not as a sociologist but as a priest. He concurred that the film in question "may or may not be anti-

Semitic," but reminded his listeners that "anti-Semitism exists." He wondered if the problematic scenes within the film might be turned upon themselves and asked how the movie might be used to combat the anti-Semitism present in the world today. He challenged the mostly undergraduate audience, "How does the movie help us to be the people God wants us to be?" He then added, "We cannot be against one another; we must be with one another," and expressed his concern that a film like *The Passion* might prevent society from realizing that end.

Jeffrey Hyson, the final panelist, began his remarks with an overview of Jesus in American cinema. He noted that the Christ figure has been portrayed on film since the late nineteenth century and has continued to be a popular subject of filmmakers through the decades. He underscored this contention with still photographs and synopses of a variety of such films, from long forgotten "silents" to more recent extravaganzas such as *Godspell, The Greatest Story Ever Told,* and *Jesus Christ Superstar*, offering critiques of each film while also evaluating them in terms of historicity. He then turned his attention to *The Passion* and, specifically, to four prominent themes within the film: the centrality of violence and suffering, the absence of references to either Jesus' life story or his teachings, the role of Mary, and the portrayal of "Romans as brutal and the Jews as evil."

Mel Gibson has gained international fame and fortune for his performances in two decades of action films—the *Mad Max* and *Lethal Weapon* series and *Braveheart* being the best known—in which his character is frequently the recipient of beatings and torture.[2] Hyson described this as "Gibson's 'Martyr Complex'" and contended that *The Passion* is part of this genre, in which Gibson tends to "portray himself and his actors as martyrs." Aware of this tendency, Hyson noted Gibson's use of extreme close-ups, contrasts of light and shadow, slow motion, flashbacks, music and dialogue as "moving and even manipulative" to the audience. He cited the scene in which the hideously scourged Jesus, struggling under the weight of the cross, falls and his mother, Mary, runs to his side as a culminating example of many of these manipulative techniques.

The final portion of the event was devoted to audience questions and comment. These ranged from requests for more specific details of biblical history and Jewish understandings of the Messiah to criticisms of the film's violence, and statements of personal faith. No one rose to give witness of having his or her faith reaffirmed by *The Passion,* although some were puzzled why a "religious film" would cause such worry within the Jewish community. Prior to the discussion, many had been willing to accept Gibson's claims of historical accuracy at face value, without necessarily associating Caiaphas, the other priests, and the mob with contemporary Jews. Some of the more "conservative" questions were pointed, but there were no attacks—either personal or religious—directed toward the panelists.

A website maintained by the Drexel Library on campus offered a homepage with readings and reactions pertaining to the film. Over the next several weeks, additional discussion sessions were scheduled to continue the conversation with students, faculty, and staff. Soon, however, final examinations and graduation reduced discussion of *The Passion* to an insignificant place in campus life. When students returned to campus in late August, concern about *The Passion* was gone.

Saint Joseph's University students are taught to think in terms of the Ignatian commitment to "a life lived for others." Students attend retreats in which they undertake spiritual exercises, involve themselves in fund-raising events for a variety of charities and promote neighborhood programs. Many spend their vacations working in Mexico, Latin America, Appalachia, on Indian reservations, or with Habitat for Humanity. Some dedicate a year after graduation to volunteer work with religious agencies. Religious ideas and idealism permeate their lives. Within the classroom, there is a genuine interest in other religions. Students often attend religious services outside their own faith as part of their theology course requirements and respond to their experiences in a positive manner. On the surface, then, there appears to be a contradiction between this religious activism and a relative detachment and indifference to *The Passion*.

It is my contention that the Gibson film made students more curious than committed; curious as to the extreme violence and wondering why so great a degree of negative publicity was being generated months before the film's release. Students who had studied Judaism or the Holocaust as part of their theology requirement may have been sensitized to potential Jewish reactions to *The Passion*, while the published clarification of the Vatican's position—including the denial of Gibson's claim that the pope had endorsed his film—may have established a satisfactory set of understandings for many of the students on this Catholic campus, who viewed the film as violent entertainment rather than religious witness. On this campus, at least, I would say the long-lasting effects of *The Passion* are nonexistent.

Discussion Questions

1. What was Mel Gibson's purpose in making *The Passion*?
2. In what way(s) was interfaith dialogue harmed by the film? How may it have been advanced?
3. How did the composition of the faculty panel at Saint Joseph's University affect discussion of *The Passion*?
4. The author has suggested that the particular religious atmosphere at this Jesuit institution may have weakened the strident effect of the film among the student audience. What other factor(s) may have contributed to the relatively tepid student response?

Notes

1. An article on the panel discussion appeared in *The Hawk*, the student newspaper, on March 26, 2004. All quotations of panelists have been drawn from that article.
2. Even his most comedic character, Bret Maverick, is beaten, shot at and goes over a cliff.

Mel Gibson's *The Passion of the Christ*

A Protestant Perspective

James F. Moore

Mel Gibson's *The Passion of the Christ* is a film. This has two meanings for the essay response that I am writing. First, it is merely a film and not any more. Thus, any analysis of the film requires a general sense of popular culture and how such films impact the popular mind. Second, it is a film of the Passion story and is in this way like so many other films and forms of presenting this story. That is, it is a Passion play, and Protestant Christians (for that matter all Christians) must think about the film in the context of its being another Passion play. There is a history of such plays, and most of us who have thought about Passion plays in a post-Shoah world believe that telling the story of the Passion must be done in a post-Shoah framework, with full knowledge that the Passion is set alongside of the stories of Auschwitz and understood in that context. I believe that few who watched the film actually consciously did that, but it is not the failing of the filmmaker but the failing of the churches that so few would actually see the film in the context of a post-Shoah reading. Finally, a focus on the story, that is how the story is told, is precisely what is central to a Protestant Christian approach and this is approach that I will take in offering my reflections in this essay.

The Film

I was disappointed that film critics Roger Ebert and Richard Roeper in their syndicated television show wanted us to see this movie as cinema and then proceeded to praise the movie for its cinematic achievement. They must have been ready to do this as a response to those who wanted to make the movie into theology. While they have a point, I was surprised that both so fully wanted to do theology in order to persuade us to think about the film as cinema. The movie is poor theology and cannot pretend to be a profound theological reflection; I believe they tried too hard to balance the act. My point is, however, to think about the telling of the story of the Passion not so much to critique the film but to ask what a Protestant would want to say in telling this story in a post-Shoah world.

My judgment is that there is little or no creativity in this film in the actual telling of the story. The filmmaker, indeed, argues that his intent is to stay true to the text (even if this, like other Passion plays, is a mixing of the Gospel texts done with a very specific point of view introduced by the filmmaker). But for me, such an effort is already problematic because the various episodes of the actual Gospel texts include elements that, if read without a post-Shoah perspective, do reinforce what Jules Isaac has called "the teaching of contempt."[1] I do not expect Mel Gibson to know this or be ready to consider it as he makes films, but I do imagine that Christians would be prepared to see that the Gospel texts can produce false teaching which has emerged in Christian history in which the Pharisees are viewed as the enemies of Jesus, Jesus is not seen as a Jew but as distinct from the Jewish culture of his time, that Jews were principally responsible for the death of Jesus, which means that Pilate, the Roman governor, is regarded as innocent. The churches have denounced all of these teachings, but the film does not attempt to minimize them as ways of thinking about this story.

A Theological Response

This is not the most significant matter, however. What is more central is the "theological" view that Jesus takes on the sin of the world especially through his physical suffering. Cinematically, Gibson has a serious problem with this choice, since he has to produce an image that surpasses all other possible forms of suffering. This effort leads Gibson into an absurdly violent telling of the Passion narrative in which the scenes become increasingly violent and ultimately cartoon-like. The scenes at the cross are over the top. But then, Gibson needed to outdo his own portrayal of the heroic William Wallace in *Braveheart.* The problem is that visually this effort is impossible, since little could possibly be done to make Jesus' suffering more than the final scenes of the torture of William Wallace. Thus the film becomes nearly pornographic in its violence, and this is hardly what Christians would want as "their" story. But I was amazed to hear so many say that when they saw the film they realized "what Jesus really went through." That is, most were able to screen out the violence or, worse, accept the violence as a real part of the story.

Protestant theologians should have a problem with this telling of the story. The efforts by Martin Luther (surely a man with problems about attitudes about Jews) to disown this kind of theology, a theology of sacrifice, are echoed by two important Protestant thinkers of the twentieth century, Helmut Gollwitzer and Dietrich Bonhoeffer. Both thinkers were active in resisting Nazi ideology and tactics. Neither thinker considers sacrifice to be the defining element of the Passion. The "theology of the cross" that is so characteristic of Protestant thinking focuses not on the suffering of Jesus but on the reconciling love which is revealed in Jesus and about the God that Jesus proclaims as his "father." Bonhoeffer gives this as the foundation for moral action in his *Ethics*, a work that predated the Nazi dominance.[2] In his later fragmentary work, *Letters and Papers from Prison*, Bonhoeffer is even more dubious about church theologies and looks to a view in which the church does not have sole possession of the truth. It is still the reconciling work of love and the power of resistance that is at the heart of Bonhoeffer's thought.[3] Gollwitzer's *An Introduction to Protestant Theology* is also careful to both include other religious views and recognize the power of Auschwitz as a dark cloud over theologies like the sacrificial theology portrayed in Gibson's film. Again Gollwitzer opts for a view in which respect for the other and reconciliation are central to the image of Jesus he portrays.[4] It is the violence of the sacrificial model that so troubled the changed Luther, who realized that adding more suffering does not produce salvation. The telling of the story as Gibson has done so centrally focused on this sacrificial model should be a serious problem for Christians. But the fact is that the Catholic Gibson actually telling his own version of a Catholic view (I leave it to John Pawlikowski and others to deal with Gibson's version of Catholicism) finally appeals through this film to an astounding number of Protestant leaders and audiences. The churches seem to have failed in getting the message across.

Post-Shoah Reflection

But more to the point is a post-Shoah reading of this film and the Protestant challenge to this telling of the Passion narrative. I have tried to address how the Passion story can be read in a post-Shoah world.[5] I simply challenge any telling of the Passion story which makes suffering the key to how we understand Jesus or God. Suffering is not salvific, and we know this absolutely after Auschwitz. My conclusion in my book *Christian Theology after the Shoah* is that the image of the cross can no longer be an image of sacrifice along the lines of the Akeda (Gen 22) but must rather be the political/moral image of resistance is the only direction that makes sense given a post-Shoah reading of the crucifixion.[6] Those who suffer because they have chosen to resist evil and to intervene to rescue those who would be victims can be salvific (that is, some can be saved from the evil intentions of the oppressor, like the Nazis), but what is saving in this context is the act of resistance and/or the act of rescue. More to the point, what is saving is the attitude of respect for the other, which is linked with the act for the other. If we take the wisdom of Emmanuel Levinas to heart, then it is especially in the one who is truly other that such an act can be redeeming.[7] Such a view seems in keeping with a Protestant telling of the Passion and necessary for a post-Shoah response.

Of course, this means that the issue is how Christians are willing to tell the story of the Passion and not really the Gibson film itself. What remains for us is not so much to undo the filming of *The Passion of the Christ* but to continue to transform the teaching of the churches so that any general response to the Christian stories can become sensitive to a post-Shoah reading. In addition, my sense is that, for Christians, the central issue is not just our concern for how a teaching of contempt can re-emerge but the necessity of moving away from theologies of sacrificial suffering toward theologies of respect for the other as the central redeeming act. In that we will be true both to our Protestant principles and to our commitments to open and respectful dialogue with our Jewish colleagues.

Discussion Questions

1. The issue that may be of most concern for Protestants regarding the Mel Gibson film *The Passion of the Christ* is the picture of Jesus' suffering. Why are Protestants so ready to accept the violence depicted in Jesus' suffering according to the film?
2. Why is it that so many Protestants can see this film and say that now they know how it really was?
3. Does the picture of a God demanding such brutality as "payment" for sin really coincide with the image of God that Protestants want to confess?
4. To what extent do Protestants who see this film recognize that the image of the suffering Jesus is precisely the teaching which the Catholic theologian Rosemary Ruether has called "the left hand of anti-Semitism?" Do you think they are aware of the way that Jewish observers feel and respond to this history of a "teaching of contempt"; and how would such awareness change the reaction of Protestants to this film?

Notes

1. Jules Isaac, *The Teaching of Contempt* (New York: Holt, Rinehart and Winston, 1964).
2. Dietrich Bonhoeffer, *Ethics* (New York: The Macmillan Company, 1955), pp. 188ff.
3. Dietrich Bonhoeffer, *Letters and Papers from Prison* (New York: The Macmillan Company, 1967).
4. Helmut Gollwitzer, *An Introduction to Protestant Theology* (Philadelphia: Westminster Press, 1982), pp. 62ff.
5. James Moore, *Christian Theology after the Shoah* (Lanham, MD: University Press of America, 1993, 2004).
6. Moore, pp. 85ff.
7. See, for example, Emmanuel Levinas, "God and Philosophy," in *The Postmodern God*, ed. Graham Ward (Oxford: Blackwell Publishers, 1997), pp. 52–73.

Jewish "Officialdom" and *The Passion of the Christ*

Who Said What and What Did They Say?

Steven Leonard Jacobs

Introduction

Among the falsely perceived myths, not only of this historical American Jewish experience but the contemporary one as well, is that of a singular American Jewish community, seemingly united by such common factors as religious faith and belief; love of and support for a continuously beleaguered State of Israel; higher educational agendas for the young; support for defensive organizations against the ongoing post-Holocaust/Shoah specter of anti-Semitism; politically left-wing, liberal, primarily Democratic voter identification; uncanny fund-raising abilities; opposition to inter-religious or mixed marriages; socio-economic concerns associated with middle-class to upper-middle-class to upper-class lives, and the like. The reality of the American Jewish community is, however, quite the opposite. While certain concerns may assume dominating positions momentarily only to be replaced by others, the myth of unity is precisely that: myth. American Jews remain divided along religious lines, have strong and varied opinions about the State of Israel and its political and military behaviors, are divided about how best to confront anti-Semitism both in the American context and elsewhere, continue to be conflicted about the best course of action in response to increasing intermarriage rates, find themselves increasingly both protective and preservative of their achieved socio-economic status, and the like.

Commensurate with this historical and contemporary divisiveness is the one question that, in truth, has been the bane of the American Jewish experience: *Who, in fact, speaks for the Jews?* Who best represents on the national and international stages Jewish concerns? The plethora of Jewish organizations—more than 600 according to the 2003 edition of *The American Jewish Yearbook* published by The American Jewish Committee—dramatically and graphically supports the contention that there are many representative voices at the table purporting to speak for American Jews, some louder than others depending upon the issue and context, and more often than not, upon membership numbers. Thus, just as the Jews of the United States do not form a unified community, so, too, do their representative spokespersons not speak with one voice *regardless* of the issues before them.

Enter Hollywood icon Mel Gibson and his religio-cinematic blockbuster *The Passion of the Christ*, pre-screened in February 2004, released to coincide with the Easter season, and complete with an end-of-August DVD availability. Though much ink has already been spilled about every possible aspect of this film and its implications by every possible commentator, the one truism that speaks loudest is the following: Jews and Christians, in the main, whether or not they sat together or saw the film together, saw two very different movies out of their, ultimately, divergent concerns. For many Christians, the film was a religiously cathartic experience, truly expanding their understanding as never before of the loving gift of the Christ's willing suffering and life-sacrifice, and re-affirmed for many the culpability and guilt of *all* humanity responsible for His death. For Jews, the continuously negative portrayals of the Jewish leaders, primarily priests, and the Jewish populace were, quite simply, the newest adumbration of anti-Semitism—a modern, technological Passion play not radically other than that produced once every decade in Oberammergau, Germany; the very same play which saw Adolf Hitler in attendance and confirming for him and others of his ilk the Jew as eternal and perpetual enemy. Thus, for these same Christians the film was a *religio-theological* experience; for Jews the film was an *historical* experience. And into the fray came any number of Jewish organizations and Jewish leaders and their Jewish concerns. Who said what and what they said are the foci of this essay.

The Findings

Beyond any question, the one American Jewish organization which "led the fight" against the perceived anti-Semitic agenda of the film and its co-writer and producer was and remains the Anti-Defamation League of B'nai B'rith under its national director, Dr. Abraham H. Foxman, Holocaust survivor and author of *Never Again? The Threat of the New Anti-Semitism* (San Francisco, CA: HarperCollins, 2003). Second was the Los Angeles–based Simon Wiesenthal Center in the person of its founding dean, Rabbi Dr. Marvin Hier. Neither of these organizations is positioned within the various religious denominational streams of American Jewry, though Rabbi Hier is himself an Orthodox Rabbi. The third is the Union for Reform Judaism under the leadership of its president, Rabbi Eric Yoffe. The remaining eleven organizations examined, while issuing (and *not* issuing) important statements, did not see this issue as among their primary concerns, based upon their actual numbers of statements and documents issued.

Anti-Defamation League

Beginning with an original letter of 24 March 2003 directly to Gibson from Abraham Foxman that the upcoming movie "not give rise to the old canard of charging Jews with deicide and anti-Semitism," which elicited no response and was followed up by a second letter 23 January 2004 which did (30 January 2004),[1] the ADL has made publicly available a host of official documents, including letters defending its stance and active involvement, and both attacking and correcting such public figures as conservative Catholic theologian Michael Novak (3 September 2003), conservative Jewish thinker and film critic Michael Medved (22 July 2003 and 2 February 2004), Hollywood columnist Liz Smith (15 September 2003), William F. Buckley, Jr. (29 January 2004), Bill O'Reilly (24 February 2004) in a variety of newspapers (e.g. *New York Times, New York Sun, New York Jewish Week, Forward*), as well as individual letter writers in those same and other publications. Also included are a variety of press releases expressing concern regarding the papal statement "It is as it was," later repudiated by Vatican officials (22 September 2003 and 17 December 2003); praising German bishops for expressing their concerns over the potential anti-Semitic *use* of the Gibson film (23 February 2004); two op-ed pieces both by Foxman (4 August 2003 and 10 March 2004), the first defending ADL's position, and the second expressing appreciation for the support of evangelical Christians; several articles and essays by various authors (17 December 2003, 3 February 2004, and 6 April 2004); three important statements (24 June 2003, 25 February 2004, and 2 April 2004); lengthy texts of actual quotations by Gibson himself (9 February 2004), acknowledged Christian and Jewish leaders about *The Passion of the Christ* (1 April 2004), and, interestingly enough, Minister of Islam Louis Farrakhan (5 May 2004).

With regard to the official statements issued by ADL, the first (24 June 2003) strongly urged Gibson to take seriously the analysis of an early version of the screenplay in April 2003, by a distinguished panel of nine Christian and Jewish scholars and incorporate their concerns into any revisions.[2] With regard to the second official statement, issued by both Foxman and (Reform) Rabbi Gary Bretton-Granatoor, ADL advisor on interfaith affairs, having now seen the film, *The Passion of the Christ* is "a potential setback for Christian-Jewish relations" because of "Mr. Gibson's failure to make alterations to the film and its unambiguous portrayal of Jews as being responsible for the death of Christ." The last is a piece by Rabbi Bretton-Granatoor entitled "Why Jews Worry About *The Passion*," and articulates ADL's concerns with being falsely accused of potentially fuelling anti-Semitism, attacking Mel Gibson, addressing the problems Jews have with Christian Scriptures (i.e., the New Testament Gospel accounts and portrayals), and of being anti-Christian. He does, however, accuse Gibson of re-creating images akin to Fagin (Charles Dickens's character in *Oliver Twist*) or Shylock (William Shakespeare's character in *The Merchant of Venice*), and raises the question "What images will the next generation of Christian faithful see when they open their Scriptures to study the core teachings of their faith?"

By the end of 2003, the ADL had already labeled the film prior to its release "among the issues most affecting the Jewish community" (30 December 2003). Of noteworthy concern was the use to which it could be put by those who would seek to do harm to the Jewish people. On 13 August 2003, ADL posted "a representative sample of the dozens of hateful email messages received," and followed it up on 4 March 2004 with an equally representative sampling of various electronic postings from a number of Internet websites (e.g. Angry White Female web-page, Vanguard News Network, Christian Identity website, Stormfront Neo-Nazi website, National Alliance website, Aryan Nations website, and Church of the Sons of Yaveh website).[3]

Summarily, ADL's position with regard to *The Passion of the Christ* may best be seen in its own "ADL and Mel Gibson's *The Passion of the Christ* Frequently Asked Questions" (undated), where it (1)explicitly states its ongoing concern regarding the consequences of this film, especially with regard to those "unfavorably disposed" toward Jews; (2) denies ever accusing Gibson of being an antisemite; (3) acknowledges the outpouring of hate already received as a result of raising issues; (4) denies any attempt to censor Gibson; and (5) denies any attempt to urge either a boycott of the film or preventing Christians from telling "their story," though it does suggest it can be told "without disparaging the Jewish people."

Simon Wiesenthal Center

Between 7 March 2003 and 24 February 2004, the Simon Wiesenthal Center in Los Angeles, under the leadership of Rabbi Hier, issued seven different press releases relating to *The Passion of the Christ,* addressing a number of themes similar to those articulated by the Anti-Defamation League, and creating, in the process, a unique document.

In its initial release, again, prior to the actual release of the film (7 March 2003), it expressed its own concern that "going back to pre-Vatican II may give rise to anti-Semitism." Three months later (22 June 2003), it informed Gibson that the "Passion of Christ—the crucifixion and hours leading up to it—has been used by bigots, including popes and kings, to inflame anti-Semitism through the ages," and urged Gibson to consider the "political context" before completing his work. Two months later (12 August 2003), Rabbi Hier announced "an unprecedented wave of hate mail and calls to the Jewish human rights group over the Center's endorsement of changes to the film proposed by Christian and Jewish scholars" (aligning himself and the Center with Foxman and the ADL).

In February 2004, the Simon Wiesenthal Center sent a lengthy "Appeal to People of Faith" together with an even lengthier "Background to a Dilemma" to select (and unidentified) leadership of all branches of the Christian faith. According to the press release, the threefold purpose of the appeal was:

- To address the spate of misinformation regarding Jewish sentiment to the film.
- To reiterate the Jewish community's gratitude for decades of work on the part of the Christian community to distance itself from the religious roots of anti-Semitism.
- To encourage the Christian community to proclaim that the crucifixion's message is not one of violence or blame and that there is no room in Christian teaching to support the notion that today's Jews should be seen as the killers of God.

The purpose of the inclusion of the background document was to detail "the progress of Jewish/Christian relations in the twentieth century and how the recent worldwide resurgence of anti-Semitism threatens to undermine much of that progress."

No follow-ups whatsoever have been thus far issued regarding the success or failure of this endeavor, and, thus, there is no way to gauge its impact.

The remaining three press releases concerned (1) condemnation of Mel Gibson's father Hutton Gibson's denials of the Holocaust (19 February 2004); (2) urging the Denver, Colorado, Christian community to rebuke the Lovingway United Pentecostal Church and its pastor for posting a sign stating "Jews Killed the Lord Jesus . . . Settled!" (the sign was ultimately removed, though there is no indication whatsoever that the SWC had any influence in that event); and (3) announcement of a meeting (24 February 2004) at the SWC Museum of Tolerance between Rabbi Hier and other Jewish community leaders and Pastor Ted Haggard of New Life Church, Colorado Springs, Colorado, and president of the National Association of Evangelical Christians "to address Jewish concerns and fears of anti-Semitic fallout over the film." Again, no follow-up information has surfaced regarding the meeting and its outcome.

Thus, though Hier and his institution, the Simon Wiesenthal Center, have been strongly active and vocal in publicizing their concerns, they chose to focus on only two areas: (1) anti-Semitism, including Holocaust denial, and (2) Jewish-Christian relations, falling a distant second to the work of the ADL and its national director, Abraham Foxman.

Union for Reform Judaism

(Reform) Rabbi Eric Yoffe, president of the Union for Reform Judaism, in a conference call to his constituency on 26 February 2004 addressed three points: (1) "Mel Gibson's role has been despicable" as someone who has "exploited and fomented controversy in order to sell movie tickets." (2) "I have no patience with those who say we should have remained silent." (3) "Until yesterday, this film was the domain of the critics, the scholars, the columnists, and the talk show hosts. But now it belongs to the people and the community." He then went on to urge the avoidance of "hysterical and over-heated rhetoric" and, a hallmark of Reform or liberal Judaism in the arena of Jewish-Christian relations, namely coalition building.

The bulk of this denominational religious community's response was turned over to its Commission on Interreligious Affairs which, in addition to providing Internet links to publications, speeches, and a lengthy listing of additional resources (including news articles and reports, materials by and for rabbis, opinion articles, Jewish perspectives and resources about the movie, Christian perspectives and resources about the movie, articles about Christian missionary efforts) made available "Ten Steps You Can Take in Advance of the Release of Mel Gibson's 'The Passion of the Christ'" (directed primarily to rabbis); two commentaries by Dr. Michael J. Cook, Sol & Arlene Bronstein Professor of Judaeo-Christian Studies, Hebrew Union College-Jewish Institute of Religion, Cincinnati; a set of resource materials specifically directed to young people; and a series of letters and commentaries by individual rabbis addressed specifically to their own congregations but, obviously of value to the larger liberal community. Among the most innovative is that of Rabbi Stephen Forstein of Kalamazoo and Battle Creek, Michigan, whose "Guide for Small Community Jews" for those who remain decidedly in the minority and whose interactions with non-Jews, presumably, would loom largest.

The arenas of concern here, too, tend to be those of anti-Semitism both today and tomorrow, overreaction and misreading and misgauging the responses to the movie of the larger non-Jewish/Christian community, and reaching out to non-Jews, clergy and laity alike, historic staples of this uniquely American liberal religious movement whose own pioneering work in interfaith relations has, in truth, set the parameters of these ongoing conversations among all Jewish religious denominations in the United States.

"Everybody Else"

With only one noteworthy and important exception—the 41-page Resource Manual produced by The American Jewish Committee and made available both online and in hard copy—none of the remaining eleven organizations examined has contributed significantly to either the intra-Jewish communal conversations regarding *The Passion of the Christ* and issues of Jewish concern, nor engaged the larger non-Jewish/Christian community in conversations over these issues.

Aish HaTorah chose to make available seven scholarly articles by important writers.

Allen C. Brownfeld, editor of the *Special Interest Report* of the American

Council for Judaism, chose to summarize the positions of others with little commentary or insight on his part.

The American Jewish Committee also issued a press release (22 January 2004) calling the film "A disturbing setback to Christian-Jewish relations," and a second press release (12 February 2004) "deeply troubled by its anti-Jewish elements and potential for polarization among people of different faiths." It further issued a formal statement by its executive director, David A. Harris, (25 February 2004) recognizing that the film's "potential to heighten misunderstanding . . . could set back temporarily the extraordinary advances in interreligious dialogue and cooperation that have taken place in recent decades."

Americans for Peace Now in its *Middle East Peace Report* (5[31]: March 1, 2004) referenced the controversy over *The Passion of the Christ* under the title "The Lamest Story Ever Told."

B'nai B'rith International chose to post the critique, observations, and reactions of its executive vice-president, Dan Mariaschin, and his concerns regarding "the potential harm its loathsome portrayal of Jews may have," and sent letters to several prominent Christians (e.g., Jerry Falwell and Pat Robertson), but noted "the only response received by BBI came from [Apostolic Nuncio Archbishop Gabriel] Montalvo [at the Embassy of the Vatican in Washington, D.C.], who suggested that we contact the American Conference of Bishops."

Hillel: The Foundation for Jewish Campus Life issued a press release (19 February 2004) entitled "Gibson Film Spurs Dialogue" and then followed it up with "Talking Points about the Passion," "10 Responses to the Passion," and a letter from Avi Weinstein, its senior educational officer, urging his professional colleagues "to create new opportunities for Jewish and Christian collegians to come to mutual understanding."

National Conference on Soviet Jewry: Advocates on behalf of Jews in Russia, Ukraine, the Baltic states, and Eurasia simply chose to make available four columns from other sources.

The Orthodox Union issued a press release summary of a video symposium with Rabbi Hersh Weinreb, executive vice-president; Professor David Berger of Brooklyn College; and Rabbi Michael Skobac, education director of the Toronto branch of Jews for Judaism, which was to be distributed to its member congregations, collectively expressing their concern about both the negative psychic and spiritual impact upon Jews.

United Jewish Communities (formerly the United Jewish Appeal) simply made available three previously published columns.

The World Jewish Congress referenced *The Passion of the Christ* in its online newsletter *Dialogues: Discussions Between Jews, Christians, and Muslims* (April 2003) under the title "Old Wine in New Bottles?"

Lastly, the Zionist Information News Service of the Zionist Organization of America, in its March/April, 2004, issue, reprinted two pieces from *The De-*

troit News, one by Episcopal priest Harry T. Cook entitled "Gibson's Delusion" and one by Jewish writer Mitch Albom entitled "The *Passion* or the Hatred? The Son Must Refute Father's Hateful Rants."

None of the many, many other Jewish organizations even appeared to address *The Passion of the Christ*, the person of Mel Gibson, the issues of anti-Semitism, Jewish-Christian relations, or anything else connected to these, or other topics, for that matter.

Conclusions

As suggested at the outset, regardless of the issue(s) at hand, there is no one voice which speaks for American Jews, just as there is no one American Jewish community. In this context, the loudest voice remains that of the Anti-Defamation League, a primary leader in defense of Jews, challenging anti-Semitism wherever and whenever it appears and educating the larger non-Jewish/Christian communities about Jewish concerns. That position appears to have not changed either positively or negatively as a result of its outspoken leadership with regard to *The Passion of the Christ.*

Neither Jewish religious nor Jewish secular organizations dominate these conversations; each has a role to play in the larger arena, addressing both similar and different constituencies. In the case of *The Passion of the Christ*, the audiences and/or recipients of these public pronouncements were both fellow Jews and non-Jews as well, clergy and opinion-makers and ordinary citizens.

Dominating Jewish concerns across the board, however, were, time and time again, the *potential* for anti-Semitic response, backlash, harm in this American context (which has not proven to be the case), and the fear of a retrogression in Jewish-Christian relations (which, equally, has not proven to be the case). With regard to this latter point, the reverse appears to be more the case; an unintended consequence of *The Passion of the Christ* seems to be a renewed energy in the arena of Jewish-Christian relations, including a thorough re-examination of the actual historic events of which this cinematic epic attempts to claim accuracy.[4]

Thus, the American democratic experiment continues to defy historical precedents. What was negatively the experience of Jews in a Europe dominated for two thousand years by various forms of Christianity in collusion with various governmental power structures, once again, appears not to have been transplanted to these shores. And those who attempt to predict a Jewish future based on that past are, again, proven wrong.[5]

Discussion Questions

1. Given what you know now about the history and evolution of the American Jewish community, and the current political-cultural situation, is the author's assessment of the response of Jewish "officialdom" as, ultimately, little more than a "tempest in a teapot" accurate or inaccurate?

2. From your own vantage point, has Mel Gibson's *The Passion of the Christ* further contributed to the global increase in anti-Semitism or not? Is it a part of an ongoing global, post-Holocaust re-assessment of Jews and Judaism and the place of both in the contemporary world heightened by increasingly negative assessments of Israel's political and military actions?

3. What agenda would you develop for contemporary and future Jewish-Christian relations after *The Passion of the Christ?* What issues and topics should/ must be addressed?

Notes

1. On 23 January 2004, Foxman again wrote Gibson, having now seen the pre-released film, urging him to "consider a movie postscript with you coming on the screen at the end to implore your viewers to not let the movie turn some toward a passion of hatred." Gibson acknowledged receipt of the letter on 30 January 2004, agreeing with Foxman that "diplomacy by press release is no diplomacy at all," (Foxman's original phrase), but not otherwise responding to either Foxman's concerns and/or suggestions. In a follow-up letter dated 2 February 2004, Foxman chided Gibson far more strongly for not addressing "any of the issues we raised in our most recent correspondence, and the concerns that we have been raising all along since we first reached out to you in March 2003." No other letters if they have been sent, received, and/or elicited a response have been made available.
2. Here, too, a bit of controversy surrounds the actual acquisition of the early screenplay. The scholars, all reputable, continue to believe the copy they received was one provided to them from Gibson and ICON Pictures upon request. Gibson, however, has argued that it was a "stolen" copy, pirated away and unauthorized.
3. Among the most vicious of documents to have thus far come forth is a flyer produced by the National Vanguard, headquartered in Hillsboro, WV, entitled (in bold type) "They Almost Killed This Film," and includes the following text:

   > Jewish pressure groups like the misnamed Anti-Defamation League (ADL) have gone to great lengths to keep you from seeing *The Passion of the Christ.* From pressuring the film's distributors not to support the film to defaming Mel Gibson and his family, they have cried "anti-Semitism" throughout the entire production process.
   >
   > Jewish groups even went so far as to steal a copy of the script and demand that certain scenes be removed or edited. The ADL's chairman Abe Foxman, posed as a pastor from a fake church to sneak into a screening of the film, and, despite signing a non-disclosure agreement, ran to the press about the "anti-Semitic nature" of the film.

   The flyer also includes Gibson's statement to CNN: "They wrote a document to say change this scene, take this scene out, change this dialogue, do this, do that.... This is not communist Russia. Does anybody realize that my rights as an American, as an artist, as a human being... are being violated here?" It then concludes with the caption (again in bold type) "Are you tired of minority groups telling Whites what we can see, read, publish, and enjoy? YOU ARE NOT ALONE."
4. On this question of dialogue as an unintended consequence of the film, see my own essay "Can There Be Jewish-Christian Dialogue after *The Passion,*" in S. Brent Plate, ed., *Re-*

Viewing The Passion: Mel Gibson's Film and Its Critics (New York: Palgrave-Macmillan, 2004), pp. 64–76.

5. This is a somewhat truncated version of the original and much longer paper, including the omitted section "Investigative Methodology." Readers interested in the full report may contact the author at sjacobs@bama.ua.edu.

A View from the Pew on Gibson's *Passion*

Stuart D. Robertson

By the time this book is published Gibson's once front-page-news movie may have the lingering interest most front-page stories retain. The heavy publicity preceding the movie's release, and the record ticket sales in the early showing, which are the kind of details often catching the media's ephemeral fascination, do not completely overshadow the issues that arise from the composition, filming, watching, and effects of *The Passion of the Christ*. My task here is to critique something of the ordinary Christian's response to the movie. In particular, did *The Passion* stir up anti-Jewish sentiment? And did it add fuel to supersessionist tendencies among Christians? Other questions arise from the flash of popularity the movie aroused.

Why did numerous conservative Protestant churches pay out some of their people's tithe money to buy up whole showings of this R-rated film, produced by an arch-conservative Tridentine Roman Catholic? Why did being overwhelmed by the movie become nearly an act of faith for many devout Christians, Protestant and Catholic? Watching the movie was for many Christians tantamount to standing by in Jerusalem, watching Jesus suffer and die. But I remind my Christian friends that Gibson's *Passion* is not a documentary, but a movie, replete with dramatic license. The Pope may have said, "It is as it was," but in a number of ways it was not as it was.

The view from the pew is well mixed. Some Christians feel seeing the movie is virtually an act of faith. By contrast, a devout Scots lady in my congregation would not see it because she saw it as another evidence of the Gibsonian fascination with violence. In *The Passion* he tried to out-violate *Braveheart*. William Wallace and Edward I faced off in a wee section in the north of the British Isles. Jesus took on the devil in eternity. Jerusalem in 30 C.E. just happened to be the earthly time and site where this cosmic battle took place.

It was the shadowy figure of the devil who lurked in a number of scenes in the movie with whom Jesus really did battle. Heaven engaged hell as Gibson saw it. It was a harbinger of the Apocalypse, Armageddon. *Braveheart* instigated some dreadful deeds by hot-headed young Scots against Englishmen who happened to be at the same pub in my Scots friend's Glasgow suburb. Not only Jews, but Christians too feared that *The Passion* would fan the smoldering embers of the age-old evil of anti-Judaism. Happily, the fear that *The Passion* would trigger anti-Jewish violence has not materialized—in the United States. What might develop in parts of Europe or the Middle East where the movie might nourish existing anti-Jewish fermentation remains to be seen.

Those in my flock and my city who most appreciated Gibson's movie responded with zero anti-Jewish sentiment. The climate is not the same as when medieval Passion plays provoked attacks against Jews. The dark shadow of the Holocaust remains long. Even if Gibson had created an English byline of the blood-libel line from Matthew's Gospel, I doubt that this would have awakened the un-Christlike behavior against Jews that it once did. Christians have taken to heart the grotesque images of the Crusades, the medieval pogroms, and the Holocaust. Many wonder how the idea of revenge ever contaminated the way begun by Jesus, who said, "Come learn of me for I am lowly and gentle of heart." Tragically religion may instigate the best and the worst behavior. The worst is the corruption of the best.

Some aspects of the movie stirred me deeply. The serpent's slithering to Jesus' feet in the Garden of Gethsemane immediately alerted me that there was an apocalyptic moment coming. Here Gibson depicted the Christian view of the fulfillment of Genesis 3:15, where God says to the serpent, "He shall bruise your head, and you shall bruise his heel." Rashi saw no apocalyptic prediction in this verse, but Christians have since early in Church history. The serpent, the devil, would not let his head be crushed without a fight.

I was troubled that Gibson depicted the devil with an androgynous figure, more woman than man. This is an ancient Christian canard against women. In the Hebrew of Genesis 3:15, the personal pronoun, "you," is masculine when God speaks to the serpent because the word for serpent is masculine. Gibson took up the Augustinian view of Eve as the medium by whom sin entered human history, making the serpent a hybrid of Eve and the devil. Eve was not a Jew, and in the movie this shadowy figure of evil is not a Jew. She/it lurks in the background, distinct from all of Jesus' tormentors.

The serpent episode in the Garden was, to my mind, the most significant Christian statement in the movie. It depicted the significance of a Divine forecast at the start of human history, the fulfillment of which transcended religious boundaries. It was the Second Adam, to use St. Paul's term, crushing the source of evil and death.

Gibson was careful to show that it was Sadducees rather than Pharisees who promoted Jesus' execution. The movie does not depict "rabbis" or "Pharisees" pursuing Jesus, as some reviewers have written. I saw no phylacteries on any of Jesus' tormentors. Josephus the Jewish historian would have given Gibson an A+ for his depiction of Caiaphas and his minions who were Sadducees. Josephus described a later high priest, the younger Ananus, whom Caesar appointed high priest. Ananus had summarily executed James the brother of Jesus, a deed that resulted in his being replaced immediately. Josephus writes: "[He] was rash in his temper. . . . He followed the school of the Sadducees, who are indeed more heartless than any of the other Jews" (*Antiquities* 20, 199).

When we remember that the Temple priests were political appointees, it provides some context for the cruelty of Caiaphas and the others we see with cruel looks on their faces in the movie. These parvenus of the Romans, whose chief was referred to by the Essenes as "the wicked high priest," did not walk the high road of Pharisaic Judaism.

Furthermore, crucifixion, though obscenely cruel to us, was commonly used in the ancient world until the fourth century C.E. Alexander Jannaeus, the Hasmonean king and high priest (103–76 B.C.E.), nicknamed "Thrakidas" (the Cossack) for his cruelty, crucified eight hundred of his fellow Jews while their wives and children were butchered before their eyes (*War* 1, 97–98). Though the cruel scourging and stark violence of nailing Jesus to the cross astounds us, people in Jerusalem had long been exposed to this. Furthermore there were many then who shared Josephus's less than savory view of the Sadducees. They were not popular. Gibson is in line with Josephus in his portrayal of Jesus' Sadducean tormentors.

Of course, these distinctions are not common knowledge today, which leads many viewers to believe Gibson impugned all Jews in depicting the Sadducees who goaded Pilate to crucify Jesus.

It is the emotions the movie stirs that are its biggest draw. In a very affluent and materialistic country deep emotions are hard to come by. *The Passion* aroused deeper emotions than sports or patriotism. Gibson taught Christians to cry again over something at the heart of their faith. The cross has become an ornament to dangle from earlobes and around the neck even for non-religious folk. Christians have mostly lost the sense of what really happened on Calvary. They forgot that crucifixion was a horrible way to die. The lingering flagellation Gibson accentuated in the movie, and the zoom-lens glimpses of the details of Jesus' crucifixion shocked staid Christians. All of a sudden, eureka! The crucifixion really hurt. Tears of sympathy and perhaps of gratitude flow.

Few Christians remembered that only a few women and the Apostle John actually stayed with Jesus in his crucial hour, and that those who fled him then were apostles who had left everything to follow him for three years. A moment's introspection might remind the throngs of movie-goers that they would not have been there either at the moment Jesus suffered, a reflection that might well temper their enthusiasm to see this celluloid dramatic reproduction of Jesus' passion.

The Passion has been criticized for not being true to the Gospels. This simply does not matter to the person in the pew. She sees the overall impact of the movie. Indeed, in culling details from all four Gospels, it was inevitable that Gibson would not reflect any one of the Gospels perfectly. That Gibson borrowed so freely from Sr. Anna Katharina Emmerich's nineteenth-century meditations on Christ's Passion does not matter to Protestants. Some are puzzled at the boy-demons who hound Judas to death, and at Jesus being flung over the bridge on the way to Golgotha. But most accept these additions as dramatic license. The teardrop from heaven at the end draws mixed responses. Some appreciate this as a reminder that it hurt God the Father to see his Son suffer. Others saw it as simply tacky, and even theologically incorrect.

When it comes to contemplating the cross Catholics and Protestants have common cause. Even the focus on Mary, so marvelously played by Maia Morgenstern, a Jewish mother-in-waiting, drew scant criticism. Every Protestant pilgrim to Rome stands in rapt silence before Michelangelo's *Pietà*.

What about the impact of Gibson's *Passion* on Christian supersessionism? Supersessionism is the view that God rejected his covenant with Israel, replacing it with a covenant with the Church. It is the view that Christ's sacrifice on the cross is both the fulfillment of and the replacement of the sacrifices that took place in the Tabernacle in Moses' days, and in the subsequent Temple, with the result that the New Covenant has replaced the Old Covenant with Israel. Has the contemplation of the cross that Gibson ignites in this movie added any ammunition to supersessionism?

Jan Levinson's book *The Death and Resurrection of the Beloved Son* suggests that Christianity shows its indebtedness to Judaism in its supersessionism because the story unfolding in the Hebrew Bible tells of the younger continually superseding the older. After all, did not Abel supersede Cain in virtue, and Isaac replace Ishmael, and Jacob get the promise instead of Esau, and Joseph eclipse his older brothers, and Ephraim the younger get Jacob's right hand of blessing instead of Manasseh? I suspect that no Jew quibbles at a theory of supersessionism in Christianity since even within the history of Judaism various sectarian expressions claim superiority to others. It's part of the stuff of religious disagreement.

Perhaps it is useful to observe that not all Christians are happy with the word "supersessionism." There is a difference between seeing the sacrifice of Christ on the cross as a fulfillment of the sacrifices that were offered under the Covenant with Israel, and affirming that God has rejected his Covenant with Israel in making a new covenant in Christ. The Apostle Paul wrote, "The gifts and callings of God are irrevocable" (Romans 11:29). In the great doctrinal treatise of Romans this pioneer in Christian reflection argues that God used Israel as a means of blessing to the world. In the drama of the history of salvation God fosters reciprocal influence between Jews and Gentiles to accomplish the fulfillment of his Great Plan for reclaiming a world infected with sin and death.

The anti-Judaism that arose in the fourth century, illustrated in the sermons of some of the greatest preachers of that century, produced immeasurable harm. But Gibson did not feed at their trough. His *Passion* proposes no anti-Jewish corollaries to the fact of Jesus' suffering. He tries to depict the brutal facts, including the various *dramatis personae* mentioned in the New Testament, and the imaginative embellishments of devout visionaries. It is not a theological movie nearly so much as it is a visceral contemplation of the agony of Jesus' willing sacrifice. It may become one of the classics in this genre, shown on the networks during Holy Week. But I suspect that its brutality may diminish its appeal, so that more suggestive, less explicit movies of Jesus' Passion may secure lingering pride of place between Palm Sunday and Easter.

Discussion Questions

1. Is there cultural, moral, or spiritual value in trying to depict graphically moments in history with monumental religious significance?
2. Gibson's movie does not seem to have incubated widespread anti-Jewish sentiment. Why not?
3. The early part of Gibson's *Passion* takes place in the Garden of Gethsemane. Might it be seen that the real theme of the movie, rather than being supersessionist, Christianity superseding Judaism, is really a depiction of apocalyptic fury as the serpent tries to crush the heel of the seed of woman, only to have its head crushed as death is conquered in the resurrection?

The Passion of the Christ and Congregational Interfaith Relations

Joseph A. Edelheit

By the time you read this we will be in the midst of the next installment of how *The Passion* will impact Jewish-Christian relations since the DVD was released on August 31, 2004. As of this writing you can find competing discounts for as low as $17.50 and bulk orders through churches are going to boost sales even before it is released. Mel Gibson's violent, darkly personal interpretation of the final twelve hours of the life of Jesus continues to be a fascinating measurement of the *Zeitgeist*. The flurry of charges and counter-charges about the film's anti-Semitism are now being dismissed, because there were no pogroms causally linked to the film.

Whether the film's violent portrayal of Jews and their role in the death of Jesus ultimately has an impact on how people feel about and relate to Jews today, only time will provide the perspective and necessary anecdotes as evidence of such negative behavior. Here is what we can state without equivocation: *The Passion of the Christ* will continue to provoke serious conversation and confusion among Jews and Christians who want meaningful relations between the communities through their synagogues and churches.

Immediately prior to the film's release in theaters and for the first few weeks prior to Easter 2004, there was an outpouring of Jewish-Christian dialogues, programs, sermons, editorials, reviews, panel discussions, workshops, and clergy association meetings. Out of all those programs came a renewal of important relationships that have both an immediate and significant influence on Jews and Christians within their congregations. Even in communities without organized interfaith programming, one could find real concern and at least a new openness to old fears. Then the movie amazed everyone with its success at the box office, $370.3 million with equally amazing numbers of viewers worldwide. All of this without any significant episode of public rage against Jews for the crime of deicide, God's death. But now as the DVD comes out in the final days of summer, there will be little of the polarizing media or renewed interfaith education which the public experienced last winter.

Yet, the release of the DVD and VHS tape is a moment which requires serious reflection for the future of the very programs that seemed so successful just six months before. The questions raised by the film are not new questions; rather they are the classic issues of anti-Judaism and anti-Semitism which have remained during the last 1,900 years. The film and now DVD version depict spectacular violence as the suffering of Jesus which is the key to why this film is a vital barometer of the *Zeitgeist*. Though created by a traditionalist Catholic who relies on the writings of a recently beatified Catholic mystic, Anna Katharina Emmerich, *The Passion of the Christ* has galvanized the Protestant Evangelical communities. The film invites the viewer to experience the physical sacrifice that Jesus went through as the Savior. This is not some visual subtlety as the film begins with a verse from Isaiah 53:5 "But he was wounded for our transgressions, crushed for our iniquities; upon him was the punishment that made us whole, and by his bruises we are healed" (NRSV). Gibson forces his viewer to experience that the Christ event is *transcendent suffering:* violent, unrelenting, bloody, cruel, merciless and mesmerizing.

The many questions raised by reviewers, scholars, and the public about the film's anti-Semitism are now the fodder of future academic papers. Whether there is an anti-Semitic affect/effect when the film is shown privately in homes, youth meetings, church adult-ed classes, seminaries, missionary meetings in foreign lands and among clergy may well be beyond calculation. Much of the Christian community prepared its followers for the film with educational material which reviewed its particular denomination's teachings about Jews, Judaism, and the death of Jesus. The release of the DVD will not include any study guide or commentary, and one must ask whether the same Christian education preparation will be offered or provided as the film leaves the public domain. Whether or not one agrees with the polarized views of scholars about the film's portrayal of Jews, no one can argue that the film is not visually provocative about Jews. How will those who view this alone or in groups without professional guidance understand the meaning of Gibson's interpretation of Jews?

One of the most benign examples illuminates this point. In one of the early scenes of the film, Caiaphas, the high priest, and the Sanhedrin are shown negotiating with Judas for the thirty shekels of silver. Gibson, the director, chooses to visually emphasize the role of the money by having the leather pouch thrown across the room in slow motion and then fall on the floor scattering the pieces of silver so that Judas is shown on the floor groveling for the money. This scene has nothing to do with the role of the Jews and the death of Jesus, yet it is a classic stereotyping of Jews and their relationship with money. I have recently led several workshops for faculty at a state university on issues of anti-Semitism, in which I asked them to comment on the use of the idiom, *to*

Jew someone down. Many among the more than 650 faculty acknowledged knowing and even using the idiom, yet they were surprised to find that the use of the word "Jew" as a verb is found in a dictionary defined as being cheap and deceitful. When seeing Gibson's Judas on the floor in a panic trying to retrieve his thirty shekels, are people aware of the depth of the classic anti-Semitic stereotyping or of their own participation in that negative perception of Jews? Similarly, Gibson's portrayal of the Pharisees as being those who goad the Romans and later the crowd is merely an affirmation of the meaning of the word "Pharisee" as a hypocrite. While some might argue that such examples are not intended as anti-Semitic or obvious to the unschooled viewer, I will argue that Gibson's intent is not the issue, but rather the impact of the film as a visual/virtual confirmation of people's perception of Jews and Judaism.

Now that millions, possibly even hundreds of millions of copies of this film will be sold, given away, shown, used, and viewed multiple times and all of it without any commentary, the issue of its anti-Semitic influence is left to be evaluated in the years to come. It is the personal/private use and viewing of the Gibson film that cannot be ignored by those responsible for congregational and communal interfaith relations. Interfaith relations have primarily been a communal endeavor with the neutral safety of public venues. While there have been smaller groups in homes that have experienced the more intimate human dimensions of conversation, it was still a communal project. The private and personal use of Gibson's film as a spiritual/visual experience creates an area of religious reality that does not open to dialogue. How do we discuss *"my" experience* of Christ's suffering in the broader context of Jewish-Christian relations?

As a barometer of the *Zeitgeist,* Gibson tapped into an unexpected pool of Christians who claim that they have had profound spiritual experiences because of the film. As the film moves from the public into the private venues, one can only imagine that there will be increased profound spiritual experiences stimulated by the dark violence of Gibson's highly stylized interpretation of the Suffering Christ. How are Christians who have such an experience going to be understood by Jews with whom they try to share their newfound virtual confirmation of what really happened to Jesus? How are Jews, who often know very little about first-century Judaism or the role of Jews in the origins of Christianity, going to understand how Christians spiritually internalize the suffering? Are Jews and Christians capable of having cognitive conversations about such affective experiences without being defensive and reactive? How will Jewish and Christian clergy use the film or ignore its effect/affect in their ongoing interfaith relations?

Mel Gibson's *The Passion of the Christ* requires that Jewish and Christian institutions, synagogues, churches, schools, seminaries, and clergy associations now make public statements about the core questions and values raised by the film. The classic issues of deicide, anti-Jewish polemics in Scripture, traditional anti-Jewish teachings in early Christianity, and the history of Jews and Judaism of the period must now be integrated into the norm of congregational interfaith relations. Synagogues cannot be constantly reactive to the fear of anti-Semitism, but rather must now educate their members about the positive meaning of Christianity and the significant differences of the two faiths, including the difficult area of how suffering is a positive source of religious meaning to Christians. Jewish leaders must take the time to change opinions and stereotyping among Jews about Christian beliefs. The obligation within the Jewish community is absolutely necessary if we expect similar work to be done in the Christian community.

Will Jews who were frightened by the prospect of the movie now be willing to spend time to learn about Christian beliefs, especially the role of suffering? This question is critical in determining the value of interfaith relations in the years ahead. If every time Jews react to classic issues of anti-Judaism, they remain isolated and insular in their own communities, then Christians have less reason to re-read their own traditions as being a source of grave fear for Jews. In other words, the unexpected popular acceptance of the Gibson interpretation now demands careful long term responses from those committed to interfaith relations. The frenzy of the last nine months with its polarizing verbal engagements will not foster better relations between Jews and Christians. If the Jewish community finds the issues raised by the film to be unsettling then we must take the time and make the effort to educate our own community about its own history and beliefs and then accept the even riskier challenge of teaching more about the positive experiences of Christians and Christianity. The unexpected diversity of opinions among Christians requires a more thoughtful intra-Christian conversation, especially among those for whom interfaith relations are essential.

Maybe the best way to begin the next stage of congregational and communal interfaith relations is to risk dismissing the polarizing diversity of views about the film. What brings us together as people of the same God, the same local and even national communities? Are there significant shared values that we can and should acknowledge which came before and remain after the polarizing experience of the film? What is the starting point of knowledge we have of each other's faiths and how does the ignorance we acknowledge distort our understanding of each other? What are the past positive experiences we have shared that can be used as a foundation for the challenges of the future?

Jewish and Christian institutions cannot ignore the impact of the Gibson film as a mere "event" in the *Zeitgeist*. The film's influence, both positive and negative, will only be fully understood when we have gained perspective over time, but our immediate tasks require that we acknowledge a common view of learning, patience, and renewal. Just as the Passion plays of medieval Europe, Gibson's film has affirmed once again that as long as some Christians pursue a traditional relationship to Scripture and a theology of suffering, their view of

Jews will stimulate fear and marginalization. The issues raised by the Gibson movie are not new, and will always be present near the core of any serious interfaith dialogue. Our task remains that given the permanence of these issues, the Gibson movie is a provocative mandate for a renewed Jewish-Christian dialogue.

Discussion Questions

1. How does the inherent anti-Jewish polemic of the Gospels become dangerous in the Passion story? Can Jews understand the fear that Christians experience when Jews "reject" the "good news" of the Christ?
2. Why is the suffering depicted in the Gibson movie so important to Christians who want to feel what Christ did for them? How can Christians help Jews understand the value of suffering as an agent of "salvation"?
3. What scenes make Jews feel the echo of anti-Semitism from centuries ago? Why do Christians not feel it? How can we help each other to empathize with each other?

Bibliography

Avi-Yonah, Michael. *The Holy Land from the Persian to the Arab Conquests 536 BC–640 AD: An Historical Geography.* Grand Rapids, MI: Baker Book House, 1977.

This is a classic of the historical geography of the Holy Land by a preeminent historical geographer. There may be found a good look at the confused situation in Palestine during the period in Mel Gibson's film.

Barbet, Pierre, M. D. *A Doctor at Calvary: the Passion of Our Lord Jesus Christ as Described by a Surgeon.* Garden City: Doubleday & Co., 1963.

Dr. Barbet examines the physiological aspects of the ordeal of crucifixion in general, and the additional psychological and physical trauma undergone by Jesus from his arrest in the garden Gethsemane until his death. This volume also includes a detailed discussion of the Shroud of Turin, of interest here because of its purported Testament of Blood, which impresses Gibson considerably.

Berger, David. "Jews, Christians, and 'The Passion.' " *Commentary* 117.5 (May 2004), pp. 23–31.

The reaction to *The Passion* by a scholar who is an authority on the debates between Jews and Christians during the High Middle Ages. Berger carefully avoids the extremes of utterly condemning or defending the film and concludes that Gibson's assault on Jews in the film results not from anti-Jewish malice but from a Manichean vision reinforced by the anti-Semitic stereotypes that he imbibed with his father's milk.

Brandon, S. G. F. *Jesus and the Zealots.* New York: Charles Scribner's Sons, 1967.

The author explores the relationship between Jesus and the Jewish case against Roman occupation in Judea in the first century, including the Zealot movement. He provides a fundamental reinterpretation of a great part of the Gospels' narrative as they were shaped by political and social forces two generations after the crucifixion of Jesus.

Bulgakov, M. *The Master and Margarita.* D. Burgin, K. O'Connor, trans.; New York: Vintage, 1995.

The best, most reliable English translation of *The Master and Margarita.*

Burnham, Jonathan, ed. *Perspectives on The Passion of the Christ: Religious Thinkers and Writers Explore the Issues Raised by the Controversial Movie.* New York: Miramax Books, 2004.

Contributions by Jon Meacham, Paula Fredriksen, Philip Cunningham, Mary Boys, John Pawlikowski and others. Far broader than solely a collection of "academic essays," these eighteen contributions address many of the same issues but include two senior editors at *U.S. News & World Report,* the *Dallas Morning News,* and *The New Republic,* as well as a concluding "Epilogue" by noted actor Steve Martin. By doing so, one gains an additional sense of the impact of *The Passion of the Christ* "out there" in the larger community.

Chilton, Bruce D. *Rabbi Jesus.* New York: Doubleday, 2002.

A revolutionary approach to the life of Jesus, in which narrative of the inner life of Jesus correlates the events and activities portrayed in the Gospels with the teachings of Jesus as his life unfolded.

Corley, Kathleen E., and Robert L. Webb, eds. *Jesus and Mel Gibson's "The Passion of the Christ": The Film, the Gospels and the Claims of History.* New York: Continuum, 2004.

Excellent articles by Helen K. Bond, "Pilate and the Romans"; John D. Crossan, "Hymn to a Savage God"; Craig A. Evans, "The Procession and the Crucifixion"; Scot McKnight, "The Betrayal of Jesus and the Death of Judas"; Mark Allan Powell, "Satan and the Demons"; Alan F. Segal, "The Jewish Leaders"; W. Barnes Tatum, "The Passion in the History of Jesus Films"; Robert L. Webb, "The Passion and the Influence of Emmerich's The Dolorous Passion of Our Lord Jesus Christ"; and seven others. There is also a useful glossary and a list of suggested books for further research.

Crossan, John Dominic. *Who Killed Jesus: Exposing the Roots of Anti-Semitism in the Gospel Story of the Death of Jesus.* San Francisco: Harper 1996.

An important text to understand a core Christian belief and its perceived anti-Semitic fallout, written by a radical Catholic New Testament scholar.

Crossan, John Dominic. *The Birth of Christianity: Discovering What Happened in the Years Immediately after the Execution of Jesus.* San Francisco: HarperSanFrancisco, 1998.

A major analytical statement on major events in the advent of Christianity.

Crossan, John Dominic and Ben Witherington III. "Scholarly Smackdown." http://www.beliefnet.com/index/index_525.html.

A discussion.

Cunningham, Philip A. "Gibson's The Passion of the Christ: A Challenge to Catholic Teaching." http://www.bc.edu/research/cjl/metaelements/texts/reviews/gibson_cunningham.htm.

The author is executive director of the Center for Christian-Jewish Learning at Boston College. His presentation offers many statements by Pope John Paul II and the U. S. Conference of Bishops.

Cunningham, Philip A., ed. *Pondering the Passion: What's at Stake for Christians and Jews.* Lanham, MD: Rowman & Littlefield, 2004.

More of an historical-theological contextual analysis, these fifteen essays are subdivided into the categories of (1) First-Century History; (2) Bible; (3) The Arts; (4) Theology; and (4) *The Passion of the Christ* (i.e. the movie itself).

Cunningham, Philip A. *A Story of Shalom: The Calling of Christians and Jews by a Covenanting God.* New York/Mahwah: Paulist Press/Stimulus Books, 2001.

This book presents a new pluralistic vision of the relationship of Christianity and Judaism from a Christian perspective. The articulation is thoughtful, constructive and healing.

Dabrowa, Edward. "The Frontier in Syria in the First Century AD," in Philip Freeman and David Kennedy, eds., *The Defence of the Roman and Byzantine East, Proceedings of a Colloquium Held at the University of Sheffield in April 1986.* British Institute of Archaeology at Ankara Monograph No. 8. BAR International Series 297 (Part i), 1986, pp. 93–108.

This essay, included in a volume of essays related to the volume's title, is an important source for Roman imperial policy during the time in Gibson's film.

"Dabru Emet: A Jewish Statement on Christians and Christianity from the National Jewish Scholars Project." http://www.icjs.org/what/njsp/dabruemet.html.

This document sets out in a very clear and direct fashion important perspectives from the Jewish community on the parameters of Christian-Jewish relations.

Efroymson, David P., Eugene J. Fisher, and Leon Klenicki, eds. *Within Context: Essays on Jews and Judaism in the New Testament.* Philadelphia: The American Interfaith Institute, 1993.

This focused collection of eight strong essays is the result of a dialogue among Jews and Christians who are keenly aware of the problems involved in teaching and preaching about the other person as a person of faith. The tone is set by the words of Irvin Borowsky in his "Foreword": "If the gospel writers had known that the invective and anger they expressed in the context of an internal struggle within the Jewish community would be later used to justify hatred, violence and even murder of Jesus' people, they would not have allowed such language into the canon."

Emmerich, Anne Catherine. *The Dolorous Passion of Our Lord Jesus Christ.* Rockford, IL: Tan Books, 1983.

Sister Anna Katharina was a German nun (1774–1824), famous for her extraordinary visions of Jesus' suffering and death. Bedridden herself, she recounted her vivid and detailed visions to the German romantic author Clemens Brentano, who had them published. Mel Gibson based much of the detail in his film on these visions, rather than on the Gospel texts. Sister Anna Katharina was beatified on October 3, 2004 by Pope John Paul II, an important step toward sainthood.

Farmer, William R., ed. *Anti-Judaism and the Gospels.* Harrisburg: Trinity Press International, 1999.

This collection of essays, together with responses, is the fruit of a three-year research project sponsored by the University of Dallas on the subject of anti-Judaism and the Gospels. It focuses on three questions: 1) When and under what circumstances did the Gospels begin to serve anti-Jewish ends? 2) Can it be said that the evangelists were anti-Jewish? 3) Are there texts in the Gospels originally intended to injure the Jewish people or their religion?

Fasching, Darrell. *Narrative Theology after Auschwitz: From Alienation to Ethics.* Philadelphia: Fortress Press, 1992.

This text is among the first to think about the Christian narratives in a post-Shoah context for Protestants. The analysis of the Christian biblical narratives gives clear alternative ways of thinking that show how Christians can think and talk differently after the Shoah.

Fredriksen, Paula. *Jesus of Nazareth, King of the Jews: A Jewish Life and the Emergence of Christianity.* New York: Alfred A. Knopf, 1999.

This volume provides good historical information regarding the important issues of Jesus in the context of the Jewish experience.

Friedman, Saul. *The Oberammergau Passion Play: A Lance against Civilization.* Carbondale, IL: Southern Illinois University Press, 1984.

A history professor provides a strongly critical assessment of the unreformed Passion play. With few exceptions, the text of the 1984 play was the same as the one that Adolf Hitler had seen and loved in 1934.

Garber, Zev, and Bruce Zuckerman. *Double Takes: Thinking and Rethinking Issues of Modern Judaism in Ancient Contexts.* Studies in the Shoah, vol. 26. Lanham: University Press of America, 2004.

For a collection of articles that considers themes similar to those raised in Zuckerman's contribution.

Greenberg, Irving. "Cloud of Smoke, Pillar of Fire: Judaism, Christianity and Modernity after the Holocaust." In *Auschwitz: Beginning of a New Era?* edited by Eva Fleischner, 7–55, 441–6. New York: KTAV, 1977.

This article presents a major statement of the way in which the Holocaust challenges all the affirmations in Judaism, Christianity and modernity, and demands new thinking in theology, ethics and cultural life.

Greenberg, Irving. *For the Sake of Heaven and Earth: The New Encounter between Judaism and Christianity.* Philadelphia: Jewish Publication Society, 2004.

This book offers a powerful argument for religious pluralism in the context of a comprehensive, affirmative Jewish theology of Christianity. The author articulates how traditional Jews and Christians can uphold their own religion's authority claims even as they correct past dismissals and denials of each other. The book includes a strong critique of the past Christian teaching of contempt for Judaism (of the type exemplified by Mel Gibson's *The Passion of the Christ*).

Hengel, Martin. *Crucifixion.* Philadelphia: Fortress Press, 1977.

This brief book (99 pages) has become the classic monograph on this topic. With his characteristic thoroughness in surveying all the relevant ancient sources, Hengel provides both a useful summary of what can be known and enormously rich footnotes to guide the reader's own research.

Isaac, Jules. *The Teaching of Contempt: Christian Roots of Anti-Semitism.* New York: Holt, Rinehart, and Winston, 1964.

This is the classic portrait of the record of Christian supersessionism and denigration of Judaism, and the ugly consequences of the teaching in terms of anti-Semitism and hostility. The book shaped Pope John XXIII's opening to Judaism and to the world.

Kermode, F. *The Genesis of Secrecy: On the Interpretation of Narrative.* Cambridge: Harvard University Press, 1979.

For a classic study that considers the inability of a reader to "get behind" a narrative to find the meaning of a text (ancient or otherwise).

Klausner, Joseph. *Jesus of Nazareth: His Life, Times and Teaching.* New York: Macmillan, 1925; second edition (with a new foreword by Sidney B. Hoenig), New York: Menorah Publishing Co., 1979.

This book is a determined pioneering effort by a Jewish scholar, who taught modern Hebrew language and literature at the Hebrew University in Jerusalem, to reclaim Jesus as a Jew in the vital period of the "Parting of the Ways." The author portrays first century Judaism as "a national world outlook with an ethico-religious basis."

Knight, Henry. *Confessing Christ in a Post-Holocaust World: A Midrashic Experiment.* Westport, CN: Greenwood Press, 2001.

This book is a collection of essays by a Protestant theologian and pastor that allow the readers to see a distinctly different picture of Jesus which is both genuinely Christian and faithful to our awareness that Jesus was a Jew. In this way, the book is an invitation to dialogue with a confession of Christ which leads to a teaching of respect.

Landres, J. Shawn, and Berenbaum, Michael, eds. *After the Passion Is Gone: American Religious Consequences.* Walnut Creek, CA: AltaMira Press, 2004.

Twenty-one distinguished scholars, including Karen Jo Torjesen, Jeffrey Siker, David Morgan, Susannah Heschel, Richard L. Rubenstein, Elliot Dorff, and Mark Juergensmeyer, reflect on the context and reception of Gibson's film. The authors approach the subject from the perspectives of history, scriptural interpretation, theology, aesthetics, Jewish-Christian relations, ethics of faith-affirmations in a multi-religious world, American culture, and the war in Iraq as a significant context for the way movie-goers experienced this film.

Lesser, Wendy. *Pictures at an Execution: An Inquiry into the Subject of Murder.* Cambridge: Harvard University Press, 1993.

The writer deals with relations between governance and citizen through television as a transmitter of messages which are absorbed gradually. Lesser studied some cases of execution, their televised reports and the audience reactions to the images. The author concludes that the viewer becomes indifferent to death, as he is not experiencing a real execution but seems to watch a fictional Hollywood one. Here, in the author's opinion, lies the real danger: blurring between reality and fiction, numbness and the belief that the punishment will never come and therefore the deterrence effect of the sovereign vanishes. Those were not the reactions of the sympathetic viewers of Mel Gibson's *Passion.*

Levenson, Jon D. "The Beloved Son Between Zion and Golgotha." In section 3 of *The Death and Resurrection of the Beloved Son: The Transformation of Child Sacrifice in Judaism and Christianity,* 173–232. New Haven: Yale University Press, 1993.

Levenson's book was written a decade before Gibson's movie, but he recognizes the theme that runs through Jewish history of "the suffering servant," and describes how this ancient Jewish theme is also found in the death and resurrection of Jesus, whom Christians see as God's Beloved Son.

Maccoby, Hyam. *Revolution in Judaea: Jesus and the Jewish Resistance.* New York: Taplinger Publishing Co., 1981.

This book provides an insightful view that argues that Jesus aspired to be king of the Jews, not in a metaphoric sense but in fact. In arguing his point, Maccoby reexamines the positive, not negative, roles of Barabbas and Judas Iscariot in the scriptural account of the Passion. A demonstrated mastery of Jewish and Roman history, with the goal to show that the New Testament interpretation of Jesus cannot possibly be correct.

Meier, John P. *A Marginal Jew: Rethinking the Historical Jesus*, vol. 1: *The Roots of the Problem and the Person.* New York: Doubleday, 1991.

This scholarly work, the first of three volumes, is marked by a bold and sober assessment by a Roman Catholic priest who deals objectively with the Gospels, Josephus, and other Jewish and pagan writings about Jesus. He sets up plausible criteria to determine what in the Gospels comes from Jesus.

Moore, James. *Christian Theology after the Shoah.* Lanham, MD: University Press of America, 2004.

This book is an introduction to a new way of doing Christian theology based on a post-Shoah midrashic approach. The text also gives clear alternative ways of reading the Passion story (the narrative of Jesus' death) which can be genuinely Protestant and avoid the crass imagery projected by Mel Gibson's film.

Moore, James, ed., Zev Garber, Steven L. Jacobs, Henry Knight. *Post-Shoah Dialogues: Rethinking our Texts Together.* Lanham, MD: University Press of America, 2004.

This book is a collection of dialogues between two Jewish and two Christian scholars reading sacred texts together. The reading of texts in this is a model showing Christians another way that avoids the exclusivism that is so apparent in the image of Jesus in the Gibson film. In addition, the text provides insight into how reading sacred texts can be done in a way sensitive to dialogue.

Neusner, Jacob. *A Rabbi Talks with Jesus* (2d ed.: Montreal and Kingston, McGill-Queen's University Press, 2000; and Ithaca: Cornell University Press, 2000).

This book shows how a rabbi argues with the Jesus represented in the Gospel of Matthew. The volume has been translated into six languages.

———. *Rabbinic Judaism: The Theological System.* Boston and Leiden: E. J. Brill, 2003.

This book contains a systematic reconstruction of the theology of the Rabbinic writings of the first six centuries C.E. from the Mishnah through the Talmud of Babylonia and shows how the diverse teachings of the Rabbinic classics form a coherent statement of monotheism, with stress on the justice of God.

Nickelsburg, George W. E. *Ancient Judaism and Christian Origins: Diversity, Continuity, and Transformation.* Minneapolis: Fortress, 2003.

This is an important core text for a college course on the origins of Christianity—well-written scholarship accessible even for laypeople.

"Nostra Aetate, Vatican II, The Catholic Churches Statement on Jews and Judaism." http://www.vatican.va/archive/hist_councils/ii_vatican_council/documents/vat-ii_decl_ 19651028_nostra-aetate_en.html.

"Nostra Aetate" is the pioneering statement of the Catholic Church inspired by Pope John XXIII on Jews and Judaism reversing centuries of Christian anti-Jewish feeling based on the unjustified accusation of deicide against the Jewish people. This document launched an unprecedented period of Jewish Catholic dialogue.

O'Malley, John, S.J. "A Movie, a Mystic, and a Spiritual Tradition," *America: The National Catholic Weekly,* March 15, 2004.

A Jesuit scholar, O'Malley describes the historical background of Sister Anna Katharina, including a dispassionate account of the anti-Jewish attitudes which were common during her lifetime and which were reflected in her visions.

"The Passion of the Christ; A Jewish Response" http://www.amygreenbaum.com/passion.htm.

A collection of Jewish (and Christian) reactions to the film.

"The Passion" Study Guide, National Catholic Reporter, February 20, 2004.

A pamphlet of questions covering all aspects of the film.

Pawlikowski, John T. *Jesus and the Theology of Israel.* Collegeville, MN: The Liturgical Press, a Michael Glazier book, 1989.

This book contains a section on how Jesus' Passion and death are to be understood within the social dynamics of the period.

Pawlikowski, John T., with Reginald H. Fuller, Donald Senior, et al. *The Passion, Death and Resurrection of Jesus.* Special issue of *Chicago Studies* 25:1 (April 1986).

Contributors discuss critical issues dealing with the foundation belief drama of the Christian faith.

Plate, S. Brent, ed. *Re-Viewing the Passion: Mel Gibson's Film and Its Critics.* New York: Palgrave Macmillan, 2004.

These twelve essays, all by noted and reputable scholars, are divided into four sections: I. Jewish-Christian Relations: Reviewing Anti-Semitism; II. Christian-Christian Relations: Reviewing *The Passion* in Christian Theological History; III. Visual Theologies and Verbal Theologies: Reviewing the Image of Jesus; IV. Media Approaches to *The Passion:* Personal Devotion and Public Discourse.

Prothero, Stephen. *American Jesus: How the Son of God Became a National Icon.* New York: Farrar, Straus and Giroux, 2003.

This book portrays the uniqueness of the American religious scene whereby Jesus as "the Christ" is not so subtly adapted by various Christian and non-Christian communities to serve other ends.

"A Sacred Obligation: Rethinking Christian Faith in Relation to Judaism and the Jewish People, A Statement of the Christian Scholars Group on Christian Jewish Relations." http://www.bc.edu/research/cjl/meta-elements/partners/CSG/Sacred_Obligation.htm.

With both a Catholic and a Jewish statement on Christian-Jewish dialogue in place this document from a primarily Protestant group of theologians and scholars represents the most developed and positive Christian statement on Jewish-Christian relations and acts as a guideline for Christian responses.

Sarat, Austin. *When the State Kills: Capital Punishment and the American Condition.* Princeton, NJ: Princeton University Press, 2001.

The author bases his book on criminal law and trials. He chooses to describe the phenomena of the death penalty in the United States by means of the relations between the citizen and the state and governmental violence towards its citizens in the guise of law and order. In chapter 7 Sarat chooses to examine the death penalty in its cultural, social, and legal aspects. This is achieved by examining three movies: Frank Darabont, *The Green Mile* (USA, 1999); Bruce Beresford, *Last Dance* (USA, 1996); and Tim Robbins, *Dead Man Walking* (USA, 1995). Sarat eventually reached the conclusion that there is a direct link between religion and capital punishment, between religion and cinematic narrative, and between trials and culture. Later, additional research led Sarat to the conclusion that religion and capital punishment, religion and cinematic narrative, and law and culture are well connected, a conclusion which does not surface in this book.

Sarna, Jonathan D. *American Judaism: A History.* New Haven, CT: Yale University Press, 2004.

Sarna's book is the latest, and, quite possibly, the best historical overview and assessment of the American Jewish experience, and provides a *contextual* "framework of understanding" Gibson's film in the context of the American Jewish experience.

Schweitzer, Albert. *The Quest of the Historical Jesus: A Critical Study of Its Progress from Reimarus to Wrede.* Trans. W Montgomery; introduction by James M. Robinson. New York: Macmillan, 1968.

Published in 1901, this book traces the quest of eighteenth- and nineteenth-century European scholarship to understand the life of Jesus. Schweitzer's ability to analyze these various works and adduce their underlying assumptions established his reputation as a scholar and religious thinker.

Schurer, Emil. *The History of the Jewish People in the Age of Jesus Christ (175 B.C.–A.D. 135)*. Revised edition by Geza Vermes and Fergus Millar. Volume 1. Edinburg: Clark, 1973.

This is a classic and standard. The sections on Judea in the time of Jesus are particularly important for an understanding of the background to Gibson's film.

Shapiro, James. *Oberammergau: The Troubling Story of the World's Most Famous Passion Play*. New York: Pantheon, 2000.

A professor of English and comparative literature, Shapiro explores the tradition of the Oberammergau Passion play, from its inception in 1633 to the eve of its 2000 season. He is rightly critical of the traditions of anti-Jewish stereotyping in the nineteenth century, traditions which began to be reformed only in the 1980s. He spent time with the villagers as they prepared the reformed play of the year 2000, a version which was purged of overtly anti-Jewish traditions.

"Special Edition on Mel Gibson's *The Passion of the Christ*," *Journal of Religious & Society*, 6 (2004): http://moses.creighton.edu.

An online journal which addresses a number of historical and contemporary issues presented by Mel Gibson's religious film.

Stern, Richard C., Clayton Jefford, and Guerric Debona. *Savior on the Silver Screen*. Mahwah, NJ: Paulist Press, 1999.

A look at a variety of portrayals of Jesus in a variety of film types, from silent, to epic, to musical. The book includes discussion questions.

Tatum, W. Barnes. *Jesus at the Movies: A Guide to the First Hundred Years*. Santa Rosa, CA: Polebridge Press, 1997.

A well-rounded viewer's guide to a variety of films that try to depict the life of Jesus. The book combines biblical scholarship, theological sophistication and a keen eye for cinematography.

Vila, Bryan, and Morris, Cynthia, eds. *Capital Punishment in the United States: A Documentary History*. Westport, CT: Greenwood Press, 1997.

A collection of documentation on all aspects of death penalty in the United States. Sources go back to ancient times through England and colonial America up to the present. The book also contains a wide review of the discourses on statehood and religion, and pro-con death penalty, legislation and deterrence. The book does not take a stand on the controversial issue of the death penalty in the United States, though the documentation and sources in it are self-evident.

Walsh, Richard. *Reading the Gospels in the Dark: Portrayals of Jesus in Film*. Harrisburg, PA: Trinity Press International, 2003.

Walsh, a professor of religion, looks at a number of films about Jesus and divides them into five basic types, each related to a particular period in the twentieth century. Like Schweitzer, he argues that the depictions of Jesus in these films is really a reflection of their times.

Whealey, Alice. *Josephus on Jesus: The Testimonium Flavianum Controversy from Late Antiquity to Modern Times.* New York: Peter Lang, 2003.

This work traces objectively the history of scholarship dealing with the passage about Jesus in Josephus and, in particular, the much-debated question whether the passage is a forgery in whole or in part. She suggests that among the early modern critics, Protestants were particularly receptive to the new critical intellectual currents of the Renaissance and the Reformation.

Wright, N. T. "The Reason for Jesus' Crucifixion." In *Jesus and the Victory of God,* 540–611. Minneapolis, MN: Fortress Press, 1996.

Wright is both a dispassionate historian who examines the sources of information on Jesus' life critically, and a Christian who holds to the traditional understanding of the meaning of the Passion of the Christ.

Zeitlin, Solomon. *The Rise and Fall of the Judaean State: A Political, Social and Religious History of the Second Commonwealth.* Vol. 2: *37 BCE–66 CE.* Philadelphia: Jewish Publication Society of America. 1969.

This is another classic treatment and important for the era of Jesus' Judaea.

Zuckerman, Bruce. *Job the Silent: A Study in Historical Counterpoint.* New York: Oxford University Press, paperback edition, 1998.

This book is a study of Job that considers its underlying story as a case of "super reality."

Contributors

S. Scott Bartchy is a professor of history at UCLA and director of the Center for the Study of Religion. His research focuses on the effects of religious beliefs, practices, and institutions on the formation of cultural values and social codes. Among his recent publications are "The Historical Jesus and Honor Reversal at the Table"; and "Who Should Be Called 'Father'? Paul of Tarsus between the Jesus Tradition and *Patria Potestas.*"

Joseph A. Edelheit has served for twenty-eight years as a rabbi in reform congregations. The first rabbi to complete a doctoral program in Christian theology, he is director of Jewish Studies and an associate professor of philosophy at St. Cloud University. He is currently working in multifaith coalitions doing HIV/AIDS work in India.

Carol Edelman is associate dean of the College of Behavioral Sciences and a professor of sociology at California State University, Chico. She is co-director of the State of California Center for Excellence on the Study of the Holocaust, Genocide, Human Rights, and Tolerance and received the Corporation for Public Broadcasting Award for Outstanding Documentaries in the Humanities for her documentary on cultural responses to genocide.

Samuel Edelman is a professor of Jewish studies and communication studies at California State University, Chico. He is the founder and current director of the program in Modern Jewish and Israel Studies at CSU Chico. He is also the coordinator of the California State University Statewide Modern Jewish Studies BA Degree. He is, with Carol Edelman, co-director of the State of California Center for Excellence on the Study of the Holocaust, Genocide, Human Rights, and Tolerance.

Louis H. Feldman is a professor of classics at Yeshiva University. He is the editor of *Josephus, Antiquities, Books 18–20* and the author of a number of books, most recently *Josephus's Interpretation of the Bible; Flavius Josephus, Judean Antiquities, 1–4;*

and *Remember Amalek! Vengeance, Zealotry, and Group Destruction in the Bible according to Philo, Pseudo-Philo, and Josephus.*

Zev Garber is a professor of Jewish Studies and Philosophy at Los Angeles Valley College and has served as the Visiting Rosenthal Fellow of Judaic Studies at Case Western Reserve University and as president of the National Association of Professors of Hebrew. He is co-editor of *Shofar,* and co-author of *Post-Shoah Dialogue: Re-thinking Our Texts Together* and *Double Takes: Thinking and Rethinking Issues of Modern Judaism in Ancient Contexts.*

Irving Greenberg is president of the Jewish Life Network/Steinhardt Foundation, whose mission is to create new institutions and initiatives to enrich the inner life of American Jewry. Rabbi Greenberg has published articles on Jewish thought and religion and on American Jewish history. His books include *For the Sake of Heaven and Earth: The New Encounter between Judaism and Christianity* and *Living in the Image of God: Jewish Teachings to Perfect the World.*

Peter Haas is the Abba Hillel Silver professor of Jewish Studies and director of the Samuel Rosenthal Center for Judaic Studies at Case Western Reserve University in Cleveland, Ohio, where he has chaired the Department of Religion since 2003. Among his publications are a number of books and articles on Rabbinic legal and moral literature as well as on the Holocaust.

Klaus Hödl is head of the Centre for Jewish Studies at the University of Graz in Austria. He is editor of the journal *Transversal* and the author of several book, most recently *Wiener Juden—jüdische Wiener? Identität, Gedächtnis und Performanz im 19. Jahrhundert.* His fields of interest include Eastern and Central European Jewish history in the nineteenth century.

Richard Holdredge is a professor of education at Los Angeles Valley College, where he is currently chair of the Media Arts Department and the director of the Institute for Developing Entertainment Arts and Studies (IDEAS), which trains and retrains entertainment industry professionals in digital media tools. He has produced many video programs in medical education.

Steven Leonard Jacobs holds the Aaron Aronov Endowed Chair of Judaic Studies at the University of Alabama, where he is an associate professor of religious studies. His primary research foci are in biblical studies and the problematics of translation, and Holocaust and genocide studies. He is the author of a number of articles and books, including *In Search of Yesterday: The Holocaust and the Quest for Meaning* (2005).

Yvonne Kozlovsky Golan is in the Department of Film and Television Art at Sapir Academic College in Hof Ashkelon, Israel. She is a fellow at the International Institute for Holocaust Research at Yad Vashem, Jerusalem, and has recently published "The Shaping of the Holocaust Visual Conscience by the Nuremberg Trials."

Richard Libowitz is a member of the theology faculty at Saint Joseph's University and the Intellectual Heritage Program at Temple University. His many publications on the Holocaust include *Methodology and the Academic Teaching of the Holocaust.* His current research is on Holocaust-related films.

James F. Moore is a professor of theology at Valparaiso University and is the author of *Christian Theology after the Shoah, Post-Shoah Dialogues,* and *Toward a Dialogical Community.* Professor Moore is co-director of the HIV workshop for the Zygon Center for Religion and Science in Chicago and is on the board of the Wyman Institute and the Studies in the Shoah series for the University Press of America.

Gordon R. Mork is a professor of history and a member of the Jewish Studies Program at Purdue University. He specializes in German history and the Holocaust. He is the author of a number of studies on the *Oberammergau Passion Play* and editor of *The Homes of Oberammergau: A Series of Twenty Etchings, Together with Notes from a Diary by Eliza Greatorex.*

Jacob Neusner is a research professor of theology at Bard College in the Jewish Studies Program. He is the author of a number of books, including *Death and Birth of Judaism: The Impact of Christianity, Secularism, and the Holocaust on Jewish Faith; Religion Theology of the Oral Torah: Revealing the Justice of God;* and *Theology of the Halakhah.* He is also a senior fellow at the Institute of Advanced Theology at Bard College.

John T. Pawlikowski is a professor of social ethics and director of the Catholic-Jewish Studies program at Catholic Theological Union in Chicago. He is president of the International Council of Christians and Jews at the Martin Buber Haus in Heppenheim, Germany. He is the author of *Christ in the Light of the Christian-Jewish Dialogue.*

Stuart D. Robertson is the pastor of Faith Presbyterian Church in West Lafayette, Indiana, a lecturer in biblical Hebrew in Purdue University's Department of Foreign Languages and Literatures, and an adjunct professor in the Jewish Studies Program.

Penny Wheeler holds a doctorate in history from the University of Southern California. She is the translator from the French of Noel Wanlin's *The Shepherd.* She is cofounder of the Institute for Historical Studies and is the author of various articles and reviews.

Gordon D. Young is an associate professor in the Department of History at Purdue University, where he specializes in ancient Near East and Mediterranean history. He is the former director of the Jewish Studies Program at Purdue University.

Bruce Zuckerman is a professor in the School of Religion at the University of Southern California. His collection of essays, co-written with Zev Garber, *Double Takes: Thinking and Rethinking Issues of Modern Judaism in Ancient Contexts,* was published in 2004. He heads the West Semitic Research and InscriptiFact Projects at USC and is director of the Casden Institute for the Study of the Jewish Role in American Life.

Index